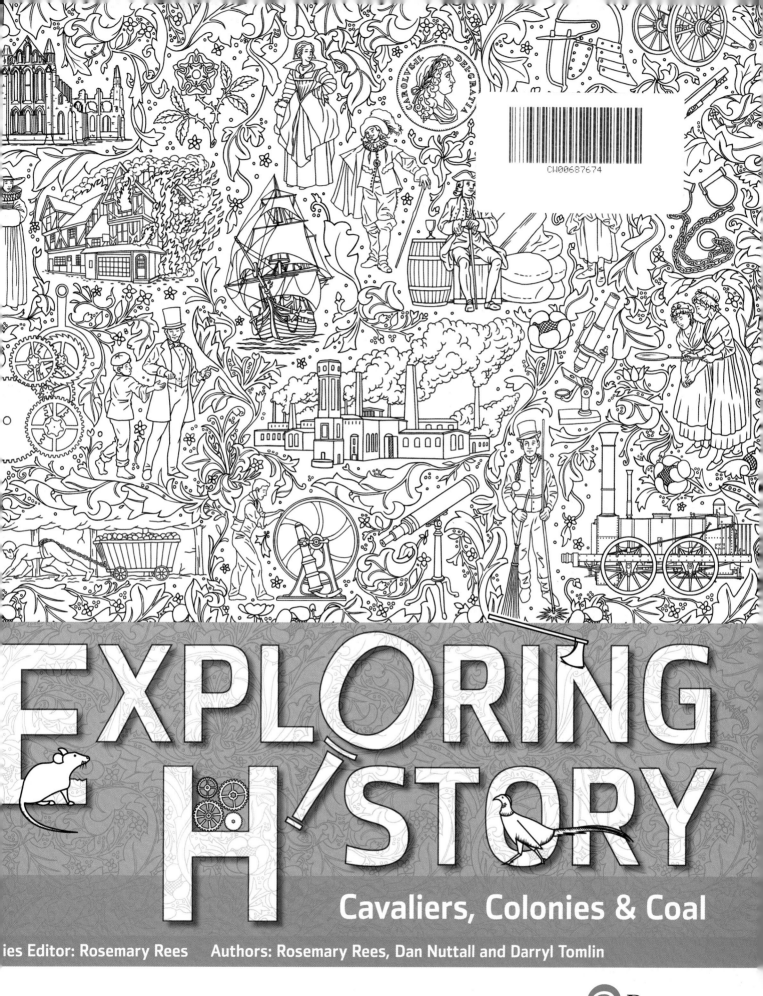

EXPLORING HISTORY

Cavaliers, Colonies & Coal

Series Editor: Rosemary Rees   Authors: Rosemary Rees, Dan Nuttall and Darryl Tomlin

Pearson

Published by Pearson Education Limited, 80 Strand, London WC2R 0RL.

www.pearsonschoolsandfecolleges.co.uk

Text © Pearson Education Limited 2018
Series editor: Rosemary Rees
Designed by Poppy Marks, Pearson Education Limited
Typeset by Hart McLeod Ltd
Original illustrations © Pearson Education Limited 2018
Illustrated by KJA Artists Illustration Agency and Beehive Illustration
Cover design by Poppy Marks, Pearson Education Limited
Cover photo/illustration © 381Mike@kja-artists

The rights of Rosemary Rees, Rob Bircher and Darryl Tomlin to be identified as authors of this
work have been asserted by them in accordance with the Copyright, Designs and Patents Act 1988.

First published 2018

21 20 19
10 9 8 7 6 5 4 3

British Library Cataloguing in Publication Data
A catalogue record for this book is available from the British Library

ISBN 9781292218717

Printed in Italy by Lego S.p.A.

Websites
Pearson Education Limited is not responsible for the content of any external internet sites.
It is essential for tutors to preview each website before using it in class so as to ensure that the
URL is still accurate, relevant and appropriate. We suggest that tutors bookmark useful
websites and consider enabling students to access them through the school/college intranet.

Note from the publisher
Pearson has robust editorial processes, including answer and fact checks, to ensure the accuracy
of the content in this publication, and every effort is made to ensure this publication is free of
errors. We are, however, only human, and occasionally errors do occur. Pearson is not liable
for any misunderstandings that arise as a result of errors in this publication, but it is our
priority to ensure that the content is accurate. If you spot an error, please do contact us at
resourcescorrections@pearson.com so we can make sure it is corrected.

In order to ensure that the content in this book is accurate and to
the highest standard possible, Chapter 4 has been reviewed by the
Holocaust Educational Trust (www.het.org.uk).

Contents

How to use this book

This book is the second in a series of three designed to help you study history at Key Stage 3.

Book 2, *Cavaliers, Colonies & Coal*, looks at the period of history between 1485 and approximately 1900 (see the timeline on pages 6–7).

The content has been carefully chosen to cover important background knowledge relevant to the Edexcel GCSE (9–1) History units. The book has depth, breadth and thematic topics to prepare you for the types of history you'll study at GCSE.

Features

As well as exciting history, the book is full of useful features to help you improve.

Enquiry questions

Every few weeks, you'll start looking at a new enquiry question. This will help you focus your learning within each chapter on a few key questions.

At the end of each enquiry, you'll find an activity that will help you to return to the enquiry question and reflect on what you have discovered.

Learning objectives

At the start of each section, you'll be set some learning objectives. These tell you what you should know and understand by the end of the section. You might cover the objectives in one or two lessons.

What do you think?

These questions give you the opportunity to show what you already know and think about what more you would like to discover about the topic.

Key terms

Where you see a word followed by an asterisk, like this: heretic*, you'll find a Key term box nearby that explains what the word means.

All the key terms are listed alphabetically in the Glossary at the end of the book.

Your turn!

Every few pages you'll find a box containing activities designed to help check and embed knowledge and get you to think carefully about what you have studied. The activities may start with some simple questions, but they get more challenging as you work through them!

Checkpoints

These help you to check and reflect on your learning at the end of a section, reinforcing the knowledge and understanding you have gained and ensuring you are familiar with the basic ideas and skills.

What do you think?

Why do you think people were criticising the Catholic Church? Think back to what you have already learned.

Key term

Heretic*: A person with religious views that disagree with official Church teaching.

Sources and interpretations

So you can really understand and explore this period of history, the book contains a lot of pictures and texts from these years, showing what people at the time said, thought or created. These are known as **sources** – you'll need to interrogate these to discover the past.

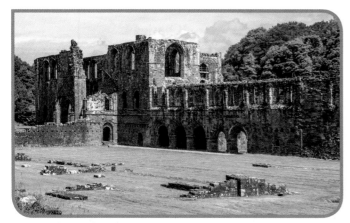

Source A: The ruins of Furness Abbey, Cumbria.

Also included are extracts from the work of historians, and other reflections of the past like poems, plays and film, which show how modern people have interpreted historical events. These are known as **interpretations**.

You'll need to examine both sources and interpretations during your work on the history of this period.

> **Interpretation 2:** From *A History of Britain* by Simon Schama, 2000.
>
> Whatever heat had been generated between the king and queen had gone through a prolonged cooling-off […]. Although he paid his queen all due respect in public, the king made little effort to hide his disappointment that the Spanish princess, whose fruitfulness had been so heavily advertised, had proved incapable of providing a male heir.

Did you know?

These features contain interesting additional information that adds depth to your knowledge. Some are useful, some are just fun!

> **Did you know?**
>
> One of the most important pilgrimage sites was Walsingham in Norfolk. It was believed that a vision of Mary, the mother of Jesus, had appeared there in 1061.

What have you learned?

In the middle and at the end of each chapter you'll find pages designed to help you reflect on the chapter as a whole and think about what you have studied in a more analytical way.

There is also a **quick quiz** at the end of each chapter, ideal for checking your knowledge of the whole chapter. The answers are supplied at the end of the book.

Writing Historically

Alongside the 'What have you learned?' sections are pages to help you improve your writing skills. These include simple techniques you can use to help you write better, clearer and more focused answers to historical questions. Many of these pages embed skills you'll need for GCSE.

> ## Pearson Progression Scale
>
> The Pearson Progression Scale has been used to determine the difficulty of content as students progress through the course and to provide coherent differentiation. Where questions are aimed at a particular Step on the Pearson Progression Scale, we have added a small icon to indicate the Step. This gives an idea of how hard the question is – the higher the Step, the harder the question:
>
> 1 Look at Source A. What do buildings such as these suggest about the Catholic Church?
>
> 2 Look at Source B. Explain why many people criticised the sale of indulgences.
>
> We have used another icon to indicate where skills relevant to GCSE are being developed. This example indicates that the content is moving students towards being able to answer GCSE-style inference questions:
>
>
> Inference questions

Tudor to 1900 Timeline

Edward V:
1483
(April to June)

Richard III:
1483–1485

Henry VII:
1485–1509

Edward VI:
1547–1553

Henry VIII:
1509–1547

Mary I:
1553–1558

Elizabeth I:
1558–1603

James I:
1603–1625

Charles I:
1625–1649

Charles II:
1660–1685

William III:
1689–1702

Mary II:
1689–1694

James II:
1685–1688

Monarchs

| AD 1485 | AD 1500 | | AD 1600 | |

Events

1559
Act of Supremacy

1517
Martin Luther pins
95 theses to the
door of Wittenberg
castle church

1530
Henry VIII makes
tennis popular and
builds a tennis
court at Hampton
Court Palace

1536–1540
Destruction of
the monasteries

1534
Act of
Supremacy

1605
Gun-powder
Plot

1588
Spanish
Armada

1642–1651
English
Civil War

1649
Execution of
Charles I

1649–1660
The Common-
wealth of
England

1688
Gloriou
Revolutio

1666
Great Fire
of London

1665
Great Plague
of London

1662
Long, curly
wigs become
fashionable
for men

1660
Restoration of
the monarchy

1684
Alice
Molland is
hanged in
Exeter, the
last person
executed for
witchcraft in
Britain

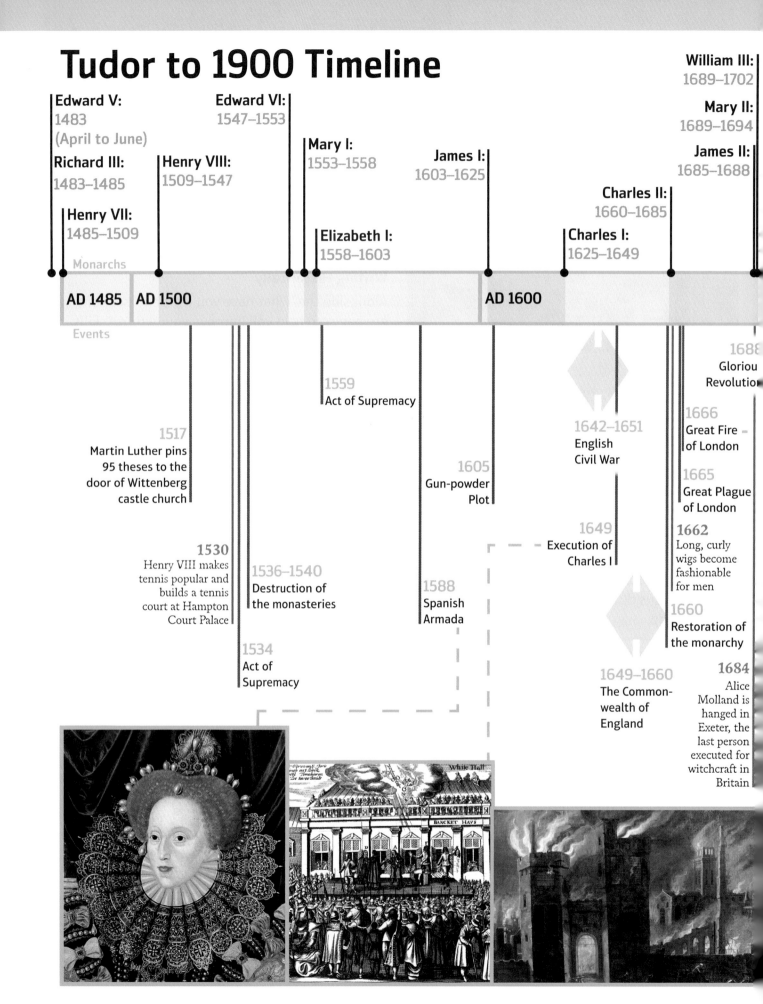

Anne:
1702–1714

George I:
1714–1727

George II:
1727–1760

George III:
1760–1820

George IV:
1820–1830

William IV:
1830–1837

Victoria:
1837–1901

AD 1700

AD 1800

AD 1900

1833
Slavery
Abolition
Act

1857
Indian rebellion
against the East
India Company

1685–1815
The Enlightenment

1760–1840
Industrial
Revolution

1776
Thirteen colonies
declare independence

1823
The sport
of rugby is
invented at
Rugby School

1851
Great
Exhibition

1718
Ice cream is
invented

1804
Invention
of the
steam train

1764
Invention of the
spinning jenny by
James Hargreaves
in Lancashire
allows faster
spinning of cotton
for weaving cloth

1807
Abolition of
the Slave Trade
Act 1807

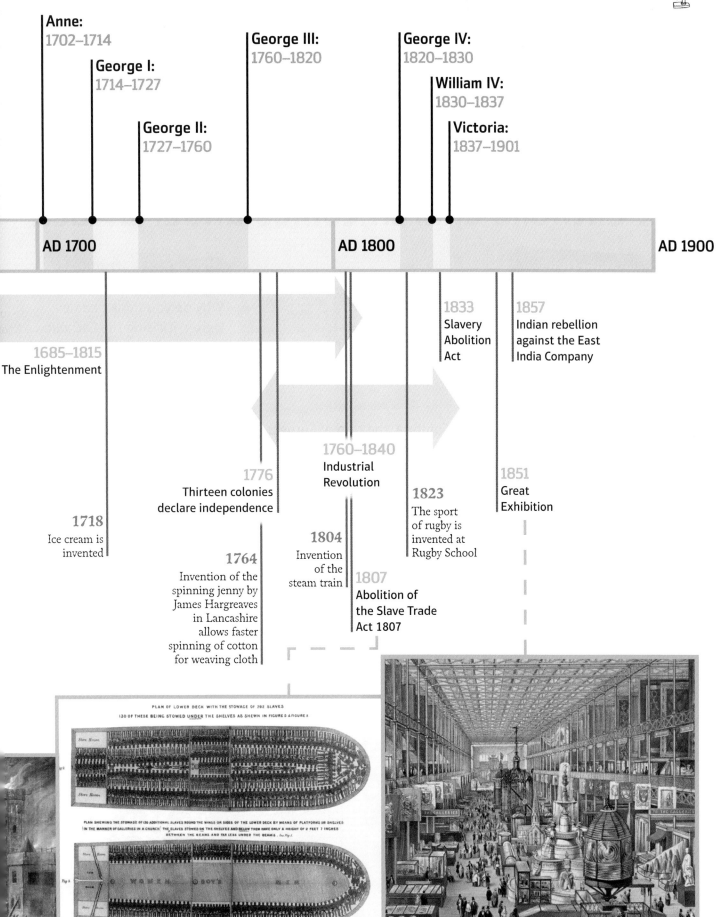

Was the Reformation 'a good thing'?

In the 16th century, the power of the Church came under attack. This led to one of the most important and turbulent periods in history – the Reformation. This section of the book will look at:

- why people became increasingly critical of the Catholic Church in the 16th century
- who Martin Luther was, and why he was important
- how these criticisms led to the European Reformation.

The Catholic Church comes under attack

Learning objectives

- Understand the criticisms of the Catholic Church that were being made in the 16th century.
- Know who Martin Luther was, and his role in the Reformation.

What do you think?

Why do you think people were criticising the Catholic Church? Think back to what you have already learned.

Key term

Abbot*: The head of an abbey.
Relic*: Part of the body or clothing of a holy person.

In Cumbria, the ruin of Furness Abbey can be found near the town of Barrow-in-Furness in Cumbria. Much of the abbey has long since disappeared. There is no roof, vegetation grows on the walls, and stairs lead to nowhere. However, you can still sense what a grand and important building this once was as you walk around the ruins.

In 2012, archaeologists discovered at the site the grave of a former abbot*, who probably died during the 12th century. They found the remains of the abbot's golden staff and a ring, which at one time may have contained a fragment of a holy relic*. The abbot must have been a very rich and powerful man.

At the time of the abbot's death, Furness Abbey was one of many rich monasteries in England. The Catholic Church was richer and more powerful than ever. People tried to avoid the agonies of purgatory through praying to saints, and going on pilgrimages to worship holy relics.

Within a few hundred years, however, many of the most sacred pilgrimage sites in England had been destroyed, with precious relics and statues of saints smashed and scattered. England seemed to have abandoned Catholicism.

Source A: The ruins of Furness Abbey, Cumbria.

Why were people criticising the Catholic Church?

By the start of the 16th century, there was growing criticism of the Catholic Church across Europe, not only from those who attended services, but also from some priests. Figure 1.1 contains a summary of some of the doubts that people had about the Church.

Key term

Heretic*: A person with religious views that disagree with official Church teaching.

Why are ordinary people forbidden from reading the Bible, and why must the Bible and all of the church services be in Latin, when few people understand it?

The rich can pay to remove their sins, no matter how bad they are, through buying indulgences. This doesn't seem right.

People are getting carried away with superstitious nonsense such as worshipping statues. This has nothing to do with the worship of God.

Why is the Church so rich when so many people are so poor? It doesn't say in the Bible that we should worship God by building palaces for bishops!

The taxes the Church asks us to pay are too high and we can't afford them as well as feeding and clothing our families.

Figure 1.1: Criticisms of the Catholic Church in the 16th century.

At the time, speaking such doubts aloud could lead to harsh punishments, including execution as a heretic*. As the new century progressed, however, these criticisms intensified, particularly over the issue of **indulgences**.

Indulgences were sold by the Catholic Church, and allowed the holder to reduce their time in purgatory, for a fee. The invention of the printing press around 1440 meant that copies of indulgences could be cheaply and easily produced. Many people were critical of these indulgences, including a German priest called Martin Luther.

Your turn!

1 Look at Source A. What do buildings such as these suggest about the Catholic Church?

2 Look at Source B. Explain why many people criticised the sale of indulgences.

3 What sort of changes do you think people would have liked the Catholic Church to make? Discuss this and jot down some examples.

Source B: A woodcut by Hans Holbein the Younger in the early 16th century, showing the sale of indulgences in a German marketplace.

Martin Luther and the '95 theses'

Key terms

Basilica*: A type of building, usually a church, given special status by the pope.

Dominican friar*: Monk following the rule of St Dominic. Friars were monks who could travel around, instead of staying in a monastery.

Reformation*: A movement in the 16th century which led to the founding of Protestantism. A Protestant is a type of Christian whose beliefs are different from those of the Catholic Church.

In 1516, the basilica* of St Peter's in Rome, which was considered one of the most holy buildings in Christendom, needed rebuilding. Johann Tetzel, a German Dominican friar*, was dispatched back to his homeland with indulgences to try to raise money for the work.

Source C gives an example of what supposedly happened when one person purchased one of these indulgences.

Source C: Description of an incident involving Johann Tetzel, written by Martin Luther and published in the early 16th century.

After Tetzel had received a substantial amount of money at Leipzig [a city in Saxony], a nobleman asked him if it were possible to receive a letter of indulgence for a future sin. Tetzel quickly answered [yes], insisting, however, that the payment had to be made at once. This the nobleman did, receiving thereupon letter and seal from Tetzel. When Tetzel left Leipzig the nobleman attacked him along the way, gave him a thorough beating, and sent him back empty-handed to Leipzig with the comment that this was the future sin which he had in mind. Duke George [of Saxony] at first was quite furious about this incident, but when he heard the whole story he let it go without punishing the nobleman.

Interpretation 1: A 19th-century engraving of Luther pinning his '95 theses' to the door of All Saints' Church in Wittenberg, Germany.

The reaction of Martin Luther

Many were angry at what they saw as the latest abuse of power by the Catholic Church. In 1517, in the university town of Wittenberg, a professor of theology, Martin Luther, approached the heavy doors of All Saints' Church and nailed a piece of paper to the door. This piece of paper became known as the '95 theses' and was to prove one of the most explosive documents in history. It would help to set in motion the Reformation* and change many countries forever.

Who was Martin Luther?

Martin Luther was a former monk who, by 1517, was Professor of Theology at the University of Wittenberg. He had become deeply disillusioned with the Catholic Church, and began to argue that salvation* could not be achieved through indulgences, charity or the worship of relics. In Luther's mind, only God had the power to grant absolution*.

These doubts led Luther to post his famous '95 theses' (see Source D), which summarised many of his criticisms of the Catholic Church.

> **Source D:** Extracts from Luther's '95 theses', 1517.
>
> 32. Those who believe that they can be certain of their salvation because they have indulgence letters will be eternally damned, together with their teachers.
>
> 62. The true treasure of the church is the most holy gospel of the glory and grace of God.
>
> 86. Why does not the pope […] build the basilica of St. Peter with his own money rather than with the money of poor believers?

Source E: A portrait of Martin Luther, painted by Lucas Cranach the Elder, c.1532.

Although the '95 theses' were only meant to reform the Catholic Church, they were to have devastating consequences. The existence of the prinitng press meant that copies were widely read meant that copies were widely read. German peasants, inspired by Luther's words, revolted against their Catholic rulers. As a result, the pope branded Martin Luther a heretic and he was excommunicated* in 1521. Some German princes sided with the peasants, leading to a civil war in which thousands of peasants died. The revolt ultimately failed, but Luther's ideas spread and soon Protestant rulers across a large proportion of Europe were inspired to denounce Catholicism, resulting in the Protestant Reformation.

Key terms

Salvation*: Deliverance from sin and its consequences.

Absolution*: The forgiving of a person's sins.

Excommunicated*: Cut off or banished from a religious group, in this case, the Catholic Church.

Your turn!

1 What does the story in Source C suggest about why people were criticising the Catholic Church and the practice of indulgences?

2 What criticisms does Luther make of the Catholic Church in Source D, and why? How did Luther believe people could achieve 'salvation'?

3 Luther wrote the description in Source C. How might this affect how you would treat it as a source?

Checkpoint

1 List two criticisms made of the Catholic Church in the 16th century.

2 Who was Martin Luther?

3 What were the '95 theses'?

4 List two consequences of Luther's actions.

What were the major events of the Reformation?

Learning objectives

- Gain an understanding of the chronological order of events from 1381 to 1603.
- Be aware of some of the most significant events in this time period and what caused them.

You have now had an introduction to the events that helped to trigger the Reformation. It is a fascinating, tragic and often moving story that still impacts our lives today. To help you to understand all the different twists and turns, it will be useful to gain an overview of the topic first.

Timeline

Medieval

Tudor – Henry VIII

1381 – The Peasants' Revolt
The peasants try to rebel against the king, but the rebellion is crushed and its leaders are executed.

1455–85 – The Wars of the Roses
Disputes over the leadership of Henry VI lead to a civil war in which the rival houses of Lancaster and York fight each other for the throne of England. The wars end in 1485 when Richard III is killed in battle and Henry VII becomes king. He unites the two warring houses by marrying Elizabeth of York in 1486, founding the Tudor dynasty.

1509 – Henry VIII becomes king
After the death of his father, Henry VIII becomes king of England. He marries Catherine of Aragon, widow of his brother Arthur.

1517 – The '95 theses'
Martin Luther nails his criticisms of the Catholic Church to the church door in Wittenberg, starting the European Reformation and Protestantism.

1524–31 – Religious wars break out in Europe
Wars break out in Germany (1524–25) and Switzerland (1529–31) between Protestants and those who want to defend the Catholic Church.

1528–33 – Henry ends his marriage
Henry and Catherine fail to produce a male heir. He asks the pope for an annulment so that he can marry Anne Boleyn. The pope refuses. Henry declares his marriage illegitimate and marries Anne Boleyn.

1534 – Act of Supremacy
Henry declares himself head of the new Protestant Church of England and breaks with the Catholic Church.

1536 – Destruction of the monasteries
Henry begins to close down and destroy monasteries. By 1540, all are closed.

Figure 1.2: A timeline explaining the major events of the European and English Reformations, 1381–1605.

Change questions

Your turn!

1 Choose five of the most significant dates from the timeline in Figure 1.2. Remember, this section is about the religious Reformation, so try to pick those that are about religious change or causes of religious change.

2 Looking at the timeline, discuss the points below.
   a What was the biggest change during this time period?
   b What appears to have caused the change? Was it driven by certain individuals or by other factors?
   Write up your answers in a short paragraph.

3 Why was there so much change in the 16th century? Why did these changes not happen earlier, or later? Discuss this with a partner, and bullet point some of your ideas.

Tudor – Edward VI and Mary I	Tudor – Elizabeth I	Stuart – James I

Tudor – Edward VI and Mary I

1547–52 – The Reformation accelerates
King Edward VI introduces radical new changes to the English Church, making it more Protestant.

1553 – Edward dies, Mary becomes queen
Lady Jane Grey is proclaimed queen but loses support after only nine days. Mary becomes queen amid scenes of jubilation.

1553–58 – Return to Catholicism
Mary reintroduces Catholicism. 300 people are burned at the stake for refusing to accept the changes.

1558 – Death of Mary, succession of Elizabeth
Mary has no children with her husband Philip II of Spain and dies with no direct heir. Mary's half-sister Elizabeth is declared queen.

Tudor – Elizabeth I

1558–59 – Elizabethan Religious Settlement
Elizabeth tries to steer a 'middle way' by keeping some Catholic and Protestant traditions.

1568 – Start of the 'Eighty Years War' in the Low Countries
Dutch Protestants rebel against the rule of Catholic Spain, beginning a struggle that lasts for decades. Elizabeth is pressured to intervene.

1587 – Mary, Queen of Scots is executed
Elizabeth feels increasingly threatened by Mary, who is a Catholic rival to the throne. After years of imprisonment, Mary is beheaded.

1588 – The Spanish Armada
The Spanish attempt to invade England. The invasion fails.

Stuart – James I

1605 – The Gunpowder Plot
A group of Catholics attempt to blow up parliament to kill the king. The attempt fails, and the plotters are horribly executed.

1618–48 – The 'Thirty Years War'
Fighting breaks out in Europe between Catholic and Protestant states, resulting in millions of casualties.

What was religion in England like before the Reformation?

To understand change, you need to know what things were like both before and after the change. You may have already learned about the medieval Catholic Church – Figure 1.3 provides a quick recap.

The pope
The pope is the leader of the Catholic Church and of all Christians in Europe. He is considered to be God's representative on Earth, and more powerful than any monarch.

The afterlife
The Church teaches that life continues after death, and that people will be sent to purgatory if they have not made amends for their sins.

Church services
Churches are richly decorated and services are at the centre of people's lives, celebrating baptisms, marriages, funerals and holy days.

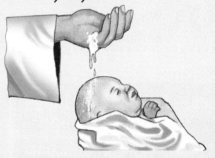

Mass
The most holy service in the Catholic Church. People believe the bread and wine actually turns into the body and blood of Christ – a process known as transubstantiation*.

Charity
Good works are believed to help a person get to heaven, so people help the poor and leave money in their wills to build hospitals.

The Bible
Ordinary people are forbidden from reading the Bible, which is written only in Latin.

Monasteries
Communities of monks and nuns exist to praise God. They also look after the poor and sick, and educate people.

Saints and relics
People have a strong belief in the power of saints. They are worshipped and shrines, often containing relics, are built to honour them.

Indulgences
People can pay to have their time in purgatory reduced through buying indulgences.

Figure 1.3: The Catholic Church before the Reformation.

Key term

Transubstantiation*: A belief held by Catholics that, when a priest blesses the bread and wine during mass, they transform into the physical body and blood of Christ.

Did you know?

One of the most important pilgrimage sites was Walsingham in Norfolk. It was believed that a vision of Mary, the mother of Jesus, had appeared there in 1061.

Power, wealth and influence

The Catholic Church was very rich and powerful. Everyone had to pay a tax to the Church, known as a tithe. However, unlike almost everyone else in England, the Church did not have to pay taxes. This meant that the Church was extremely rich – richer even than the king. The taxes it received helped to fund the monasteries. There were many of these throughout England and, as well as worshipping God, monks also farmed land, educated people, and looked after the poor and the sick.

Church appearance

English churches were much more colourful at the start of the 16th century than they appear today. Interpretation 2 shows a recreation of how a French cathedral looked in medieval times. It is likely that most cathedrals in England would have looked like this too.

At the start of the 16th century, few could have foreseen the violent changes to come. Within a few decades, many of the familiar features of the Catholic Church would be swept away forever.

Interpretation 1: Peterborough Cathedral. Before the Reformation, this was one of the richest monasteries in England and was home to 120 monks.

Key features questions

Your turn!

1 Create a concept map of the main features of the Catholic Church at the start of the 16th century. Include sections on beliefs, avoiding purgatory, monasteries, church appearance and services.

2 Imagine a time traveller from our time were to go back to England at the start of the 16th century. What would they need to know and understand about the role of the Catholic Church at the time to fit in? Design a leaflet giving them advice on the features you covered in your concept map.

Checkpoint

1 Why was the pope so powerful in medieval times?
2 What was 'transubstantiation'?
3 What role did saints play in people's lives?
4 Give two ways in which people's lives were connected with the Catholic Church.

Interpretation 2: A recreation of the exterior of Amiens Cathedral in France as it would have appeared in the 13th century.

What was the king's 'Great Matter'?

Learning objectives

- Understand the reasons why Henry VIII wanted to end his marriage.
- Know what decisions were made to enable Henry to marry Anne Boleyn.
- Understand the consequences that Henry's actions had for England.

By 1528, Henry VIII was deeply unhappy and frustrated. On the surface, the king had much to be proud of. Since becoming king and the second Tudor monarch in 1509, his armies had triumphed over the French and the Scots in battle, resulting in an uneasy peace.

In 1521, Henry, a devout Catholic, had been disturbed enough by the criticisms of the Catholic Church and the rise of Protestantism to write a book criticising Luther and giving his support to the Catholic Church. The book, entitled *Defence of the Seven Sacraments*, earned him the title 'Defender of the Faith' from the pope. Source A gives an idea of what Henry thought of the ideas of Luther.

> **Source A:** From Henry VIII's book, *Defence of the Seven Sacraments*, published in 1521. In this extract, Henry is criticising Martin Luther.
>
> [He] is ashamed of nothing, fears none, and thinks himself under no law. [He] condemns the ancient [ideas] of the church, and [criticises] the new ones [...]. Finally, he so undervalues customs, doctrine, manners, laws, decrees and faith of the church (yea, the whole church itself) that he almost denies there is any such thing as a church, except perhaps such a one as himself makes up of two or three heretics, of whom himself is chief.

Henry appeared to be ruling England as a devout Catholic, as his predecessors had for hundreds of years.

Despite such success and popularity, Henry was unhappy. The root of this unhappiness was an issue that has troubled monarchs for centuries – that of ensuring they had a male heir. Although Henry had been married to his wife, Catherine of Aragon, for almost 20 years, they still did not have a son.

Henry's attempt to find a solution to this issue was to have huge consequences for the future of England.

Source B: Portrait of the young Henry VIII, c.1520, painted by an unknown artist.

Henry's marriage to Catherine of Aragon

Henry was never intended to become king. Instead, his elder brother Arthur, as the Prince of Wales*, should have inherited the throne. In preparation for his role, Arthur had married Catherine of Aragon in 1501. As daughter of the king and queen of Spain, and a devout Catholic, she seemed like an ideal match. Unfortunately, Arthur was struck down by illness and died. Henry became king instead, and decided to marry Arthur's widow, Catherine, in 1509.

Initially, their marriage appears to have been relatively happy. However, Catherine was not able to give Henry the male heir that he desired, although she had given birth to a healthy baby girl – the future Mary I. By the 1520s, it was clear that the queen was past childbearing age and Catherine fell out of favour.

Henry had already been unfaithful to Catherine, and in 1519 his mistress, Elizabeth Blount, had given birth to a healthy boy. Unfortunately, as the child was illegitimate, Henry was unable to name him as his successor.

Henry now became increasingly obsessed by one of Catherine's ladies-in-waiting – Anne Boleyn.

> **Interpretation 2:** From *A History of Britain* by Simon Schama, 2000.
>
> Whatever heat had been generated between the king and queen had gone through a prolonged cooling-off […]. Although he paid his queen all due respect in public, the king made little effort to hide his disappointment that the Spanish princess, whose fruitfulness had been so heavily advertised, had proved incapable of providing a male heir.

Key term

Prince of Wales*: Since the 13th century, this title has been given to the eldest son of the monarch, who is the heir to the throne.

Interpretation 1: Portrait of Catherine of Aragon, painted by an unknown artist in the early 18th century.

Your turn!

1 Draw a flow chart showing the events that led Henry to seek a divorce. Start with Arthur's marriage to Catherine.

5th 2 What does Interpretation 2 suggest about why Henry became unhappy in his marriage to Catherine of Aragon?

6th 3 Pick a phrase that Simon Schama has used to suggest that Henry's marriage to Catherine had broken down.

Henry attempts to have his marriage annulled

Henry became besotted with Anne Boleyn. By 1526, he was writing love letters to Anne, such as the one quoted in Source C.

Source C: Extract from a love letter written by Henry VIII to Anne Boleyn, 1526.

Seeing I cannot be present in person with you, I send you the nearest thing to that possible, that is, my picture set in bracelets... wishing myself in their place, when it shall please you.

Henry now began to look for ways to end his marriage to Catherine of Aragon, in the hope that marriage to Anne Boleyn could provide him with the male heir he wanted. Henry, who was a keen scholar of the Bible, became obsessed with a section of the Bible that seemed to support this theory (see Source E).

Source E: Extract from the Old Testament of the Bible, (Leviticus Chapter 20 Verse 16).

If a man shall take his brother's wife, it is an impurity; he hath uncovered his brother's nakedness; they shall be childless.

Source D: Portrait of Anne Boleyn, painted by an unknown artist in the 16th century.

As a result, Henry began to argue that Catherine's pregnancy problems were a punishment from God for the sin of marrying his brother's widow, and that his marriage was both sinful and illegal. Whether Henry really believed this, or whether he was just looking for ways to secure his succession, is for you to decide!

Henry told Cardinal Thomas Wolsey, the pope's representative in England and one of the most powerful people in Henry's court, to convince the pope of the rightfulness of his argument and persuade him to grant Henry an annulment* of his marriage to Catherine. Henry argued that, as his marriage was not legal, he did not need a divorce.

Henry's attempts to convince Pope Clement VII to grant him an annulment could not have come at a worse time. In 1527, Rome had been invaded and plundered by the troops of the Holy Roman Empire, and the pope was essentially a prisoner of the emperor, Charels V – Catherine's nephew. The pope was hardly likely to grant Henry an annulment under such circumstances.

Key term

Annulment*: Declaration that something is invalid.

Henry breaks with Rome

In 1529, Cardinal Wolsey held an inquiry to examine the legality of Henry's marriage before representatives of the pope. Catherine of Aragon made a moving speech criticising Henry's attempts to end their marriage, which so embarrassed Henry that he stripped Wolsey of his power and accused him of treason. Wolsey died before he could be executed.

Henry then came under the influence of some of his advisers, including Thomas Cromwell and Thomas Cranmer, the future Archbishop of Canterbury. They persuaded the king to embrace the Protestant faith, reject the pope and appoint himself as the head of a new, independent Church in England. It is easy to see how taking control of the power and wealth of the Church in England would have been very appealing to Henry.

In 1534, parliament passed the Act of Supremacy* which declared that Henry was the Supreme Head of the Church of England. Henry married Anne Boleyn and ignored the protests of the pope.

Interpretation 3: Painting of Catherine of Aragon's appeal before representatives of the pope at Blackfriars, London in 1529. The painting was made between 1846 and 1848.

Interpretation 4: From *The Reformation* by Patrick Collinson, 2005.

[…] no Reformation [would have occurred] if Henry's first wife, Catherine of Aragon, had borne him several healthy sons, or even just one. Henry's need to be released from a marriage that could not provide him with a male heir was the cause […] of a religious revolution […].

Key term

Act of Supremacy*: An act passed by parliament in 1534 which made Henry and his successors Supreme Head of the Church of England. It was abolished by Queen Mary and a new Act of Supremacy was passed under Elizabeth I in 1559.

Your turn!

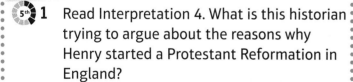

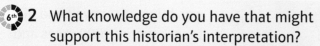

1   Read Interpretation 4. What is this historian trying to argue about the reasons why Henry started a Protestant Reformation in England?

2   What knowledge do you have that might support this historian's interpretation?

3   Do you think Henry was motivated more by religious or political issues to start a Protestant Reformation in England? Explain your reasons.

Checkpoint

1   Why did the pope name Henry 'Defender of the Faith' in 1521?

2   Make a cause and effect diagram showing what factors led Henry to break with Rome, and what impact that had.

3   What did Henry VIII do that allowed him to end his marriage?

4   Write a speech from Henry explaining why he made himself Head of the Church of England.

What impact did Henry's decision have on England?

Although Henry had managed to end his marriage, he pressed ahead with changes to the Catholic Church, with the help of Thomas Cromwell and Thomas Cranmer. As a result, the Protestant Reformation was taken further than perhaps even Henry intended. The clergy and the nobility were forced to swear an oath of allegiance to Henry, supporting his changes. Those who refused were executed. Most agreed to swear the oath.

Inspecting the monasteries

Soon, the attentions of Henry and Cromwell turned towards perhaps the richest prize of all – the monasteries of England. There were compelling reasons for Henry to destroy them. Not only were monks some of the most loyal servants of the pope, and therefore most likely to stand in the way of the Reformation, but the monasteries were also extremely rich. Some people were critical of the monasteries, arguing that they had strayed too far from their original purpose of allowing monks to praise God and live simple lives, and were instead simply business enterprises filled with sin and corruption.

As Henry wanted an excuse to destroy the monasteries, he sent Cromwell with a team of inspectors to report on the activities of many of the most important monastic houses in England. The scope of the survey was huge – Cromwell and his team covered 1000 miles and visited 121 religious houses. The evidence that they compiled was damning (see Source A).

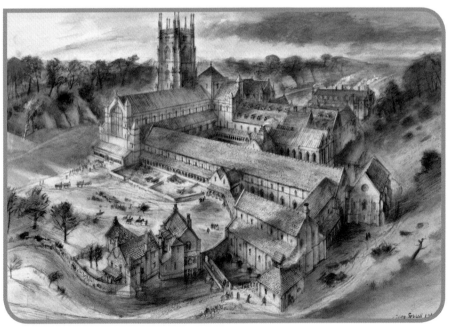

Interpretation 1: A reconstruction of how Fountains Abbey in Yorkshire might have looked before its destruction.

Although some of the report may have been exaggerated, it served its purpose. Parliament was shocked, and in 1536 passed an Act that paved the way to destroy the monasteries. From 1536 to 1540, 800 monasteries were closed through a combination of intimidation, violence and generous retirement offers, and their land was sold off at bargain prices. A thousand years of monastic life in England were coming to an end.

Interpretation 2: The ruins of Fountains Abbey, as they appear today.

Key term

Coffer*: A strong box used to store money or valuable items.

> **Source A:** Extracts from the report to Henry VIII, in 1535. Each name (for example, Lichfield) refers to a monastic house.
>
> Lichfield: 'two of the nuns were with child'
>
> Bradley: 'prior hath six children'
>
> Abbotsbury: 'abbot wrongfully selling timber'
>
> Pershore: 'monks drunk at mass'

> **Interpretation 3:** From *A History of Britain* by Simon Schama, 2000.
>
> For the tens of thousands of men and women [living in the monasteries and] cast out into the world, what happened in 1536 and the years that followed was no joke [...]. Priories [...] were offered at bargain prices, and [...] former residents were soon forgotten or reduced to family legends of headless nuns and spectral monks. And by filling the Crown's coffers* with the proceeds, the dissolution gave Henry the [money] to stand up to the worst that the Catholic powers could throw at him.

Your turn!

1 Draw a flow chart summing up the chain of events from the Act of Supremacy to the final destruction of the monasteries.

2 What caused these changes? Was it just Henry's actions, or were other factors involved? Explain your answer.

3 Explain in your own words why many people consider the dissolution of the monasteries to be such an important change in English history. Think about the role the monasteries had performed for hundreds of years.

What were the consequences of the Reformation in England?

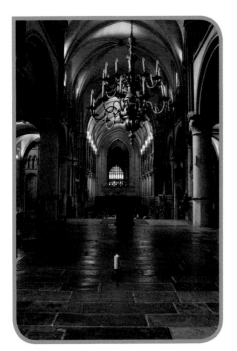

Interpretation 4: A candle marks the spot where the shrine to Thomas Becket stood in Canterbury Cathedral.

One historian estimates that no more than two per cent of the population of England were Protestant by the time of the 1534 Act of Supremacy. However, the changes Henry had unleashed began to have a great impact on ordinary people.

How did Henry change England?

Many of the most holy sites of pilgrimage in England were destroyed. Saint Thomas Becket, who had been made a saint after his murder by Henry II's knights in 1170, was branded a traitor in a trial. His shrine, one of the richest and most important in Europe, was destroyed. Becket's bones were dug up, burned in the centre of Canterbury, and the ashes were shot into the air from a large cannon.

Henry also made some important changes to church services. A copy of the Bible, translated into English, was to be placed in every church, so that anyone could read it. Superstitious practices, such as kneeling before images of saints, were forbidden and a new English litany* was published in 1545.

However, in other ways Henry seemed to want to hang on to aspects of the Catholic faith.

- People were still encouraged to say prayers for the dead.

- Henry ruled that the ceremony of transubstantiation was real and ordered that anyone who denied it was to be burned alive.

- Thomas Cromwell fell out of favour and was executed as a heretic on 28 July 1540.

- Henry changed his mind about allowing the people to read the Bible in English.

Interpretation 5: From *Tudors* by Peter Ackroyd, 2013.

The evidence suggests that [Henry] died, as he had lived, a Catholic. His will [called on] 'the name of God and of the glorious and blessed virgin our Lady Saint Mary'; he also ordered that daily Masses be said, as long as the world endured, for the salvation of his soul. That is not the language of a Lutheran. It suggests, although it does not prove, that the king still believed in the existence of purgatory despite the denial of it in his own religious articles.

Henry, overweight and suffering from various illnesses, died on 28 January 1547. Even Henry's wishes after his death suggest a man conflicted about the religious changes he had instigated, as Peter Ackroyd discusses in Interpretation 5.

The Reformation accelerates under Edward

With Henry's death, his son Edward became King Edward VI. Although the new king was only nine years old, he was a devout Protestant and had strong ideas about religion. His reforms went much further than those of his father, and began to have more of an impact on ordinary people.

- Clergymen were instructed to criticise the pope in church and to preach the works of Martin Luther.

- The Book of Common Prayer, published in 1549, became the first prayer book to contain prayers and services exclusively in English.

- The idea of transubstantiation was rejected and the Catholic Mass was replaced by Communion, a ceremony in which the bread and wine were regarded as purely symbolic.

- The appearance of churches became much plainer. Ornate screens, stained glass windows and colourful images of saints were removed and destroyed.

Source B: Portrait of Edward VI, painted in 1546 while he was Prince of Wales.

Your turn!

1 What does Interpretation 5 suggest about Henry's beliefs? Does this indicate that Henry was more in favour of change or continuity?

2 Explain why Henry changed the Church if he still had strong Catholic beliefs. Give two reasons.

5th 3 Go back through the pages that cover this enquiry question. Draw a table with two columns headed 'Change' and 'Continuity'. Write examples of each in the correct column.

6th 4 What do you think was the biggest change of the Reformation period? Which change would have had the biggest impact on the greatest number of people?

Checkpoint

1 Give two reasons why Henry wanted to destroy the monasteries.
2 How did Henry manage to close down the monasteries? List two ways.
3 In what ways did Edward VI continue the Reformation?
4 In what ways had England become more Protestant by the end of Edward's reign in 1553? Give three examples.

Was the Reformation 'a good thing'?

In this section, you have learned about some of the most far-reaching and important changes that have ever happened in English history. But were the changes for the best? In small groups, role-play how each of the following people might have felt about the changes: a devoutly Catholic priest; a Protestant preacher who had previously been forced out of England; a woman parishioner who was used to worshipping images of saints; a monk who had spent his life in a monastery.

In this section, you have learned:

- why the Catholic Church was being criticised, and how this helped to cause the European Reformation

- why Henry VIII started the Reformation in England

- how England changed as a result of the Reformation.

Figure 1.4: How the interior of a church might have changed from the beginning of the 16th century to the reign of Edward VI.

How far did the Reformation change England?

The Reformation led to a great deal of change in England. Imagine someone who had grown up under the rule of Henry VII, and had lived long enough to see the changes made by Edward VI – a period of about 50 years. What would have been the main changes that they observed? What would have stayed the same? How would this have affected their lives?

One of the biggest changes would have been to people's local churches. As virtually everyone went to church in medieval and Tudor times, it would have been hard to ignore these changes. Figure 1.4 gives an example of the kind of changes people might have seen.

Your turn!

1 Look at Figure 1.4. Make a list of the main ways in which the interiors of churches changed during this period. Use your notes to answer this question: 'Describe two features of a Catholic Church in the early 16th century'. You will need to describe two features in detail.

2 Explain one way in which churches and/ or church services changed by comparing features in 1500 and 1553 (the end of Edward's reign). You should focus on one aspect and compare it in detail – for instance, the appearance of churches.

Writing historically

Change and continuity

There was a lot of change brought about by the Reformation, but it is rare for any time period only to have change. Instead, there is normally a mixture of change and continuity. Let's have a look at how you might answer the following question:

'Explain one way in which religion in 1553 was similar to religion in 1500.'

To answer this question, you will need to think about continuity. In some ways, this is trickier than thinking about change. The following are a few examples you could think about.

- Religion was still not a matter of choice. The church or government dictated what people should believe.

- People could still be horribly punished for challenging Church-approved religious ideas.

- Most people still went to church regularly and most people still had strong religious beliefs.

- Religion was seen as such an important matter that the king and parliament spent a long time debating religious matters.

- The Church still had a lot of power. Religious figures served in the government and helped to advise the king and run the country.

So, what might some answers to a question like this look like?

Student 1

In the 1500s, religion was very important. There were many churches, and the Church had a lot of money. People believed if you didn't go to church you would go to hell. People paid taxes to the Church called tithes. Henry changed the Church so that he could end his marriage and have a male heir. Edward was a Protestant and changed the Church too. People had to read the Bible in English and had to criticise the pope. A lot of people didn't like this.

This answer is accurate, but doesn't answer the question. Instead, it just describes aspects of the topic.

Student 2

Religion was similar in 1500 and 1553 as the Church was powerful. Most people were religious and went to church regularly. Therefore, the Church had a lot of influence over their lives.

This is better, as it answers the question, but it could be improved by giving some more specific examples from both time periods in order to make a comparison.

Student 3

Religion was similar in 1500 and 1553 as kings continued to tell the ordinary people what they should believe. In 1500, kings were Catholic, and expected their subjects to follow their beliefs, for example believing in saints and relics. Although by 1553 England had a Protestant king (Edward), he still expected people to follow his beliefs, for example by reading the Bible in English instead of in Latin.

This is a much better answer – it compares both time periods explicitly, and gives some relatively specific examples to make the comparison.

Now write an answer to the question 'Explain one way in which religion in 1553 was different from religion in 1500', using the guidance above.

Who won: Catholics or Protestants?

Henry's break with the Catholic Church started the Reformation and unleashed a tidal wave of change. Religious upheaval continued under his successors. Who had won – the Catholics or the Protestants? This section of the book will look at:

- the events of Mary's reign and how she tried to turn England back into a Catholic country

- Elizabeth's attempt at a religious compromise

- the attempts by the Spanish to invade England with the Armada and restore Catholicism

- the Gunpowder Plot to reinstate a Catholic monarch.

The Catholics strike back – Mary becomes queen

Learning objectives

- Understand how and why Mary tried to return England to Catholicism.
- Evaluate how successfully Elizabeth managed to pursue a 'middle way' in religion.

Source A: Portrait of Queen Mary I, painted in 1554 by Anthonis Mor.

By the summer of 1553, the 15-year-old Edward VI knew that he was dying. Edward and his advisers tried to protect the Protestant England they had created by naming Edward's protestant cousin, Lady Jane Grey as his successor instead of his Catholic half-sister, Mary. On 6 July 1553, the young King Edward died and Lady Jane Grey was declared queen. However, Mary was so popular that after only nine days Lady Jane Grey was forced to give up the throne. She was arrested and later executed for treason. Mary was declared queen of England instead.

Mary's primary aim was to return England to Catholicism. To do this, parliament passed an Act that overturned all the changes made during the reign of Edward. The following are some examples of the changes Mary made.

- There was a ban on Protestant preachers and the discussion of religious matters.

- The churches were returned to their Catholic appearance and the Latin Mass was reinstated.

- Those who denied transubstantiation were sentenced to death by burning.

- Mary appointed Cardinal Pole, a Catholic, as Archbishop of Canterbury.

However, a reconciliation with the pope was not going to be easy. The pope demanded the return of Church lands stolen during the Reformation, but things had simply gone too far for this to happen, with monasteries already in ruins and the land sold off to numerous different landowners.

'Bloody' Mary?

Mary soon set about rooting out 'heretics' with great ruthlessness. Protestants were burned to death for refusing to accept the Catholic faith. High-profile figures, such as the former Archbishop of Canterbury, Thomas Cranmer, and Bishops Latimer and Ridley, were put on trial and burned alive.

Although Mary had fought to return England to Catholicism, it is debatable how successful she really was, as Peter Ackroyd explains in Interpretation 1.

> **Interpretation 1:** From *Tudors: The History of England* by Peter Ackroyd, 2013.
>
> The only shrine to be restored was that of Edward the Confessor in Westminster Abbey, and in her reign Mary never went on pilgrimage. […] There was [little] interest in saints or in the Virgin. Little was said of purgatory. Mary remained the supreme head of the Church of England, and only lip service was paid to the doctrine of papal supremacy. It was pointed out at the time that almost half of the population was under the age of twenty and thus had never experienced papal domination. It simply could not be imposed once more.

By 1558, more pressing issues were at hand. The queen, who had failed to produce an heir, was clearly dying. She reluctantly named her Prostestant half-sister Elizabeth as her successor and died on 17 November.

Did you know?

During Mary's reign, 283 people were burned for heresy. This is more than all of the other Tudor monarchs combined.

Source B: An illustration from *Foxe's Book of Martyrs*, written by John Foxe and published in 1563. It shows the death by burning of Thomas Cranmer.

Your turn!

1 Draw a mind concept summing up the ways in which Mary aimed to make England into a Catholic country again.

2 Look at Source B and Interpretation 1. What can you learn from these sources about the events of Mary's reign?

3 Read Interpretation 1. What conclusion does Peter Ackroyd come to about:
   a how far Mary was able to 'turn back the clock' and make England Catholic again
   b the reasons why this was difficult.

4 Do you think Mary deserves her reputation as 'Bloody' Mary? What are the arguments for and against this interpretation?

Elizabeth's Religious Settlement

Elizabeth had inherited a nation that was deeply divided by the religious turmoil of the last 30 years. Although she had been raised as a Protestant, Elizabeth seemed to be less passionate about religious matters than either Edward or Mary. It is believed that she once said to a French ambassador 'There is only one Jesus Christ… the rest is a dispute over trifles'. Her own preferences on religion seemed decidedly mixed. She liked the choral music and the rituals of the Catholic Church, but hated the smell of incense and called herself a Protestant. She kept a gold crucifix in the royal chapel and disapproved of married priests.

Figure 1.5: The problems Elizabeth faced at the beginning of her reign.

Elizabeth had to tread carefully to solve these issues. There was probably no single solution that was going to please everyone. Instead, with parliament's assistance through the Act of Uniformity and Act of Supremacy in 1559, the following steps were taken.

- The religious laws from the time of Edward VI were to be reintroduced and services in English were to resume.

- Edward's Book of Common Prayer was to be reintroduced, in English, but with changes to avoid offending Catholics, such as removing an insulting reference to the pope.

- The queen appointed herself as the 'Supreme Governor' rather than 'Head' of the Church of England. All public officials had to swear an oath of loyalty to her as Supreme Governor.

- The issue of transubstantiation was left open to interpretation.

How far did Elizabeth succeed in her 'middle way'?

Elizabeth had tried hard to satisfy as many people as possible, with mixed success. Only one Catholic bishop swore the oath to Elizabeth. The rest refused and were sacked. However, only four per cent of local clergymen refused to swear the oath.

So, had Elizabeth been successful in ending the religious turmoil and navigating a 'middle way' for England? Interpretations 2 and 3 give modern views on this question.

> **Interpretation 2:** From *Tudors* by Peter Ackroyd, 2013.
>
> It was a very English settlement; it was practical […]; it brought together materials that might otherwise have been considered incompatible; it introduced compromise and toleration […]. Its very lack of clarity saved it. In London the reformers preached [Protestant ideas] […] while in York the [Catholic] faithful prayed still on their strings of beads [rosaries*]. 'The difference between Catholics and Lutherans', the queen told the Spanish ambassador, 'is not of much importance […]'.

> **Interpretation 3:** From *The Reformation* by Patrick Collinson, 2005.
>
> No doubt Elizabeth was some kind of Protestant. Her origins, her claim to the throne, her foreign diplomacy, all made that a necessity […]. But certainly not hot Protestant […]. She habitually used old-fashioned Catholic oaths such as 'By God's Body!' which curdled the blood of hot Protestants. She was attached to images that hot Protestants wanted to smash. But for her, it is likely that England['s] great cathedrals would have gone the same way as the monasteries, and with them the great tradition of English church music.

Your turn!

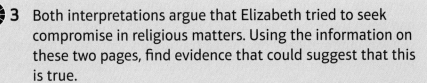

1 Create a concept map of the religious policies introduced by Elizabeth and parliament in 1559.

2 Read Interpretations 2 and 3. Pick quotes from each that suggest:
   a Elizabeth was not as devoutly religious as her predecessors
   b her religious reforms were successful.

3 Both interpretations argue that Elizabeth tried to seek compromise in religious matters. Using the information on these two pages, find evidence that could suggest that this is true.

Checkpoint

1 Name two ways in which Mary tried to make England Catholic again.

2 Why did Mary become known as 'Bloody' Mary?

3 Why was it difficult for Elizabeth to resolve England's religious problems? Give two reasons.

4 Name three changes Elizabeth made to England's religion.

How precarious was Protestant England?

Source A: Portrait of Philip II of Spain, painted c.1580.

In late July 1588, a huge fleet of 122 ships, arranged in a vast crescent formation, was spotted off the coast of Cornwall. The ships were part of what has become known as the Spanish Armada, the biggest ever invasion force up until that point, and the first serious attempt to invade England since the Norman Conquest.

The invasion force aimed to land an invading Catholic army, overthrow Queen Elizabeth and restore Catholicism to England's shores. The invasion had been launched by Philip II of Spain – Mary I's husband. How had relations between England and Spain become so bad?

What caused the tension between England and Spain?

Philip II of Spain, who had been married to Mary I, hoped to marry her half-sister Elizabeth. However, he was deeply unpopular in England and his offer was rejected.	In 1568, Spain sent soldiers into the Netherlands to crush a Protestant rebellion. Stories of Catholic atrocities reached England, putting pressure on Elizabeth to act.	Elizabeth sent English troops and money to support the Protestant rebels, angering Spain. In 1570, the pope promised heavenly rewards for anyone who assassinated Elizabeth.

Figure 1.6: Events leading to the Spanish Armada.

How did Catholics react to the Reformation in Europe?

During this time, the Catholic Church went through a period of change as it responded to the challenges of the Reformation. It made new efforts to enforce Catholic practices and force Protestants back to the Catholic faith. This was known as the Counter-Reformation*. In response to this, Elizabeth, who had previously been relatively tolerant towards Catholicism, began to persecute Catholics. From 1585, any English Catholic priest who had been trained abroad since 1559 and was found on English soil was automatically deemed a traitor and sentenced to death. Punishments for not attending Protestant services were increased to 20 pounds, a huge sum in those days.

Key term

Counter-Reformation*: Reforms to the doctrine and beliefs of the Catholic Church in response to the Protestant Reformation, starting in 1545. It also involved attempts to enforce Catholic practices and convert Protestants back to Catholicism.

The most important of the monastic orders were the Jesuits, who were organised along military lines and aggressively tried to convert people to Catholicism.

The education of priests was improved, since some did not even understand Latin.

England became a target for Jesuits keen to return Catholic influence. In 1580, the first Jesuits began to arrive in England.

New monastic orders were introduced in Europe to try and return monks to their original spiritual purpose.

Figure 1.7: How the Catholic Church responded to the Reformation.

Interpretation 1: From *Reformation: Europe's House Divided* 1490–1700 by Diarmaid MacCulloch, 2003.

In a decade between 1581 and 1590, seventy-eight priests and twenty-five laypeople were executed, with executions still numerous between 1590 and 1603: fifty-three priests and thirty-five laypeople. Seventy more priests were executed between 1601 and 1680. In fact England judicially murdered more Roman Catholics than any other country in Europe, which puts English pride in national tolerance in an interesting perspective.

Your turn!

1 Create a cause and effect diagram showing all of the reasons why England and Spain were drifting towards war by 1585. Try to include both long-term and short-term factors.

5th 2 Sum up what the historian in Interpretation 1 is arguing about the English treatment of Catholics.

6th 3 Explain why you think Elizabeth had abandoned her comparatively tolerant treatment of Catholics by the 1580s.

Mary, Elizabeth and a cauldron full of conspiracy

In the 1570s and 1580s, Elizabeth faced some of the biggest threats of her reign, from attempted assassinations to full-blown invasion attempts. Most of these centred around the figure of Mary, Queen of Scots. As Henry VIII's great-niece, Mary had a strong claim to the throne. Because Mary was Catholic, many English Catholics wanted to replace Elizabeth with Mary. It didn't help that Elizabeth had never married and so had no heir. The question of Elizabeth's succession became very important.

Mary had ruled Scotland together with her husband, Lord Darnley, but was implicated in his murder and forced to flee to England. Seeing her as a threat to the throne, Elizabeth imprisoned her for the next 18 years, during which time Mary became the centre of a string of conspiracies.

1571 – The Ridolfi Plot

The plotters: A Florentine banker, Roberto Ridolfi; the pope; Philip II of Spain; Elizabeth's cousin, the Duke of Norfolk; Mary, Queen of Scots.

The Plan: Ridolfi would try to raise support to land an army in England and provoke an uprising of Catholics. The Duke of Norfolk would then marry Mary, and they would seize the throne.

What happened: After a tip-off from spies, a courier was caught at Dover with incriminating letters. Norfolk was executed, but Ridolfi escaped abroad. Elizabeth allowed Mary to live.

1583 – The Throckmorton Plot

The plotters: An English Catholic, Francis Throckmorton; the Duke of Guise; possibly Mary, Queen of Scots; plus others.

The plan: Elizabeth was to be assassinated, while at the same time an invasion of England by the Duke of Guise aimed to inspire an uprising of Catholics and put Mary on the throne.

What happened: Throckmorton was arrested after Elizabeth's agents became suspicious. He confessed and was executed. The Spanish ambassador was told to leave. Elizabeth's court issued a symbolic Bond of Association in which they swore to protect her and vowed that no one, especially not Mary, should profit from her death.

1586 – The Babington Plot

The plotters: Charles Babington, a Catholic exile and former servant to Mary, Queen of Scots; possibly Mary herself.

The plan: To assassinate Elizabeth, free Mary and place her upon the throne.

What happened: Babington wrote to Mary proposing 'the dispatch of the usurping Competitor' (i.e. killing Elizabeth). Mary's reply was seized by agents and used as evidence of her guilt. Babington and other conspirators were executed. Under pressure from her advisers to end the threats against her, Elizabeth signed Mary's death warrant and, despite Mary's professions of innocence, she was executed on 8 February 1587.

Figure 1.8: Conspiracies against Elizabeth, 1571–86.

The Spanish Armada

In 1588, Elizabeth faced her biggest challenge yet – an attempted invasion of England.

Outraged by Elizabeth's interference in the Netherlands, her treatment of Mary, Queen of Scots and her persecution of Catholics, in 1586 Philip II of Spain orders an Armada (fleet) to be assembled. The plan is for the Armada to collect a Spanish army from the Netherlands and transport it to England to overthrow Elizabeth. In August 1588, the Armada sets sail.

The huge Armada is intercepted by English ships in the Channel, but it is too big and powerful for them to attack. Instead, English ships wait until night when the Spanish fleet is anchored and then launch burning fireships into the Spanish fleet. The terrified Spanish flee in disorder. The next day, the English attack them and inflict heavy losses.

The defeated Spanish fleet tries to sail for home. Unable to pass back through the Channel, the fleet tries to sail around Scotland and Ireland, but is caught in a storm in which many ships are wrecked. Only 10,000 of the 30,000 Spanish sailors who had departed returned home. The invasion had completely failed.

Figure 1.9: Events leading to the defeat of the Spanish Armada.

Elizabeth triumphed against the Spanish and survived the attempts on her life. Hopes of a Catholic England began to fade.

Interpretation 2: From an article on the History Extra website, by the historian Robert Hutchinson, 2016.

The failure of the Spanish Armada campaign of 1588 changed the course of European history. If the Duke of Parma's 27,000-strong invasion force had safely crossed the narrow seas from [the Netherlands] [and defeated Elizabeth] […] England would have reverted to the Catholic faith and there may have been no British empire*.

Key terms

Empire*: A group of states or countries ruled over by one monarch or government.

Your turn!

1   Some historians have argued that Elizabeth's ministers 'set up' Mary, Queen of Scots so that Elizabeth had to agree to her execution. Discuss why they might have wanted this.

5th 2   Read Interpretation 2. What does it suggest the consequences of a Spanish victory in 1588 might have been?

6th 3   Do you agree with Robert Hutchinson's interpretation? Do you think people in England would have welcomed a return of the Catholic Church at this point?

Checkpoint

1   Make a concept map of the main threats against Elizabeth up until 1588.

2   Why did many people see Mary, Queen of Scots as a serious contender for the English throne?

3   Why did the Spanish Armada's attempted invasion of England fail?

Why do people celebrate 'Bonfire night'?

Learning objectives

- Know why James I became king of England in 1603.
- Understand why some people were planning to kill the king.
- Assess the reasons for the failure of the Gunpowder Plot.

Many people take part in celebrations on 'Bonfire night'. Maybe you have wrapped up warm, watched the fireworks and stood around a bonfire. Perhaps you have even seen a 'guy' put on the fire. For many years, children in England made a model of a person and would ask for a 'penny for the guy', before putting the model onto a bonfire and burning it on 5 November. Why do we do it, what are we 'celebrating' and should we even celebrate it at all?

The end of the Tudors, and start of the Stuarts

Elizabeth I died on 24 March 1603, aged 69, after ruling for 44 years. As Elizabeth had no children, she had named James Stuart as her successor, and he became James I of England and James VI of Scotland, the first monarch of a new dynasty, the Stuarts.

Who was James I?

James was born in 1566 in Edinburgh, Scotland. He had a turbulent childhood – his father, Lord Darnley, was murdered in a conspiracy when James was only a few months old. His mother, Mary, Queen of Scots, was suspected of being involved in the conspiracy and was forced to flee to England, where she was imprisoned until her execution on the orders of Elizabeth I in 1587. James became king of Scotland at the age of one.

Scotland was ruled by regents* until James came of age. Although his mother had been Catholic, James was brought up as a Protestant. He proved to be an intelligent young man with a quick mind.

As James was the great-great-grandchild of Henry VII through Henry VIII's sister, Margaret, he was the legal heir to Elizabeth, and was crowned king of England and Scotland in 1603.

Key term

Regent*: A person appointed to rule, normally while a monarch is abroad, ill or too young to rule.

Figure 1.10: A guy on top of a bonfire on 'Bonfire night'.

What sort of king would James be?

The new king's reign was greeted with cautious optimism by many Catholics in England, who hoped for an end to the repressive laws and persecution that had been a feature of the last years of Elizabeth's reign. However, they were to be disappointed for the following reasons.

- James was a devout Protestant. He commissioned a new English translation of the Bible, known as the 'King James' Bible, which became the standard translation of the Bible for the next 250 years.

- James failed to end the fines for non-attendance at Church of England services, and instead expanded them.

- All Catholic priests were ordered to leave the country.

Source A: A 17th-century engraving showing Robert Catesby and the other key members of the 'Gunpowder Plot'.

Most Catholics were law-abiding citizens, and probably tried to do their best to walk the tightrope of remaining loyal to both their religion and their king at the same time. However, a small group of people, furious with James, began a plot that would become infamous in English history.

Who were the plotters, and what did they want?

A group of young Catholic gentlemen led by Robert Catesby met in London. They decided to assassinate James to allow his young daughter, Elizabeth, to take the throne. The method? To wait until James arrived at the palace of Westminster for the opening of parliament and then to blow the Houses of Parliament to pieces by exploding dozens of barrels of gunpowder, which they planned to hide in the cellar.

Catesby's cousin, Thomas Wintour, travelled to the Netherlands in the hope of enlisting Spanish support. Spain refused to become involved. However, Wintour did meet a young English mercenary and explosives expert, who agreed to join the plot. He referred to himself by the Spanish name 'Guido' Fawkes, which gave him the name by which he has become infamous – 'Guy' Fawkes.

Your turn!

1 Explain why James VI of Scotland became Elizabeth's successor in 1603.

5th 2 Make a flow chart explaining why Robert Catesby and his conspirators began plotting to kill the king. Start by explaining the hopes Catholics had at the time of James's coronation.

6th 3 Imagine you are one of the conspirators. Write a letter to a friend urging them to take part in the conspiracy. Remember to explain what you are angry about and what you are planning to achieve. Lastly, remember the letter could get you executed, so be careful!

How close did the plotters come to killing the king?

Step 1 – The plotters get into position

The plotters made careful plans to ensure success.

- Thomas Percy, a cousin of the Earl of Northumberland, used his influence to be appointed as a royal bodyguard. He had Guy Fawkes appointed as his servant, with the false name 'John Johnson'.

- Percy hired a cellar directly underneath the Houses of Parliament, while Catesby rented a house in Lambeth to store the 36 barrels of gunpowder, which were transferred secretly from Catesby's house to Percy's cellar.

- The attack was planned for 5 November, when the king was due to open parliament.

Step 2 – The Monteagle letter

On 26 October, a few days before the attack was due to go ahead, Lord Monteagle received a mysterious letter (see Source B).

> **Source B:** Extract from the letter to Lord Monteagle, received 26 October 1605.
>
> My lord, out of the love I bear to some of your friends, I have a care of your preservation, therefore I would advise you as you tender your life to devise some excuse to shift your attendance at this parliament, for God and man have concurred to punish the wickedness of this time […] they shall receive a terrible blow this parliament and yet they shall not see who hurts them […].

Alarmed by the letter, Monteagle showed it to the secretary of state, Robert Cecil, who passed it to the king. The king ordered the cellars under the Houses of Parliament to be searched.

Onthe night of the 4 November, the cellars were searched and the guards found a man calling himself 'John Johnson', along with a large store of firewood. 'John Johnson' told the guards the wood belonged to Thomas Percy. Suspicious, the guards investigated further and found 36 barrels of gunpowder placed directly underneath the chamber of the House of Lords. 'John Johnson' was found to have both matches and fuses on his person. He was placed under arrest.

The plan had failed. For the plotters, there was to be a dreadful retribution.

Figure 1.11: Guy Fawkes is arrested underneath the Houses of Parliament.

Step 3 – The plotters are rounded up

Guy Fawkes was taken to the Tower of London, where he was horribly tortured. Source C gives an indication of how Fawkes was affected by his brutal treatment. Broken, he confessed on 9 November. The other plotters fled to the Midlands but were surrounded at Holbeche House in Staffordshire, where a shoot-out ensued. Catesby and Percy were killed by one lucky shot, while the rest of the plotters were either killed or captured.

Step 4 – The punishment

In January 1606, the plotters were put on trial and found guilty of treason. They were sentenced to the harshest punishment possible – to be hanged, drawn and quartered. Later, James I ordered that bonfires should be lit on 5 November as a celebration. Models of the pope and Guy Fawkes were placed upon the fires and burned. The ceremony has survived almost unchanged up to the present day. The Gunpowder Plot was to be the last serious Catholic rebellion against the monarchy. Catholics were to face official discrimination for the next 200 years, and were banned from voting.

Source C: Guy Fawkes's signature before and after his torture on the rack.

Your turn!

1 Draw a flow chart showing the main events of the Gunpowder Plot. Make sure to include the following: who the plotters were and what they planned to do, what preparations they made to ensure that the plot worked, the Monteagle letter, and how the plotters were killed and captured.

5th 2 Use your flow chart to write a narrative answer to the following: 'Explain why the Gunpowder Plot of 1605 failed.'

Checkpoint

1 Why was James Stuart crowned king of England in 1603?
2 Why were some Catholics unhappy with James as king? Give two reasons.
3 What were the gunpowder plotters hoping to achieve?

Who won: Catholics or Protestants?

Divide into small groups and look back over what you have learned about in this section. Make a table with two columns, 'Catholic' and 'Protestant', and examine the evidence for who 'won' by 1605. You should consider the following.

- English monarchs – who was in charge from 1553 onwards? What were their religious views and how far did they succeed in changing England to fit their ideas?

- Dealing with threat – what internal and external threats did England face in this time and to what extent did it deal with them?

- Consequences – what were the consequences of what happened for each faith? What came after?

When you have finished, tally up the points in each column and decide who 'won'. Write a paragraph explaining who you think 'won' by 1605.

What have you learned?

Analysing interpretations

In this chapter, you have learned:

- how Mary, Elizabeth and James dealt with the difficult issue of religion in England

- the reasons for the Spanish Armada and the Gunpowder Plot, and how these were overcome.

Quick Quiz

1 Who posted the '95 theses' in 1517?

2 Why did Henry VIII want the pope to annul his marriage to Catherine of Aragon?

3 What name was given to the law passed in 1534 that made Henry VIII Supreme Head of the Church of England?

4 Who succeeded Henry VIII as king?

5 Three people served as monarch of England in 1553 – one of them for only nine days. Who were they?

6 Who became queen of England in 1558 and ruled for the next 44 years?

7 What name was given to the Spanish fleet that tried to transport an army to England in 1588?

8 Why was James Stuart – a Scot – made king of England and Scotland in 1603?

9 What alerted James I to the Gunpowder Plot in 1605?

10 What gruesome punishment was inflicted on the gunpowder plotters in 1606?

What motivated the plotters?

One of the skills you have used a lot in this section is the skill of historical interpretation. Read the following two interpretations carefully and answer the questions below.

Interpretation 1: From *Our Island Story*, a history book for children written in 1905 by Henrietta Marshall.

Although his [James's] mother, Queen Mary, was a Roman Catholic, James had been brought up a Protestant. The English Roman Catholics thought however that, in memory of his mother, James would be kinder to them than Elizabeth had been […].

The Roman Catholics soon found out that James had no intention of being kind to them, and they became very angry. So angry did they become that they formed a plot to kill the King and all the chief Protestants in the country.

Interpretation 2: From an article on the History Today website about the Gunpowder Plot, written by Pauline Croft, Professor of Early Modern History at the University of London, 2005.

[The plotters were] tragic figures, brave and deeply religious men drawn into a doubtful cause. Led by the charismatic figure of Robert Catesby, they were driven by sustained state persecution to see themselves as heroes freeing their oppressed people. Perhaps we should see the Gunpowder Plot as the last violent act of England's turbulent Reformation.

Your turn!

1 What do Interpretations 1 and 2 say about why the Gunpowder Plot happened?

2 What similarities are there between the interpretations?

Writing historically

Analysing interpretations

Interpretations are at the heart of History. Learning to understand the arguments of different historians and being able to compare and contrast them is an important task for a historian.

Comparing interpretations

We are going to consider how to answer the following question:

'Study Interpretations 1 and 2. What is the main difference between these views?'

In order to answer this question, you will need to consider the following:

- what issue both interpretations are talking about

- what view both historians have about this issue

- how the view is different in each interpretation.

Here are some examples of how students might answer this question.

Student 1

> The interpretations are different. Interpretation 1 was written in 1905, while Interpretation 2 was written in 2005. This means that Interpretation 1 is more reliable, as it was closer in time to the events.

This student is confusing sources with interpretations. You don't need to evaluate reliability when answering this question. However, you do need to think about what each historian is saying about the issue. The last statement, as well as being unnecessary, is also untrue. Sometimes new evidence comes to light that means our historical understanding is better than it was in the past.

Student 2

> The interpretations are different as Interpretation 1 says that the king should have been more tolerant towards Catholics, while Interpretation 2 says that they were 'tragic', and describes them as 'heroes'.

This is better – the student has read the interpretations and picked out two relevant quotes. However, the student needs to explain what the difference is, otherwise it is not clear that they have understood it.

Student 3

> The interpretations are different as Interpretation 1 describes the plotters as 'angry' men who wanted to kill the king to improve the lives of Catholics, while Interpretation 2 describes them as 'tragic' and 'brave'. This could suggest that the author of Interpretation 2 believes they had good reasons to try to blow up parliament and that we should feel sympathy for them.

This answer is much better. The student has understood the interpretations, has picked a relevant point of comparison, and has explained how they are different through a subtle understanding of the choice of words the historian has used.

Now write your own answer to the following question, comparing the similarities in the two interpretations: 'Study Interpretations 1 and 2. What is the main similarity between these views?'

Why did the English fight the English in 1642?

In the 1640s, England experienced one of the most violent and significant episodes in its long history – the Civil War. In this section, you will learn about:

- the reasons why relations between the king and parliament became so bad during the reign of Charles I

- the factors that led to the outbreak of war in 1642.

An unexpected guest

Learning objectives

- Start to understand the causes of the English Civil War.
- Understand the chronology of the main events that led to war.

What do you think?

Who has more power now – the monarch or parliament?

On 4 January 1642, the House of Commons, a normally busy and boisterous place, was unusually quiet. The previous day, King Charles I had demanded the arrest of five leading MPs, but the Commons refused. Now, the king himself had arrived. Not only was the king not supposed to enter the House of Commons, but he had brought soldiers with him.

The king walked across the floor of the House of Commons and sat in the Speaker's Chair. He apologised to the Commons for his intrusion, but said that the five members he sought were guilty of treason and demanded that they be delivered to him. Charles asked William Lenthall, the Speaker of the House of Commons, if he knew where they were, but Lenthall respectfully refused to help.

Charles left the stunned chamber of the House of Commons. Later, he faced such hostility from the people of London that he was forced to leave the capital for the safety of Hampton Court Palace. The king was not to return to London for another seven years, during which time war tore England apart as never before. In 1649, Charles returned to London as a prisoner of parliament. He was found guilty of treason and was beheaded in his capital.

How did England come to be at war with itself?

Interpretation 1: A painting of Charles's attempted arrest of five MPs, painted by Charles West Cope in 1866. William Lenthall is shown kneeling before the king. This painting now hangs in the House of Commons.

What was parliament supposed to do?

Over hundreds of years, traditions had developed that meant the monarch and parliament were supposed to work together. Figure 2.1 shows how this had happened.

Key term

Absolutist*: An absolutist ruler is one who has supreme authority and power.

In 1215, King John had been forced to sign the Magna Carta, a document which established that the king was not above the law and that he had to ask his barons for advice on matters such as taxation.

In the 13th century, the first real parliaments were held. It became custom for the monarch to regularly consult with the most important people in England. By the 14th century, parliament met regularly.

As time passed, it became custom that the monarch summoned a parliament when in need of money – normally when the monarch wanted to fight a war. In return, parliament expected to have a say in the running of the country, by getting the monarch to agree to laws that it felt needed passing.

Figure 2.1: The evolution of the relationship between the monarch and parliament over time.

By the time Charles I came to the throne in 1625, parliament had evolved to the point where MPs expected to be regularly consulted on matters of government. England was unusual in this respect. Most states in Europe had absolutist* monarchies. Charles I seemed to wish he had this kind of power.

One of the most important reasons for the Civil War that was about to engulf England, was disagreement about who ruled England. Was it the king, or was it parliament? It would take the deaths of thousands of people for the question to be answered.

Your turn!

1   Describe what parliament was, and what it was supposed to do.

2   Give two reasons why monarchs in the 17th century had less power than those before the Magna Carta.

3   Look back at the story of Charles's entry into the House of Commons on 4 January 1642. Explain why members of the House of Commons might have been outraged about this.

4   Explain why Charles might have been jealous of other 'absolutist' monarchs in Europe.

What were the main events that led to the English Civil War?

1625
James dies and is succeeded by his son, Charles. Charles argues with parliament over resources for war. Some also feel that he is far too tolerant of Catholics.

Charles marries the French Princess Henrietta Maria, a devout Catholic. The union causes alarm amongst many in England.

1621
James recalls parliament to discuss the 'Thirty Years War' in Europe, but dismisses it after parliament pushes for more rights, declaring that he will have nothing more to do with parliaments.

1603
James Stuart is crowned James I of England and James VI of Scotland.

1614
James recalls parliament, but dissolves it after only eight weeks when parliament wishes to discuss James raising money without parliament's consent. There was to be no parliament for the next seven years.

1624
James is forced to recall parliament to discuss raising money for a war with Spain.

1604–11
After a positive start, James quarrels with parliament over finances and whether the monarch has the right to raise money without parliament. James dismisses parliament for three years.

Figure 2.2: The main events that led to the Civil War.

1642

January
Charles attempts to arrest five MPs in the House of Commons that he feels are plotting against him. His plan fails and Charles is forced to flee London.

August
Charles raises his royal flag, or 'standard', in Nottingham to summon an army to fight parliament. The Civil War begins.

1637–39
Charles attempts to introduce a new English-style prayer book into Scotland, sparking off a rebellion and eventually war. Charles's army is humiliatingly defeated by the Scots.

1634
Charles expands a tax known as 'Ship money' to raise money without consulting parliament. Many MPs are furious.

Personal Rule

1626–29
Charles argues with parliament over religious and financial issues. In 1629, he dissolves parliament and does not call another one for 11 years. This period is known as the 'Personal Rule'.

1633
Charles appoints William Laud as Archbishop of Canterbury. Laud offends many by introducing reforms that seem close to bringing back Catholicism.

1637
The leading Puritans William Prynne, Henry Burton and John Bastwick are horribly mutilated in public for criticising Laud's reforms. There is widespread sympathy for them.

1640
Charles is forced to recall parliament to pay for the war with Scotland, but is faced with fury as parliament unleashes 11 years of complaints upon him. He dissolves parliament, but is forced to recall it again after the situation with Scotland worsens. This period is known as the 'Long Parliament', as parliament stays in session until 1660!

1641
Parliament passes the Triennial Act, requiring the king to call parliament more regularly.

October
Violence breaks out between Protestants and Catholics in Ireland. Charles attempts to raise money for an army to deal with the problem, but parliament issues the 'Grand Remonstrance' – a list of complaints against Charles.

Your turn!

1 Look at the timeline of the events leading to the English Civil War. Make a concept map and note down examples of the following.
   a When and why there were arguments over money.
   b When and why there were arguments over religion.
   c When and why there were arguments over power – for example, between the king and parliament.

2 Discuss with a partner which of the above appear to be the most common causes of tension before the English Civil War.

The role of religion

- Know why there were religious differences in England.
- Understand the role of religion as a long-term cause of the Civil War.

Key term

Rood screen*: A screen in a church that separates the area around the altar from the congregation.

The legacy of the Reformation

Britain had been torn apart in the 16th century by the Reformation. Catholicism was replaced as the official state religion by the Church of England, which was Protestant. However, the religious turmoil was not yet over, and would play an important part in the English Civil War. Although the term 'Protestant' suggests people had the same views, in fact there was widespread disagreement about what the Church of England should be like, as Figure 2.3 shows.

Puritans
Protestants who want to remove all Catholic influence

The Church of England

'High Church'
Protestants who continue many of the rituals and traditions of the Catholic Church

Rejects Catholicism ← → Protestantism → Closer to Catholicism

Figure 2.3: A diagram showing different Protestant views.

The rise of the Puritans

In the 17th century, a group known as the Puritans emerged. They were deeply religious Protestants who argued that the religious changes of the 16th century had not gone far enough. They saw the Church of England as still being too Catholic, and saw Catholicism as an evil conspiracy intent on destroying Protestantism.

Puritans had very different views from the Church of England on how religion should be conducted. They believed that:

- individuals could have a private relationship with God, without the need for priests

- the role of the clergy should be limited to conducting sermons and reading scripture

- decorations such as stained glass and rituals in church were a distraction, and that churches should be plain-looking churches.

- people should avoid alcohol, rich food and other worldly things.

Source A: A Puritan family, engraving from a woodcut, 1563.

Charles and religion

When Charles came to the throne in 1625, he did so as the Protestant head of the Church of England. However, although Charles was just as passionate about religion as the Puritans, he clearly belonged to the 'High Church'. Some people even wondered whether the king was in fact a secret Catholic.

Charles's actions only seemed to reinforce this impression. In 1625, Charles married Henrietta Maria, a French princess and a practising Catholic. Many feared her influence over the king.

Charles used his influence to promote the beliefs of the Arminians – a group within the Church who wished to roll back many of the changes of the Reformation. Charles appointed William Laud, a leading Arminian, as Archbishop of Canterbury. Laud introduced some extremely controversial reforms, such as replacing the simple communion table with a traditional stone altar and moving it behind a rood screen*. Charles favoured the return of colourful stained glass windows and images, and the wearing of rich and colourful clothes for priests.

These moves infuriated the Puritans and soon the king and the Church faced growing criticism. Three critics – Henry Burton, William Prynne and John Bastwick – published pamphlets criticising the king's marriage and Laud's reforms to the Church of England. Charles responded to the criticism with harsh punishment. The three were arrested in 1637 and sentenced to have their ears cut off in public. The punishments were witnessed by large crowds that seemed sympathetic to the men.

Charles did not seem to realise that his religious views, and punishments of those who disagreed with them, were driving a wedge between himself and his subjects.

Source B: A portrait of Charles I and his Catholic wife, Henrietta Maria, c.1630–32.

Interpretation 1: An account of the mutilation of Burton, Prynne and Bastwick, published in 1706.

The executioner cut off his ears deep and close, in a cruel manner, with much effusion of blood, an artery being cut, as there was likewise of Dr Bastwick. Then Mr Prynne's cheeks were seared with an iron made exceeding hot which done, the executioner cut off one of his ears and a piece of his cheek with it; then hacking the other ear almost off, he left it hanging and went down; but being called up again he cut it quite off.

Your turn!

1 Make two concept maps summing up the main religious ideas of (a) the Puritans and (b) Charles and the Arminians.

2 On what points were Puritans and Arminians most likely to disagree? Discuss with a partner.

3 Describe two religious reasons why Puritans might have been angry with Charles I by 1637.

4 Explain why a Puritan might have been alarmed by Charles I.

Charles's problems increase: conflict with Scotland

By 1637, Charles had already angered many of his English subjects with his religious views. However, his actions were soon to lead to conflict with the land of his birth – Scotland.

The situation in Scotland

Scotland had experienced its own Reformation during the 16th century and had abandoned Catholicism too. Scotland had, however, taken quite a different path from England. As a result, the Scottish Church had its own prayer books and services. Under James I, these differences had been respected and tolerated.

However, Charles and Archbishop Laud were determined to bring the Scottish Church in line with England and their own 'High Church' beliefs. Charles, despite his Scottish ancestry, showed little interest in the country. He ignored the pleas and advice of Scottish bishops and introduced a new English-style prayer book in July 1637.

The Prayer Book Rebellion

On 23 July 1637, a large crowd gathered in St Giles's Cathedral in Edinburgh for the first service using the new prayer book. However, as the minister began to conduct the service, violence erupted in the crowd. A woman called Jenny Geddes threw a stool at the minister, while others threw sticks and stones.

Did you know?

There was so much hostility towards the new prayer book that the Bishop of Brechin even had to threaten his congregation with two loaded pistols to keep order while he read the new service!

The prayer book faced the same hostile reaction across Scotland. Soon, Scotland was in open rebellion. The Scottish Church signed a document, known as the 'National Covenant', in which it asserted its right to a separate identity and rejected Charles's attempts to interfere with the Scottish Church. It also abolished Scotland's bishops. Charles and Archbishop Laud's plans had backfired spectacularly.

The Arch-Prelate of St Andrewes in Scotland reading the new Service-booke in his pontificalibus assaulted by men & women, with Crickets stooles Stickes and Stones.

Source C: A contemporary illustration of the riot at St Giles's Cathedral, Edinburgh, 23 July 1637.

Charles goes to war with Scotland

Charles hoped that parliament would grant him the money he needed to deal with his problem in Scotland. But Charles had been ruling without parliament for the last 11 years and soon found himself faced with hostile MPs.

Charles sent an army to Scotland to force the Scots to end the rebellion and to accept the new prayer book.

The Scots were well led and convinced of the righteousness of their cause, while the English were badly led and unhappy about fighting fellow Protestants.

Apparently it's all about some Popish prayer book.

I think the Scots have got the right idea.

After seeing how much better the Scottish army was, Charles signed a truce. Charles had no intention of keeping to his word, but wanted to buy time to defeat the Scots.

However, Charles had no money to raise more soldiers and needed new taxes.

Sire, the treasury is empty. We must recall parliament.

Charles had ruled without parliament for 11 years after dismissing it in 1629. He believed he could and should rule on his own. However, if he wanted more money, he had to recall parliament.

I've jotted down a few things I want to say to the king about the last 11 years.

Figure 2.4: Charles's attempts to deal with the Scottish rebellion.

Your turn!

 1 Make a concept map outlining the main religious problems from 1625 to 1640. Include sections on Puritans, Arminians, Archbishop Laud's reforms, religious persecution, the role of Charles, and the Scottish Prayer Book Rebellion.

 2 Imagine you are a Puritan preacher in 1640. Write a sermon criticising Charles and Archbishop Laud for their actions since 1625. Try to group your points into separate paragraphs. Use your concept map to help to structure your answer. Remember to make your speech fiery and persuasive, and finish by explaining what you want Charles to do.

Checkpoint

1 List three reasons why Puritans might have been angry with Charles by 1640.
2 What did Charles do that upset the Scots so much in 1637?
3 What was Charles forced to do in 1640 to raise money?

Why couldn't Charles get on with parliament?

Source A: An oil painting of Charles I by the Dutch artist Anthony van Dyck, 1638.

It was with great reluctance that Charles recalled parliament in 1640, but only parliament could grant him the money he needed to fight the Scots.

Charles's relationship with parliament had been bad from the start, but had deteriorated as time passed. In 1629, after arguing with parliament over his religious views and whether he had the right to raise money on his own, he had dismissed parliament and ruled without it for 11 years. This period is now known as the 'Personal Rule'.

The Court of Star Chamber

During this period, Charles had attempted to exercise what he believed was his God-given right to rule the country on his own as an absolutist ruler. Charles ruled through the Court of Star Chamber – a court that had been set up to settle legal disputes. Under Charles the Court became a substitute government, allowing him to rule without parliament by punishing those who criticised him and raising money by issuing fines.

Ship money

Charles soon needed bigger sources of income and eventually set upon the idea of expanding 'Ship money'. Ship money was a tax that was normally paid by coastal areas in return for protection against hostile foreign navies. However, in 1635 Charles expanded the tax so that inland counties also had to pay it. Those who refused to pay were threatened with imprisonment.

The tax was deeply unpopular. One person who refused to pay the tax was the MP John Hampden, who argued that the tax was illegal as parliament hadn't agreed to it. He was put on trial and, although he was found guilty, he was seen as a hero by many for standing up to the king.

As parliament gathered again in 1640 after such a long break, many must have relished the opportunity to air their grievances.

The Short Parliament

When Charles recalled parliament, he was faced with a storm of criticism over his actions over the last 11 years, which members of parliament argued were unlawful. Charles was heavily criticised in a two-hour speech by the MP John Pym, who was beginning to emerge as the leader of a group of five MPs who were particularly critical of Charles.

Furious, Charles dissolved parliament after only three weeks, leading to its nickname – the 'Short Parliament'. Riots broke out in London in support of Pym. Charles had the offices of the five MPs searched, believing they were in league with the Scottish rebels.

Meanwhile, Charles tried again to take on the Scottish rebels on his own. The Earl of Strafford proposed using Irish Catholic troops against the Scottish Protestants – but this idea outraged many. The campaign failed and the Scots occupied the North of England. Charles was now in a worse position than before, and was forced to recall parliament again to prevent a military disaster.

The Long Parliament

Charles recalled parliament in November 1640. Realising the strong position it was in, this time parliament was intent on reducing the power of the king. This session of parliament became known as the Long Parliament, as it stayed in session for the next 20 years.

Source B: A portrait of John Pym, who emerged as one of the leading critics of Charles I in parliament.

Source C: A report of a speech John Pym made in the Commons on 17 April 1640, described by Sir Thomas Peyton, a Kent baronet:

… [the king] left not anything untouched: ship-money, forests, the granting of knight-hood, the punishment of those with different religious views, the granting of monopolies*, the present inclination of our church to popery*… [I urge the House of Lords] that they would be pleased to join with [the House of Commons] in a petition to the King for redress of all those grievances.

Your turn!

1 Explain why the king felt that he could rule without parliament.

2 Explain what political and financial reasons forced Charles to recall parliament in 1640 after 11 years.

3 What were the main reasons why relations between the king and parliament deteriorated so much between 1625 and 1640? Think of at least three reasons, and arrange them in order of importance. Explain why you have put them in that order.

4 Imagine you are a Puritan MP, recalled after 11 years. Write a speech to deliver in parliament explaining why you are so angry with the king.

The Long Parliament and the outbreak of the English Civil War

The Long Parliament wasted no time in trying to put the king in his place. In a flurry of activity, parliament made up for the lack of action during the time of Charles's 'Personal Rule' by passing many important Acts of Parliament.

- Ship money was declared unlawful and abolished.

- The Court of Star Chamber was abolished to prevent Charles attempting to run the country on his own.

- Parliament passed the Triennial Act, which ensured parliaments were called at least once every three years.

- The Earl of Strafford and Archbishop Laud were arrested. After a show trial, Strafford was sentenced to death and Charles was forced to sign his death warrant. He regretted it for the rest of his life.

Unfortunately for Charles, parliament was unwilling to grant him the funds necessary to continue the fight against the Scots, with whom many MPs had sympathies. Besides, a new crisis was brewing in Ireland, which overshadowed the Scottish rebellion.

Source D: An illustration depicting supposed atrocities committed against Protestants by Irish Catholics in 1641.

The Irish Rebellion

By the 17th century, Ireland had been ruled by the English for hundreds of years. There was widespread resentment over English rule and this became worse after the Reformation, when English rulers tried to force Irish Catholics to become Protestants. In 1641, these resentments reached boiling point and Irish Catholics rose up in rebellion. In the resulting violence, many died on both sides, but lurid stories appeared in the English press depicting atrocities against Protestants (see Source C). England was horrified, and Charles wanted to send an army to Ireland to end the rebellion. For this, he would again need to ask for money from parliament.

However, parliament was again reluctant to grant the king money and were worried about the power it would bring. MPs also feared that saving the day in Ireland might boost Charles's popularity. Instead, parliament passed what became known as the 'Grand Remonstrance'.

The Grand Remonstrance

The Grand Remonstrance was organised by John Pym, who was becoming the king's biggest enemy. It was a summary of all of the criticisms that parliament had of the king. The document proposed that parliament should have control over the future reform of the Church, and that the king's choice of ministers should be approved by parliament. The Grand Remonstrance passed in the House of Commons by 159 votes to 148.

The Grand Remonstrance was the final straw for Charles. Furious, he branded John Pym and four other MPs as traitors, and ordered parliament to hand them over for arrest. When parliament refused, on 4 January 1642, Charles arrived at the House of Commons with 300 troops and tried to seize them, but John Pym and his followers had already fled. Charles left London, now convinced that only war would settle the argument between himself and parliament. He travelled to Nottingham where, in August 1642, he raised his royal standard and set about gathering a Royalist army to fight parliament. Parliament likewise began raising an army to defend its own rights. The Civil War had begun.

Interpretation 1: A modern photo of how Royalist troops might have looked when assembling to fight for Charles.

Your turn!

 1 Draw a diagram showing the long- and short-term causes of the English Civil War. Here are some factors you should include: Ship money, 'Divine Right of Kings', the Scottish rebellion, Archbishop Laud's reforms, the Grand Remonstrance, Charles's attempted arrest of the five MPs. You should also try to think of your own.

 2 Who or what do you think was most to blame for the outbreak of the Civil War? Was it the king or parliament? Consider the evidence for and against both.

Checkpoint

1 What was 'Ship money', and why did it make parliament angry?

2 Why did the Grand Remonstrance make Charles angry?

3 What did Charles do on 4 January 1642 that helped to trigger the Civil War?

Why did the English fight the English in 1642?

As a class, conduct a trial to establish who was most guilty of starting the English Civil War. Divide the class into three, representing parliament, Charles and the jury. The first two groups should look for evidence that their side is innocent and the other side is guilty. You should choose someone to represent each side – one person could be the king, while another could represent John Pym. Each will have to defend their position and accuse the other. You should also appoint a 'legal team' for each side to give advice. When you have finished, the jury should decide who was most responsible for causing the English Civil War – parliament or the king.

In this section you have learned:

• the long-term causes of the Civil War, such as religion and attitudes to the role of the monarch

• the short-term reasons that led to England going to war in 1642.

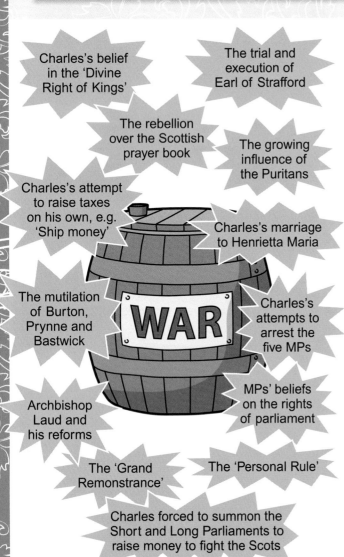

Charles's belief in the 'Divine Right of Kings'

The trial and execution of Earl of Strafford

The rebellion over the Scottish prayer book

The growing influence of the Puritans

Charles's attempt to raise taxes on his own, e.g. 'Ship money'

Charles's marriage to Henrietta Maria

The mutilation of Burton, Prynne and Bastwick

WAR

Charles's attempts to arrest the five MPs

Archbishop Laud and his reforms

MPs' beliefs on the rights of parliament

The 'Grand Remonstrance'

The 'Personal Rule'

Charles forced to summon the Short and Long Parliaments to raise money to fight the Scots

Figure 2.5: A summary of some of the factors that caused the English Civil War.

Summarising the causes of the English Civil War

Trying to understand what causes big historical events, such as the English Civil War, can be one of the most fascinating aspects of studying History. However, it can also be very complex – some historians have spent their entire careers discussing these subjects.

To grapple with a subject such as the causes of the English Civil War, it is helpful not just to know what happened, but also to be able to categorise factors. Throughout this section, you have been thinking about the long- and short-term causes of historical events. However, causes can also be arranged into **categories**.

Some of the categories you could use are summarised below, along with some ideas of what might be included in these categories.

• Political – Decisions made by the king or parliament, ideas on how the country should be run, laws passed, the appointment of important people.

• Religious – The role of religious leaders such as the Archbishop of Canterbury, as well as ideas and decisions made about church services, prayer books, etc.

• Economic – Factors related to money, trade and taxes.

Your turn!

1 Make a concept map entitled 'What caused the English Civil War?' Include three sections – political, economic and religious factors. Look at the factors above and write them into the correct category.

2 Explain why each factor helped to cause the Civil War and add your reasons to your concept map.

3 You may notice that some factors are connected. Draw links between these factors and explain what each link is – e.g. how Charles's beliefs in his own power led him to dismiss parliament.

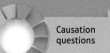

Writing historically

Causation questions

Now that you have thought about how to categorise causes, let's look at how to answer the following causation question.

'Charles's religious blunders were the main reason for the outbreak of the English Civil War. How far do you agree with this statement?'

To answer this question, you will need to look at the different reasons why war broke out and argue which was most important. Use the factors in Figure 2.5 to explain why religious reasons, such as Charles's introduction of the Scottish prayer book, helped to cause the English Civil War. You will then need to look at other reasons, such as Charles's attempts to rule without parliament.

Remember to start with an introduction, saying what you're going to argue, and a conclusion that sums up your main points. Here are some extracts from sample answers to the question, written by three different students.

Student 1

Charles introduced a new prayer book into Scotland. The Scottish didn't like it and started a rebellion. Charles was angry and sent an army to Scotland to force the Scottish to accept the prayer book. The English army was not as good as the Scottish army.

This answer shows a good knowledge of what happened, and talks about religious factors. But it isn't answering the question – it is a description. Remember to address the question: how did religion help cause the Civil War?

Student 2

Charles's religious blunders were definitely a big reason why the English Civil War started. Charles upset a lot of people by his religious changes. Some people even thought he was a Catholic. He should have been much more sensitive about religion. People got so fed up with the religious changes that they eventually started a war.

This answer is addressing the question in the first line of the answer, which is good. The student also has a general understanding of how religion helped to start the Civil War. However, the answer is very general. It would have been better to use some key words or some more specific examples.

Student 3

Charles's religious blunders were a significant reason why the English Civil War started. For example, Charles attempted to introduce a new prayer book to Scotland that reflected his own 'High Church' beliefs. This upset Protestant Scots and caused a rebellion, which Charles was unable to stop, even with military force. As a result, Charles was forced to recall parliament, which then caused a chain of events that led to the outbreak of war.

This answer is better. It clearly addresses the question in the first sentence, uses specific evidence to support the point and explains the consequences of Charles's actions. The student might go on to describe other religious factors, for example the influence of the Puritans, before explaining the role of other factors.

Now, complete the next paragraph on a different factor – e.g. a political or an economic factor.

What were the differences between the Roundheads and the Cavaliers?

Once Charles raised his standard at Nottingham in 1642, war became inevitable. The country divided into two as people opted either to support the cause of the king or to support parliament. What were both sides hoping to achieve by fighting? In this section you will learn:

- the reasons why people fought in the English Civil War
- the differences between the armies
- the reasons parliament won.

Roundhead or Cavalier?

Learning objectives

- Understand what different groups hoped to achieve by fighting.
- Know which groups sided with the king, and which with parliament.

What do you think?

Would you have supported the king or parliament?

Did you know?

The word 'Cavalier' seems to have come from words influenced by Latin, such as *Cavaliero* meaning Spanish trooper – an insulting reference to the supposed foreign, Catholic influence in the king's army. However, it was soon adopted as a term by the Royalists themselves.

Parliamentarian soldiers became known as 'Roundheads' due to their shaven heads, in stark contrast to the long hair of the king and the people in his court.

Source A: A contemporary illustration showing the two rival sides in the English Civil War insulting each other.

Who were the Royalists?

Those who supported the king were known as Royalists, although as the war developed they were also referred to by the nickname 'Cavaliers'.

The Cavaliers sought to defend the position of the king at the top of the social order. They also generally had 'High Church' ideas, with many supporting Charles and Archbishop Laud's reforms. Some vowed to defend religion against what they saw as fanatical Puritan influences.

As London was a stronghold of parliament, Charles instead based himself in Oxford. In 1643, he declared parliament an illegal assembly and set up a rival parliament, known as the 'Oxford Parliament'. This was supposed to demonstrate that, although Charles intended to defeat the rebels, he still planned to work with a version of parliament once the war was over.

Parliament's war aims

Many of those who fought for parliament aimed to protect the rights of parliament to perform its traditional role, which they saw as working with the king to decide on matters such as taxes and important laws. They wanted to reduce the power of the king by forcing him to agree to limits upon his power. This was to stop the king from ruling without parliament again.

Most parliamentarians had little appetite to make England into a Republic*. However, there were different groups within parliament who wanted very different things. The diagram on the right shows some of these different groups and what they wanted.

What happened as a result of these groups?

- The ideas of the Puritans led to a wave of destruction of religious art across England.

- Parliament ignored the Levellers' ideas (see Figure 2.6). It would take another 250 years for most of them to be acted upon. In 1649, some Levellers were involved in a mutiny and were executed.

- The landowners didn't much like the idea of sharing their land with everyone, so by 1650 the Digger movement was supressed.

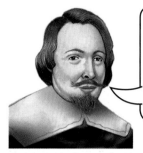

We Puritans would like to see the Church of England purified by removing all papist (Catholic) elements. The godly should destroy any superstitious statues and idols they find in churches and cathedrals.

A group of us in parliament's army call ourselves 'Levellers'. We think we should use the war to bring about massive change. We would like to see every man given the vote, and for parliament to meet every two years so we can check it is doing its job properly.

We are the Diggers. We think the Levellers' ideas don't go far enough! Let's abolish the monarchy, and share all of the land amongst the people equally. We can then work together to dig the land for the good of everybody, instead of a few big landowners keeping all the land to themselves.

Figure 2.6: Different political and religious factions within the parliamentarian side in the Civil War.

Key term

Republic*: A country that has no monarchy, and in which supreme power is held by an elected body.

Source B: Extract from a pamphlet written by Gerrard Winstanley, one of the leading Diggers, in 1649.

...[we will] lay the Foundation of making the Earth a Common Treasury for All, both Rich and Poor, That every one that is born in the land, may be fed by the Earth ...Not Inclosing any part into any particular hand, but all as one man, working together, and feeding together as Sons of one Father, members of one Family; not one Lording over another, but all looking upon each other, as equals in the Creation.

Your turn!

1 Make a concept map summing up each group (Royalists, parliament, Puritans, Diggers, Levellers), and what they wanted to achieve out of the war.

2 Look at Source B. What does this suggest about the changes the Diggers would like to see?

3 Who do you think would have been alarmed by the ideas revealed in Source B, and why?

4 Create a character – either a Cavalier or a Roundhead. Decide on what you are fighting for and what you want the war to achieve. Practise answering questions 'in character', with the help of a partner.

How did people decide who to fight for?

The start of the English Civil War forced people to make a choice – whether to support the king or parliament. This decision not only split the country in half, but also divided counties, towns and even families.

One of the first things parliament did in the Civil War was to order the army to rally to its defence. This was the first time in English history parliament had tried to pass laws without the king. As soon as Charles heard this, he issued his own orders demanding that the army rally to him. This placed officers in a terrible dilemma as to whose orders they should follow, and led to outbreaks of fighting across the country. Source C reveals how one officer reacted to the orders.

For some, the decision was easy, as they believed very passionately in the cause they were fighting for (see Source D), while for others it took some time to make up their minds (see Source E).

Source C: Letter from Sir Thomas Kyvett to his wife, 1642. Kyvett was an army officer who received two sets of orders – one from parliament and one from the king.

Oh sweete hart, I am nowe in a great strayght what to doe. Waulking this other morning at Westminster, Sir John Potts [requested] (by vertue of an Ordinance of Parliament) my campanye and command againe. I was surprised what to doe, whether to take or refuse. Twas no place to dispite, so I tooke it and desierd sometime to advise upon it. I had not received this many howers, but I met with a declaration point Blanck against it by the King.

Source D: Extract from a letter written by Edmund Ludlow, a committed Puritan who went on to become an important Roundhead commander.

I thought it my duty, upon consideration of my age and vigorous constitution, as an Englishman, and an invitation to that purpose from my father [another Parliamentarian], to enter into the service of my country, in the army commanded by the Earl of Essex under the authority of the Parliament. I thought the justice of that cause I had engaged in to be so evident that I [decided without] much difficulty.

Source E: Portraits of George Digby, 2nd Earl of Bristol, and William Russell, 1st Duke of Bedford, painted by Anthony van Dyck in 1637. Both Digby and Russell served as courtiers to the king in the 1630s, and both served in the Long Parliament. Digby was married to Russell's sister. However, Digby fought for the king, while Russell fought for parliament. Russell then changed sides to fight for the Royalists, before changing sides again!

How did the Civil War tear apart families?

Some of the most sad and tragic stories of the Civil War show how the conflict divided families. One of the best known examples is the story of the De Verney family.

The De Verneys were a rich and influential family in Buckinghamshire. The head of the household was Sir Edmund Verney. He had two sons – Sir Ralph Verney and his younger brother Sir Edmund Verney (the younger).

When the war started, the father and his youngest son Edmund felt they had to support the king, although they had deep doubts about Charles.

> I wish the king would talk to parliament, but I've served him for 30 years – I can't betray him!

However, his eldest son, Sir Ralph Verney, decided to fight for parliament.

> Goodbye father. May the lord protect you.

The elder Sir Edmund Verney carried the king's standard at the Battle of Edgehill in 1642, where he was killed. Family legend states that the younger Edmund sent his servant to find the body, but all that could be found was his father's hand, still clutching the flag.

Ralph lost faith in parliament's cause and fled to France, not returning until after the war was over. His younger brother Edmund was killed leading Royalist infantry at the Battle of Drogheda in Ireland.

Figure 2.7: The story of the De Verney family in the English Civil War.

Your turn!

 1 Read Source D. Explain why Edmund Ludlow was so convinced that he had picked the right side. What reasons might he give?

 2 Look at Sources C (it may help to read this aloud), E and the story of the De Verney family. Why was it so difficult for some to decide who to fight for? How do you think they made their decision?

3 Write a letter from Sir Ralph Verney to his father, explaining why he had decided to fight for parliament instead of the king. Think about what he might say, and how he might try to convince his father that he had backed the wrong side.

Checkpoint

1 What were the main aims of the Royalists and parliamentarians?

2 Where did Charles base himself and his rival 'parliament' during the war?

3 Who were the Levellers, and what did they want?

4 Who were the Diggers, and what did they want?

5 Give two reasons why it was difficult for soldiers to know who to fight for.

Who had the better army in the English Civil War?

Learning objectives

- Understand the differences between the Cavalier and Roundhead armies.
- Know about the New Model Army.
- Assess the role the New Model Army played in parliament's victory.

The first three years of the war saw both sides settle into the areas of the country in which they had most support. Several major battles were fought, the first being the Battle of Edgehill on 23 October 1642. However, despite thousands of deaths, no single battle dealt the decisive blow that was needed to end the war.

Table 2.1: Major Civil War battles, 1642–44

Battle	Outcome	Key detail
The Battle of Edgehill 23 October 1642	Draw	After a successful cavalry charge, the Royalist cavalry gallop off in pursuit of loot, leaving their own army unprotected and losing their advantage.
Adwalton Moor 30 June 1643	Royalist victory	Royalists try to surround a trapped Roundhead army, but the Roundheads pick a spot of rough terrain, which makes it difficult for the Royalist cavalry to attack. However, the Roundheads are forced to retreat.
Roundway Down 13 July 1643	Royalist victory	Parliamentary forces attack a Royalist army, but stop to rest. The Royalists gather reinforcements, attack and drive the Roundheads from the battlefield.
Marston Moor 2 July 1644	Roundhead victory	An outnumbered Royalist army is caught off guard and attacked before it is ready. The Roundhead cavalry, led by Oliver Cromwell, successfully defeat the Royalist cavalry.
Second Battle of Newbury 27 October 1644	Roundheads win, but allow Royalists to escape	The Roundheads make a daring attack on the Royalists, forcing them to retreat. Cromwell is stopped from chasing and destroying them by his army commanders.

Key ◼ Royalists ◻ Parlamentarians

Figure 2.8: A map showing the key battles and areas controlled by the king and parliament, 1642–44.

The creation of the New Model Army

By mid 1644, no battle had decisively defeated the king's army. A parliamentary general named William Waller began to argue that there were problems with the Roundhead army that were preventing them from landing a 'knock-out blow' to the Royalists. His ideas were taken up by a promising young MP and cavalry officer called Oliver Cromwell.

To change the army, in 1645 parliament passed two very important laws.

- The 'Self-Denying Ordinance': this said that MPs were not allowed to command soldiers in the army. Instead, officer positions were to be filled with men who had shown their talent on the battlefield.

- The 'New Model Army Ordinance': up to this point, soldiers had joined regional armies and had been reluctant to fight outside of their own region. Now they were to join a professional national army called the 'New Model Army' and could be sent anywhere in the country. Discipline was to be strictly enforced amongst the infantry and cavalry, so that soldiers would do exactly as they were told on the battlefield. In return, soldiers were to be paid regularly to ensure their loyalty and were expected to be strictly religious.

These changes created an army that would decisively defeat the king's army in the battles to come.

Source A: Oliver Cromwell describes his views on leadership in the army to Sir William Spring, in a letter dated September 1643.

I had rather a plain russet-coated captain that knows what he fights for and loves what he knows, than that which you call a gentlemen, and is nothing else.

Source B: Extracts from the 'Soldier's Catechism' (1644), a pamphlet that was given to every soldier in the New Model Army and which they were expected to read. It was written by Robert Ram, a chaplain in the army.

Q – *What is it that you chiefly aim at in this war?*

A – At the Reformation of a most corrupt, lazy, infamous, superstitious, soul-murdering Clergie.

At the advancement of God's kingdom and the purity of his Ordinances.

At the bringing to Justice the enemies of our Church and State.

At the upholding of our Parliaments, which are the Subjects best inheritance, and the Crowne of our Nation.

Q – *What are the principal things required in a Soldier?*

A – That he be religious and godly.

That he be courageous and valiant.

That he be skilful in the military profession.

Your turn!

1 Read the summary of the key battles from 1642 to 1644, in Table 2.1. What can you infer about the problems in both armies, for example discipline? List as many as you can.

6th 2 Read Source A. What does this suggest about the kind of officer Cromwell wanted in his army?

7th 3 Read Source B. Explain what this source suggests about what soldiers in the New Model Army were fighting for. Use a quote to support your point.

4 Why do you think parliament placed so much importance on soldiers being religious and knowing what they were fighting for?

What was the New Model Army like?

By 1645, the New Model Army was ready to take to the field against Charles. Figure 2.9 sums up some of the types of units in the New Model Army.

Fact file

Cavalry	Infantry	Artillery
Who were they? Cavalry fought on horseback and were the elite units of the army.	**Who were they?** Infantry were soldiers who fought on foot. This included pikemen and musketeers.	**Who were they?** Artillery were the heavy guns of the battlefield.
How were they armed? They wore light armour, and carried swords and pistols.	**How were they armed?** Pikemen had pikes, which were long pointed spears. Musketeers were armed with a musket, which was an early firearm.	**How were they armed?** Cannons fired heavy cannonballs at the enemy.
What tactics did they use? They attacked the weak points of the enemy, such as the flanks. They could make unsteady soldiers flee in panic.	**What tactics did they use?** The pikemen's long poles were very effective against cavalry. Both sides used pikemen, and they sometimes fought each other. Musketeers would fire 'volleys' of musket fire at the enemy, which could be devastating at close range. However, their muskets were inaccurate and slow to load.	**What were their tactics?** Artillery could demoralise the enemy by 'softening them up' before a battle, and could punch holes through densely packed infantrymen. However, they were vulnerable to cavalry.

Figure 2.9: Different units used in the New Model Army.

The New Model Army had its first chance to enter battle on 14 June 1645, in a field in Northamptonshire, near the village of Naseby. On one side of a valley stood the main force of the Royalist army, with King Charles himself present on the battlefield, although his nephew Prince Rupert was in command.

On the other side was the as yet untested New Model Army, commanded by Lord Fairfax, with the rising star Oliver Cromwell in charge of the cavalry.

What followed would be one of the most decisive battles in English history.

The Battle of Naseby, 14 June 1645

At 10am, the battle started when the cavalry under the command of Prince Rupert successfully charged the cavalry on the left flank of the Roundheads's position. However, instead of following up their victory and supporting their infantry, Prince Rupert and the poorly disciplined Royalist cavalry charged for the Roundheads's baggage train*, looking for plunder.

Meanwhile, Royalist cavalry attacked the cavalry on the right flank of the Roundheads's position, which was under the command of Oliver Cromwell. The highly disciplined and trained Roundhead cavalry stood their ground and beat back the Royalist attack.

Seizing the initiative, Cromwell launched an attack on the Royalist infantry which, without Rupert, were leaderless. The panicked Royalist line collapsed and surrendered. The Royalist army was ruthlessly pursued and Charles's army was almost entirely destroyed. A thousand Royalist soldiers were killed and another 4500 taken prisoner. All of the king's artillery was captured. The Battle of Naseby effectively marked the end of the Royalists, and Charles surrendered the following year. The question now became – what to do with the king?

Key term

Baggage train*: People, wagons and supplies that the army needed on campaign. As well as basics, the baggage train could contain expensive personal items and plunder from previous battles.

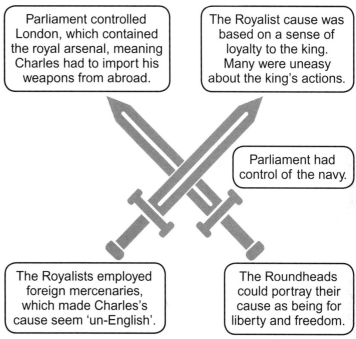

Figure 2.10: Reasons why parliament won the Civil War.

Your turn!

 1 Group reasons why parliament won the Civil War into categories – for example, discipline, leadership.

 2 Pick one reason and explain why it led to Charles's defeat. Remember to use some specific evidence to support your argument.

Checkpoint

1 Name two problems both armies had in the first battles of the Civil War.
2 Name two ways in which the New Model Army was different from the old Roundhead army.
3 What happened at the Battle of Naseby?
4 Give two reasons why Charles lost the Civil War.

What were the differences between the Roundheads and the Cavaliers?

Draw pictures of a Roundhead and a Cavalier on separate pages. Surround each with information about what they were fighting for, their religious beliefs, where they were based and the differences between them. Make sure to include information on the New Model Army and the Battle of Naseby.

Why did the English kill their king?

The Civil War was over in England, but the debate about what to do with Charles was just beginning. So how did the English end up executing their own monarch? In this section, you will learn about:

- the events that led to the trial and execution of Charles I

- how historians have interpreted the English Civil War in different ways.

Why was Charles put on trial?

Learning objectives

- Understand how and why Charles I was put on trial and executed.
- Learn how to evaluate different interpretations of the English Civil War.

What do you think?

Do you think Charles deserved to be punished?

Source A: A contemporary engraving showing Charles I in prison on the Isle of Wight.

In 1648, Charles I was imprisoned in Carisbrooke Castle on the Isle of Wight. At first, Cromwell and the parliamentary leader, Henry Ireton, tried to negotiate with Charles. However, Charles refused to cooperate. Instead, he infuriated his captors by repeatedly attempting to escape. One attempt failed only because Charles became stuck in a window!

Later, it emerged that Charles had been secretly conspiring with the Scots, who invaded England to put Charles back on the throne. The plan failed as the Scottish army was crushed by Cromwell's forces. Cromwell and other leading figures began to argue that Charles should be put on trial for treason.

Disagreement over how to treat Charles

Not everyone agreed with the need to put Charles on trial. Many in parliament preferred the idea of allowing Charles to return with reduced powers. Others questioned whether it was even legal to put the king on trial, and expressed horror at the idea of killing someone who was supposedly appointed by God.

However, Cromwell and the New Model Army were in no mood for compromise. They occupied London, and prevented all MPs who had sympathy for the king from entering the House of Commons. The remaining 154 MPs (known as the 'Rump Parliament') issued an ordinance (order) on 1 January 1649 calling for a trial of Charles. The House of Commons declared that it alone had the right to rule England without the need to consult either the king or the House of Lords. Preparations were begun to put Charles on trial for treason – against his own people.

The trial of Charles I

Cromwell, who was fast becoming the most powerful man in parliament, made plans to hold the trial of Charles I. As no one had ever put a king on trial before, the process was extremely difficult. 135 commissioners were nominated to sit in judgement on the king. However, around 50 of them refused to take part, along with the Lord Chief Justices and parliamentary lawyer Bulstrode Whitelocke. Instead, an obscure lawyer called Peter Bradshaw was appointed as the judge in one of the most significant trials in English history.

The trial began on 20 January 1649 at Westminster Hall. Thousands of members of the public crammed into the hall to watch.

The trial did not go smoothly. When the charges were read to Charles, he repeatedly interrupted (see Source C).

> **Source C:** Extract from a speech made by Charles I during his trial, January 1649.
>
> I would know by what authority I was brought [here], and carried from place to place, and I know not what: and when I know what lawful authority, I should answer. Remember, I am your King, your lawful King… I have a trust committed to me by God, by old and lawful descent.

Source B: An engraving of the trial of Charles I in Westminster Hall, made in 1688. Charles I is shown sitting on his own towards the bottom of the picture.

Charles refused to plead guilty or innocent and was therefore removed from the court and barred from taking part in the rest of the trial. Over the next few days, the court heard from witnesses who accused Charles of what would today be described as 'war crimes'. On 27 January, Charles was summoned back to Westminster Hall, where he was sentenced to death. He was again forbidden to say anything, and was removed from the court to await his execution.

Did you know?

Peter Bradshaw, the judge in the trial of Charles I, was so worried about being assassinated during the trial that he wore a steel-lined bulletproof hat!

Your turn!

 1 Look at Source A. What can you see in this image? Do you think the artist was a supporter of Charles or parliament? How can you tell?

2 Do you think Charles was treated unfairly during his trial? Make two columns and note down the arguments for and against, using the information on these pages.

3 Look at Sources B and C. How useful are these sources as evidence about whether the trial of Charles I was fair or not?

Did you know?

One account suggests that Cromwell was so nervous about signing the king's death warrant that he broke into a fit of hysterical giggles.

The execution of Charles I

It was so cold on 30 January 1649 that the Thames froze over. It was a day that would live long in people's memories – for it was the day that England killed its king.

Charles's death warrant had been signed by 59 of those who had presided over his trial, including Cromwell, Bradshaw and Ireton. A scaffold had been constructed outside Whitehall Palace in London. As with most public executions, a large crowd had gathered to watch.

Eventually, Charles emerged, dressed in a white shirt. In fact, he was wearing two shirts, as it was such a bitterly cold day that he didn't want people to think he was shivering with fear. He faced the crowd and gave the last speech of his life, in which he repeated his ideas on who had the right to rule England (see Source D).

Charles then lay down and placed his head upon the block, and stretched his arms in the shape of a cross. The executioner brought down his axe and severed the king's head with one blow. Some accounts state that when the head of the king was held aloft, the crowd made a low groan.

The king was dead, and parliament passed legislation to outlaw any succession to the throne. For the next 11 years, England, for the first and only time in its history, became a republic.

Source D: Extract from the last speech made by Charles I before he was executed, 30 January 1649.

[As for the people], truly I desire their liberty and freedom as much as anybody... but I must tell you that their liberty and freedom consist in having [the protection of] government. It is not... having [a] share in government, sirs; that is nothing [to do with] them; a subject and a [monarch] are clear different things... therefore I tell you... that I am the martyr of the people.

Source E: The execution of Charles I, 1649, from a German engraving made at the time.

How has the English Civil War been interpreted by historians?

The English Civil War is a complex but fascinating period in British history. It is a time that continues to divide historians, particularly over what we should think about the war and its legacy. Some examples of the different views are given in Figure 2.11.

It seems likely that debates will continue about the legacy of the English Civil War. How do you think it should be remembered?

In the Victorian era, historians argued that the English Civil War was part of the long march of the English people towards freedom and democracy. This is known as the 'Whig' view of History. Victorians saw Cromwell in a positive light, and produced statues and paintings showing him as a hero, such as the example shown here.

The death and destruction of the 20th century led historians to dismiss the idea that each generation is better than the last. Marxist historians, inspired by the ideas of the Russian revolution, argued that the English Civil War was part of the endless struggle between classes – in this case, between the middle class, represented by parliament, and the upper class, represented by the king.

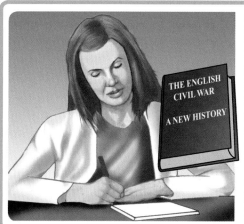

Nowadays, many historians believe that the English Civil War could have been avoided, perhaps if Charles had acted differently. More recently, people have argued that the name 'English Civil War' is misleading – after all, Ireland, Wales and Scotland took part too, and there was more than one war. Should it be known as the 'British Civil Wars'?

Figure 2.11: Some of the different ways in which the English Civil War has been interpreted by later generations.

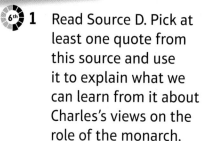

Your turn!

1 Read Source D. Pick at least one quote from this source and use it to explain what we can learn from it about Charles's views on the role of the monarch.

2 In what ways does Source D help historians to understand why the Civil War was fought? What does it suggest about Charles's views of government?

3 Look at Figure 2.11 and think about the following questions.
   a Why do you think views on the Civil War have changed so much over time?
   b Which historical interpretation do you agree with more?

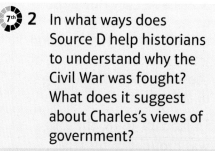

Checkpoint

1 Who did Charles try to encourage to invade England in 1648?
2 Give two reasons why some in parliament felt uneasy about putting the king on trial.
3 What was Charles accused of in his trial, and why?

Why did the English kill their king?

Now that you know about the arguments that took place over the trial of Charles I, decide as a class who deserves a statue more – Cromwell or Charles I? Or neither?

What have you learned?

In this section, you have learned about:

- the differences between the two sides in the English Civil War

- the reasons for parliament's victory

- why Charles was executed, and what later generations have made of these events.

Source A: Lucy Hutchinson wrote an account of Charles I's trial. Her husband, John Hutchinson, was one of those who signed the king's death warrant.

In January 1648, the king was brought to his trial... When he was charged with the blood spilt in the war... he smiled... His looks and gestures suggested that his only sorrow was that all the people that opposed him had not been killed... God did not signal his favour towards the King... it was therefore [my husband's] duty to [sign the king's death warrant].

Using evidence to understand the English Civil War

In History, you have probably discussed before whether a source is useful or not. However, the usefulness of a source depends on the question being asked – that is, useful *for what*?

Look at Source A.

How useful is Source A for finding out about the fighting in the English Civil War?

The answer is… not that useful! It talks about the war indirectly ('blood spilt in the war'), but not the war itself. We are asking the wrong question.

However, if we were to ask a different question, the source might appear more useful.

How useful is Source A for finding out about why Charles I was sentenced to death?

Your turn!

1   How would you answer this second question? Is Source A more or less useful for investigating why Charles I was sentenced to death?

2   Can you think of another question that Source A could help you investigate?

3   Is Source A useful? Explain your answer.

Quick Quiz

1   Why did some disapprove of Charles's marriage to Henrietta Maria?

2   Who did Charles appoint as Archbishop of Canterbury in 1633, causing tension?

3   What did Charles do in 1637 that provoked a rebellion in Scotland?

4   What name has been given to the period between 1629 and 1640 when Charles attempted to rule without parliament?

5   What did Charles try to do on 4 January 1642 that helped to cause the Civil War?

6   What name was given to the reformed parliamentary army which defeated the Royalists at the Battle of Naseby in 1645?

7   What crime was Charles accused of in his trial?

8   Why did Charles wear two shirts on the day of his execution?

Writing historically

Source utility questions

We are going to explore how to answer the question 'How useful is Source A for an enquiry into the personality of Charles I?'

When considering the utility (usefulness) of a source, you should think about:

- what the source says or shows about the issue in the question

- the reliability of the source for that issue.

To plan your answer, you could use a table like the one below. Make a copy of this table and fill it in for Source A.

	Useful as evidence about the personality of Charles I	Limitations as evidence about the personality of Charles I
Source A	It's an eyewitness account of how he behaved in the trial.	

Here are some examples of how students have approached this question.

Student 1

Source A is not useful because it is written by a woman whose husband signed Charles's death warrant. It is a contemporary source from the time. She says that the king smiled in court. The source tells us that a lot of blood was spilled in the war, which is useful.

This answer picks some relevant points from the source, and some points that are not relevant. The points are not used to answer the question about how they are useful as evidence about the personality of Charles I.

Student 2

Source A is useful as it could suggest that Charles was an arrogant man. It shows us that Charles I had no remorse for his actions and felt that he was not to blame. However, it is less useful as Lucy Hutchinson may have exaggerated Charles's unpleasant side to justify why her husband signed his death warrant.

This answer is better because it evaluates the strengths and weaknesses of the source for the enquiry. It goes beyond surface features and thinks about, not just what the source says, but who wrote the source and why.

Now it is your turn – try to use the skills you have learnt to answer the following question.

'How useful is Source A for an enquiry into whether Charles I deserved to be executed for treason?'

Remember to plan your answer – you could create a table like the one above.

Make sure your answer is relevant to the new question: did Charles I deserve to be executed for treason?

Why were kings back in fashion by 1660?

The beheading of Charles I on 30 January 1649 was, for many people, a terrifying moment. Who would rule? How would the country be governed? For other people, the killing of the king gave the country a marvellous opportunity to try out new and different ways of governing. The result was a new republic, called the Commonwealth, with Oliver Cromwell as leader. Cromwell died in 1658, and his son turned out to be a hopeless ruler. For a short time there was a real danger of another civil war. Then parliament, together with the army, decided that the only way to bring back stability was to invite Charles, son of the beheaded Charles I, to become king.

This section of the book will look at:

- what the Commonwealth was like

- the problem of who would succeed Cromwell after his death

- the events that led up to Charles becoming king.

Was the world turned upside down?

Learning objectives

- Know about England during the Commonwealth years.
- Understand the reasons why the monarchy was restored in 1660.

What do you think?

Why would a country behead its monarch and then, less than 20 years later, ask his son to become their king?

Source A: The front cover of a pamphlet published in 1647. Many people believed that, once the king was beheaded, the world would be turned upside down.

In 1649, England became a republic. With no monarch, how would power be managed? Oliver Cromwell – backed by, and sometimes controlled by, the army – took control of the situation.

How was the country governed during the Commonwealth years?

- Cromwell did not work well with any parliament and often ran the country without one. He was titled 'Lord Protector', and passed laws, called 'ordinances', when parliament was not meeting.

- Cromwell was a leading member of the army and relied heavily on it to back him up.

- Cromwell refused to become king when parliament offered him the crown, but behaved like a monarch. He was called 'Your Highness' and lived in royal palaces.

Under Cromwell, England prospered at home and abroad, but many people did not trust him. Royalists hated him, and some of Cromwell's supporters thought his reforms had not gone far enough. Cromwell ruled England in a strictly Puritan way, and this changed society in many ways (see Figure 3.1).

Banned swearing, duelling, cockfighting, horse racing and all kinds of sport

Encouraged trade by making peace with France, Holland, Portugal and Sweden

Reformed the legal system and the Poor Laws

Abolished the celebration of Christmas

Closed theatres and many inns

Allowed Jews to return to England

Outlawed religious persecution, except of Catholics and Protestant groups considered extreme, such as Quakers

Ruled with the support of the army, which he found difficult to control and which sometimes controlled him

Figure 3.1: How were people's everyday lives affected by the Commonwealth?

The problem of the succession

Oliver Cromwell died in September 1658. As agreed with parliament before his death, Cromwell's son, Richard, took over as Lord Protector. Oliver Cromwell had run England with the support of the army and the respect of parliament. Richard Cromwell had not been a soldier and didn't have the support of the army. In April 1659, he tried to persuade parliament to limit the power of the army. Army leaders met and forced Richard to retire. England was once more leaderless.

Did you know?

'Tumbledown Dick' was the nickname royalists gave to Richard Cromwell, showing what a weak and feeble leader they thought he was.

Your turn!

 1 Look at Source A. What are the 'upside down' images that the cartoonist has drawn? Discuss whether or not you think this was an effective way of getting the Royalist message across.

 2 What problems would (a) Royalists and (b) republicans have had with the way the Commonwealth was governed?

 3 Work with a partner. Use the information in Figure 3.1 to construct an argument between two people, one of whom believes their life is better under the Commonwealth and the other who disagrees. Act out the argument in front of your class.

Source B: A contemporary painting of Charles II's coronation procession, April 1661.

Why was the monarchy brought back?

A decision was made to invite Charles, son of the beheaded Charles I, to return to England and become king. How did this happen?

The timeline shows *how* Charles became king, 11 years after his father was beheaded and England became a republic. However, it doesn't show *why* the monarchy was restored. In order to find out why this happened, it is necessary to look at the background to the events in the timeline. This will uncover a number of reasons and proposed solutions, some of which are linked together.

Timeline

1658
Sept – Richard Cromwell takes over as Lord Protector on the death of his father, Oliver

1659
April – Richard and parliament try to limit the power of the army
May – Army officers force Richard to resign
Oct – Army officers quarrel with parliament and shut it down. The army runs the country
Dec – The army hands power back to parliament. MPs quarrel with each other about how to run the country and control the army

1660
Feb – General Monck, head of the army in Scotland, arrives in London with a large force of soldiers
Mar – General Monck orders elections to be held
April – Parliament meets
May – Charles makes a number of promises in the Declaration of Breda. Parliament votes to offer him the Crown. Charles returns to England as King Charles II

1661
April – Charles II is crowned in Westminster Abbey, London

Reason 1: The army and parliament

In May 1659, the army recalled parliament, thinking it would provide stable government. Instead, parliament spent a lot of time discussing how it could limit the power of the army. The army closed parliament down and ruled England through a Committee of Safety. This was very unpopular and General Monck spoke out against it. In December, parliament began meeting again but continued to argue.

Solution: Only the return of the monarchy would bring about stable government.

Reason 2: Religion in the army

Many people believed that the lower ranks of the army were full of Quakers. This was seen as dangerous because Quakers were extreme Protestants who held many ideas that challenged authority, such as not obeying Church authorities and not paying tithes (a Church tax). People were afraid that the army would increasingly act on its own, outside the law.

Solution: Bring back the monarchy and the army would have to swear loyalty to the Crown.

Reason 3: General Monck

General Monck had worked with both Charles I and Oliver Cromwell. He was greatly respected by most people on all sides. Deciding to sort out the situation, he rode down to London from Scotland. He found parliament divided and unpopular, so he closed it down and ordered elections.

Solution: Monck believed that only a restored monarchy would bring back political stability.

Reason 4: The Declaration of Breda

Charles, advised by General Monck, wrote a declaration at Breda, in Holland (where he was in exile). It consisted of promises about what he would do if he were allowed back into England as king. The most important were that he would grant religious freedom, pardon those who had fought on the parliamentarian side in the civil war, pay those in the army the wages that were owed to them and negotiate for the return of land that had been taken from the Royalists.

Solution: Charles II should govern in a restored monarchy, under certain conditions.

Source C: A contemporary painting of King Charles II in his coronation robes.

The Declaration of Breda was read out in parliament. It convinced most people that Charles would reign in a very different way from his father. Parliament passed a resolution that 'government ought to be by King, Lords and Commons'. England was once again a monarchy.

Your turn!

 1 Create a concept map of Reasons 1–4, showing as many links as you can between the reasons. Which is the most important link? Write two to three sentences to explain your choice.

 2 Look at Source B. What impression is the artist trying to create? Write down as many words as you can that could be used to describe the scene. Now do the same with Source C. The pictures were painted by different artists. Are they trying to create the same impression? Write a paragraph to explain your answer.

Checkpoint

1 What was the role of the Lord Protector?
2 Name three things that were banned during the Commonwealth.
3 Why did the death of Oliver Cromwell create a crisis?
4 What was the importance of the Declaration of Breda?

What have you learned?

In this section, you have learned about:

- the Commonwealth under the Lord Protector, Oliver Cromwell
- the ways in which the death of Oliver Cromwell led to a crisis
- the reasons why Charles II became king in 1660.

Charles writes the Declaration of Breda

Oliver Cromwell dies and his son Richard turns out to be a poor ruler

Parliament agrees to offer the crown to Charles

The army tries to run the country

General Monck arrives in London and orders elections

The army forces Richard Cromwell to resign

Figure 3.2: Events leading to the restoration of the monarchy.

Your turn!

Draw a vertical timeline from September 1658 (at the top) to April 1661 (at the bottom). Put the six events in Figure 3.2 on the timeline. Give it the heading 'Events leading to the restoration of Charles II'. Rule a column to the right of the timeline. In this column write the additional relevant detail that helps you understand the situation in more depth. Use the information on page 70 to help you.

Writing narratives

Historians often tell stories about the past. These stories are called narratives. It is important, of course, to get the chronology right. If a historian were to put the boxes in Figure 3.2 in the correct chronological order, we would have a very basic narrative of the events that led to the restoration of Charles II. However, it would simply tell us what happened. It wouldn't make connections between the events and there wouldn't be any relevant detail that would help us understand the situation more deeply.

What is relevant detail?

Think about the following two sentences.

1 When Charles II came back to England in 1660, he was wearing beautiful black leather shoes made in Flanders, with silver buckles that came from Venice.

2 When Charles II came back to England in 1660, he did so on the understanding that he would keep the promises he made in the Declaration of Breda.

Both these sentences contain details about Charles II's return to England. But which sentence contains relevant detail? Relevance depends on what the author is writing about, or what question is being answered. If a historian is writing about fashion in the 17th century, then the detail in sentence 1 would be relevant. If a historian is writing about the increasing power of parliament, then the detail in sentence 2 would be relevant.

Writing historically

Analytical narratives

We are going to explore how to answer the question 'Write an analytical narrative of the events 1658–60 leading to the restoration of Charles II'.

Planning your answer

Planning is important to help organise your ideas before you start writing. It should help you to remember everything you want to include in your answer. A plan can be a concept map, a spider diagram or a sequence of events. It is worth experimenting to find the sort of plan that suits you best.

Writing your answer

Two students have drawn up their plans and written the following answers.

Student 1

Oliver Cromwell died in 1658 and Richard Cromwell became Lord Protector. The parliament he called tried to limit the power of the army. The army closed down parliament and ran the country itself for a bit. General Monck came down from Scotland and ordered elections to be held. Charles wrote several promises in the Declaration of Breda. Parliament liked the promises. It asked Charles to be king.

There is nothing wrong here, but the student has written a narrative account, simply saying what happened. There is no relevant detail to explain events and show a deeper understanding of why the events happened.

Student 2

Richard Cromwell was born on 4 October 1626. In 1649, he got married and he and his wife had nine children. When his father died in 1658, Richard became Lord Protector. He turned out to be a weak ruler. As a result, the army forced Richard to resign and tried to run the country itself. After a short time it was clear that this wasn't working and so the army handed power back to parliament. Royalists gave Richard the nickname 'Tumbledown Dick'. General Monck decided to sort things out. He marched down to London with the part of the army he had been commanding in Scotland. The promises Charles had written in the Declaration of Breda were read out to parliament and as a result MPs decided to ask Charles to become king.

There is some relevant detail here that does show a deeper understanding of events. However, the student has also included some detail that isn't relevant in an answer to the question. Can you spot the irrelevant detail? Quite a lot of factual material is missing, too. This needs to be included, together with relevant detail.

Student 3 – you!

The death of Oliver Cromwell plunged England into a crisis. This was because his son, Richard, who succeeded him as Lord Protector, was a weak ruler. He could not...

Using these opening sentences, write your own answer, bearing in mind the points made about the two sample answers above. Don't forget to write a plan first!

What made Restoration London exciting?

The restoration of Charles II meant that London once more became a place of fun, merriment, parties and fairs, in contrast to the Puritan atmosphere of the republic. However, this came to an abrupt end when plague hit the city in 1665–66, killing up to 100,000 Londoners, followed by a fire in 1666 that destroyed most of the centre of the city. The architect Christopher Wren designed a new-look London. The ideas of the Enlightenment led to dramatic changes in the ways in which some people began to see the world. This was an exciting time – but also a dangerous one.

In this section you will:

- learn about the ways in which Londoners reacted to the plague and the Great Fire

- understand the significance of Samuel Pepys's diaries as a source of evidence

- find out about the importance of Enlightenment ideas.

What was it like to live in Restoration London?

Source A: A painting of London in about 1660.

When Charles II came to the throne, there was a reaction against the strict Puritan lifestyle imposed by Cromwell and people began to enjoy themselves again. Theatres and inns reopened; music, gambling and dancing, cockfighting and bear-baiting became popular again, as did fairs and festivals.

Source B: Extracts from Samuel Pepys's diaries about his daily life.

July 19 1662: To the King's theatre, where we saw 'A Midsummer's Night's Dream', which I had not seen before nor never will again. It is the most insipid and ridiculous play that ever I saw.

July 6 1664: Having got some bottles of wine and beer, we went to our barge at the Tower. We set out for the docks, with friends, playing at cards and other games, being pretty merry.

Plague!

London may have been a more lively place under Charles II, but it was also a dangerous one. Hundreds of houses without sanitation or fresh water, crowded around courtyards and alleys, teeming with people in the capital, were breeding grounds for disease and black rats. The fleas that lived on these rats carried bubonic plague. The plague had never completely gone after the Black Death of 1348–49 and there were occasional outbreaks over the years. In 1665, there was a massive outbreak and about 100,000 Londoners died.

No one knew what caused the Great Plague, nor how to cure it. The rich moved out of London; the poor were left to suffer and die. The Lord Mayor issued orders that included clearing the streets of rubbish and shutting the victims up in their houses, but none of this worked. The plague only ended when brown rats, which did not carry the disease, drove out the black ones.

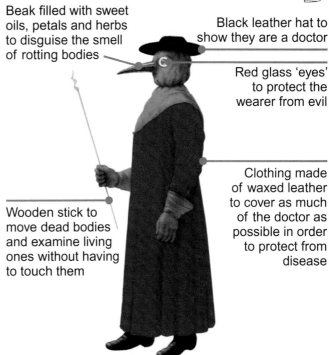

Beak filled with sweet oils, petals and herbs to disguise the smell of rotting bodies

Black leather hat to show they are a doctor

Red glass 'eyes' to protect the wearer from evil

Clothing made of waxed leather to cover as much of the doctor as possible in order to protect from disease

Wooden stick to move dead bodies and examine living ones without having to touch them

Figure 3.3: A plague doctor's uniform.

Source C: Extracts from Samuel Pepys's diary for 1665 about the plague.

June 7: I did in Drury Lane see two or three houses marked with a red cross upon the doors, and 'Lord have mercy upon us' writ there.

June 29: By water to Whitehall, where the Court full of waggons and people ready to go out of town. This end of the town every day grows very bad of the plague.

July 20: The sickness is scattered almost everywhere, there dying 1089 of the plague this week. Lady Carteret did this day give me a bottle of plague water.

August 31: In the City this week 6,102 died of the plague. It is feared that the true number of the dead this week is near 10,000: partly from the poor that cannot be taken notice of.

September 20: But Lord! What a sad time it is to see no boats upon the river; and grass grows all up and down Whitehall court, and nobody but poor wretches in the street!

Your turn!

 1 a Read Source B. What was Samuel Pepys able to do that he could not have done in the Commonwealth years?

 b In what ways is Source B useful to show what life was like for Londoners in 1660?

2 Look at the picture of the plague doctor in Figure 3.3. What can you learn from this about people's ideas about what caused the plague?

 3 a Read Source C. What did Samuel Pepys do to avoid catching the plague?

 b Imagine you are writing a book about medicine in the 17th century. How reliable would you find the information about the plague in Source C? What further questions would you need to ask about the source before you could decide if it was reliable?

4 Think back to the ways in which people dealt with the Black Death in 1348. In what ways were they the same and in what ways were they different?

How did Londoners cope with the Great Fire of 1666?

Learning objectives

- Learn about the Great Fire of London.
- Find out what Samuel Pepys's diaries and other sources can tell us about the Great Fire.

1 2 September: London burns and hundreds of people pour down to the river in order to escape by boat.

London's burning!

Between 2 and 6 September 1666, a terrible fire swept through London. The summer had been hot, with little rain, and the wooden buildings were tinder-dry. The fire is thought to have started in a bakery in Pudding Lane, near to London Bridge. It spread quickly and, before long, 300 houses had burned to the ground.

2 Samuel Pepys informs King Charles about the situation.

3 King Charles orders houses in the path of the fire to be pulled down, to create a firebreak. This doesn't work: the fire jumps the firebreak.

4 King Charles and his brother, James, Duke of York, join the firefighters, passing buckets of water to them.

5 The old St Paul's Cathedral catches fire and lead from the roof forms a molten river flowing into the street below.

6 Charles orders gunpowder to be used to blow up houses in the path of the fire and so create a wider firebreak.

7 6 September: the wind changes direction and the wide firebreak holds. The fire is out.

Figure 3.4: The events of the Great Fire of London, September 1666.

By 6 September it was over. 13,000 houses had been destroyed along with 87 parish churches, St Paul's Cathedral, the Guildhall, the Royal Exchange, 52 company halls (the backbone of London's trade and industry), as well as markets, taverns, playhouses and jails. More than four-fifths of London was destroyed.

How do we know?

We know about the Great Fire of London because people living at the time drew and painted the city in flames, and wrote about it.

> **Source A:** Extracts from Samuel Pepys's diary about coping with the Great Fire.
>
> 3 September: About four o'clock in the morning my Lady Batten sent me a cart to carry away all my money and plate and best things, which I did, riding myself in my nightgown in the cart. And Lord! to see how the streets are crowded with people running and riding, and getting carts to fetch away their things.
>
> 4 September: In the evening Sir W Pen and I did dig a pit in the garden and put our wine in it and I put in my Parmesan cheese as well as my wine and some other things.

Source B: The Great Fire of London, 1666, painted shortly after it ended.

> **Source C:** Extracts from John Evelyn's diary about coping with the Great Fire. He was an author and garden designer, and wrote diaries at the same time as Samuel Pepys.
>
> 3 September: I saw above ten thousand houses all in one flame, the noise and crackling and thunder of the flames, the shrieking of women and children, the hurry of people, the fall of towers, houses and churches was like a hideous storm.
>
> 4 September: The poor inhabitants are dispersed for several miles, some under tents others in miserable huts without a rag or any necessary utensils. I returned with a sad heart to my house, blessing the mercy of God who in the midst of all this ruin left me and mine safe and sound.

Your turn!

1 Do you find it surprising that King Charles left London during the plague, but the following year he stayed in London and helped fight the Great Fire? Discuss this in your class.

7th 2 If you had to choose only one of Sources A, B or C to tell you about the Great Fire, which would it be, and why?

3 Why is it important that historians use more than one source to tell them about the past?

Checkpoint

1 Name two things that people could do in Restoration London that they couldn't do in the Commonwealth years.

2 When did the plague outbreak start?

3 How did plague doctors protect themselves against catching the disease?

4 How did people try to save (a) themselves and (b) their possessions from the Great Fire?

5 How much of London was destroyed by the Great Fire?

Changing ideas: the Enlightenment

Source A: A picture painted by Joseph Wright in 1768 called *An Experiment on a Bird in the Air Pump*.

In Source A, a scientist (shown pointing towards his experiment) is demonstrating to a group of onlookers what happens to a cockatoo (the white bird) in a glass container when it runs out of oxygen. This kind of fascination with science and experimentation was a result of the Enlightenment.

What was the Enlightenment?

The Enlightenment is sometimes called the 'Age of Reason'. It was a time in the mid 17th and 18th centuries when new ideas swept through Europe and Britain. People began believing in the power of the human mind to explain the world by using rational and scientific thought. Enlightenment thinkers viewed the world as one governed by mathematical and scientific laws. This was a huge challenge to the traditional view that God controlled everything.

The Royal Society

Charles II was very interested in these new scientific ideas. He heard about a group of Oxford University men who had been talking about the new ideas and conducting experiments. In 1662, he granted the group a royal charter, showing his approval. In 1663, he granted another royal charter, setting up the 'Royal Society of London for Improving Natural Knowledge'. Some of the cleverest people in Britain were members: for example, the mathematician Isaac Newton, the inventor Robert Hooke, the architect Christopher Wren, as well as Samuel Pepys and John Evelyn. At Royal Society meetings ideas were discussed, academic papers were read and experiments were carried out.

Did you know?

The motto of the Royal Society was, and still is, *Nullius in verba*. This is Latin for 'Take nobody's word for it'. Everything had to be proved by experiments that could be repeated giving the same result.

The solar system and cells: Robert Hooke (1635–1703)

Robert Hooke was interested in a huge number of things: planets and fossils, light rays and metal springs, gravity, air and the workings of the human body. A lot of what he did provided clues for others to follow up. For example, his work on fossils proved that they were once living organisms and led others to think about evolution; his work on the movement of the planet Jupiter led others to think about the laws governing the solar system. Perhaps the single most important thing that Hooke did was to make a very powerful microscope. Using his microscope he discovered that plants were made up of tiny sections. He called these 'cells'. Scientists later discovered how important the understanding of cells was in the development of medicine.

Light and mathematics: Isaac Newton (1642–1727)

Most people believe that Isaac Newton was the greatest scientist of the 17th century and some say that he was the greatest scientist of all time. What did he do to win such praise and respect?

- He discovered the force that holds planets in orbit and stops them flying off into space. He called this force 'gravity'.

- He studied light and discovered the seven colours of the spectrum: red, orange, yellow, green, blue, indigo and violet.

- In 1687, he published a book, *Principia Mathematica*, which explained how the universe worked according to mathematical rules.

- He invented calculus, a mathematical way of describing change.

Source B: Robert Hooke's microscope.

Did you know?

Isaac Newton first became interested in gravity by watching an apple fall from a tree. Why, he wondered, did it fall down and not up?

Source C:
Two comments made by Isaac Newton.

If I have seen further than others, it is by standing on the shoulders of giants.

I seem to have been like a boy playing on the seashore and every now and then finding a smoother pebble or a prettier shell than ordinary, while the great ocean of truth lay all undiscovered before me.

Your turn!

1 Work in groups. Each person in your group should pretend to be one of the people in Source A and write a sentence that says what they are feeling. Compare the feelings of your group with others in your class. Is it likely that 17th-century people would be feeling the same way about experiments like this?

2 Why would the Church find the new ideas of the Enlightenment dangerous? Write a paragraph to explain your answer.

3 Hooke and Newton worked in different areas of science. What was the same about their work?

4 Most people in Britain knew nothing about the Royal Society and the new experiments that its members were carrying out. Does this mean that science wasn't very important? Explain your answer.

Key terms

Proclamation*: An official announcement on an important issue.

Architecture: Christopher Wren (1632–1723)

The Great Fire had destroyed most of the old, medieval city of London (see pages 76–77). This seemed a wonderful opportunity to build a new, modern city using the latest ideas about city planning. King Charles II issued a proclamation* promising 'a much more beautiful city than is at this time consumed'. He set up a committee to decide how the new London should look. Several people submitted plans to the committee, including Christopher Wren, Robert Hooke and John Evelyn.

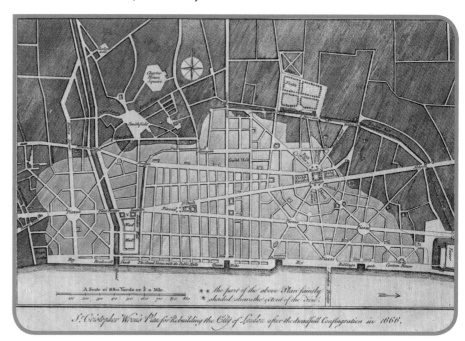

Source D: Christopher Wren's plan to rebuild London in 1666.

A new London to rival Paris?

Wren thought that this was a marvellous opportunity to clear away London's jumble of tiny, cobbled, overcrowded streets where disease and fire spread easily. He had visited Paris the previous year and had been impressed by its wide avenues and huge open squares. His design for London included these elements, laid out in a careful grid pattern. He was determined that the new London would rival Paris in magnificence.

Opposition!

Charles admired Wren's plan, but he couldn't let it go ahead. Property owners had already begun rebuilding along the lines of the old medieval streets, and there was no money available to spend on legal battles with wealthy merchants to force them to accept Wren's plan and stop rebuilding. However, the king insisted that the old roads were widened and building materials were of brick or stone.

Wren was appointed to be one of the six commissioners whose job was to oversee the building work. He was also asked to design over 50 of the city's churches and the new St Paul's Cathedral.

Building St Paul's Cathedral

The new St Paul's was the first cathedral to be built in Britain since the Reformation (see pages 12–15). Many people were shocked by Wren's designs. They were expecting a great medieval-type cathedral, with a huge steeple pointing to the sky, reminding people of heaven and life after death. What they got was something quite different!

Wren was building for the Church of England, not the Catholic Church. He wanted a building where everyone could hear the service and see the preacher. His cathedral had an enormous dome, tall elegant columns and round arches. It was a place of light.

Wren believed that true beauty came from geometry. He wanted his cathedral, and London, to be a place where simple curves, angles and squares reminded people of the order and beauty of their world.

Source E: Christopher Wren's sketch for the new St Paul's Cathedral.

Your turn!

1 Imagine you have been given the job of redesigning London after the Great Fire. How would you set about it? Draw up a plan of action.

7th 2 How far did Christopher Wren change London? Write a paragraph in explanation.

Checkpoint

1 What did Enlightenment thinkers believe governed the world?
2 What was the Royal Society?
3 Why was Robert Hooke's microscope so important?
4 Name two of Isaac Newton's discoveries.
5 Why were Christopher Wren's plans for London turned down? Give two reasons.

Did you know?

Christopher Wren is buried in St Paul's Cathedral under a simple slab of black marble. His son had an epitaph engraved: *Lector, si monumentum requiris, circumspice*, which means 'Reader, if you seek his monument, look around'.

What made Restoration London exciting?

- You are going to create a frieze that shows Year 5 pupils just how exciting it was to live in Restoration London. Start with the sort of fun things that could be done when Charles II became king, and end with the exciting ideas of Christopher Wren and the Royal Society. Don't miss out the plague and Great Fire – sometimes being scared can be exciting! Work in a group.

- Use all the information in this chapter so far to write a guidebook to Restoration London in 1660–1710. Tell people where to go, what to do – and what to avoid!

Who ran the country: Crown or parliament?

In the years to 1714, there was a gradual but steady shift of power from the Crown to parliament. Charles I's attempt to rule without parliament had ended in civil war, and yet Cromwell's attempt to govern without a monarch ended in failure and the enthronement of Charles II. It seemed that sound government needed both a monarch and a parliament. The problem was how power was to be shared between them.

In this section you will:

- learn what happened to the monarchy up to the point when Queen Anne died in 1714

- find out about the ways in which parliament worked in the reigns of George I and George II

- understand how and why power shifted between Crown and parliament.

Who controlled the succession?

Learning objectives

- Learn about the ways in which James II became unpopular.
- Understand why the birth of a son to James II created a crisis.
- Know about the Glorious Revolution and its importance.

What do you think?

Should a country be run by people who have been born, or elected, to do the job?

1660
Cromwell's rule hasn't worked. We'll ask Charles I's son to reign as Charles II.

1688
James II has been a disaster as a monarch. We'll ask his Protestant daughter Mary and her husband William to come from the Netherlands and reign.

1714
Queen Anne has died without any children to succeed her. We'll ask her Protestant relative, George of Hanover, to be our king.

1701
Must make sure that only Protestants can inherit the throne.

Figure 3.5: Who shall reign?

Between 1660 and 1714, parliament made some very important decisions about the succession – that is, about who would be the next monarch (see Figure 3.5). How had this come about?

James II: a disastrous monarch?

Charles II and his wife Catherine had no children, so, when Charles died in 1685, his brother James became king. James was a Catholic, and some people were afraid that Britain would again come under the influence of powerful European Catholic countries. However, no one wanted another civil war and so James became king without any trouble. But his reign was to last for just under four years. The main problem was religion. How could a Catholic king rule a Protestant country?

Source A: An entry in John Evelyn's diary for 5 March 1685.

To my grief, the Mass is being publicly said, and the Catholics swarming at Court with greater confidence than has ever been seen in England since the Reformation. Everybody is worried what this might lead to.

Supporting Catholics and upsetting Protestants

James did everything he could to give Catholics rights that were equal to those enjoyed by Protestants, even though it meant upsetting parliament. A more sensible monarch might have tried to introduce changes slowly, but James moved quickly.

- He appointed Catholics to be officers in the army and to positions in the government, even though this was illegal. Previously, these jobs were only given to members of the Church of England.

- Parliament refused to change the law, so James simply dissolved it and declared that anti-Catholic laws no longer applied.

- When judges disagreed with him, he sacked them.

- James said that everybody, including Catholics, could worship as they wished. The Archbishop of Canterbury and six bishops protested, saying James could not change laws without the agreement of parliament. James had them thrown into the Tower of London.

Most Protestants watched and waited. James had no sons and his heir was his daughter, Mary, who was a Protestant. Then, for the Protestants, disaster struck!

Source B: A 17th-century warming pan. Warming pans like these were filled with hot coals and used to warm the beds of rich people.

The 'warming pan' baby

On 10 June 1688, after 15 years of marriage that had not produced any children, James's second wife, Mary of Modena, gave birth to a son, also called James. Almost immediately, rumours started. Some Protestants said that the baby wasn't the king and queen's, but was another baby that had been smuggled into the queen's bed in a warming pan. A lot of rude jokes and songs circulated, and cheap newspapers spread the story. There were even playing cards made with pictures of the 'event'.

A Catholic prince was now heir to the throne. It looked as if Catholic monarchs might rule Britain for generations to come.

Source C: A playing card, produced in 1689, showing how the baby might have been smuggled into the queen's bed.

Your turn!

 1 Look at Figure 3.4. Write down one thing that changed and one thing that stayed the same.

 2 Read Source A. Why do you think John Evelyn wrote that 'Everybody is worried what this might lead to'?

3 Read about the changes made by James II. Which do you think was the most important? Why?

 4 Write two sentences, one beginning 'The warming pan story seems likely because…' and the other beginning 'The warming pan story was almost certainly made up because…'.

 5 Write a paragraph to explain the significance of the birth of the baby prince James for (a) Catholics and (b) Protestants.

Source D: A contemporary picture of James trying to escape to France.

Source E: Portraits of William and Mary by Godfrey Kneller.

The Glorious Revolution, 1688

A group of senior MPs were worried by James's actions. After the birth of the 'warming pan' baby, they were afraid about what would happen to Britain if there was a whole line of Catholic monarchs after him. They knew that James's elder daughter, Mary, was a Protestant and was married to William, the Protestant ruler of Holland. They wrote secretly to William to ask him to help them oppose James. William agreed to help. In November 1688, he landed in Devon with an army of 14,000 men. Would this lead to another civil war?

How did James react?

James's army did little to oppose William as he marched slowly to London. This was because many of James's supporters, including John Churchill, James's senior and highly skilled general, and his soldiers, changed sides. James had already sent his wife and baby son to safety in France, and he decided to follow them. Unfortunately for James, some fishermen in Kent spotted him and he was taken back to London. However, William decided to let James escape, because it was difficult to know what to do with him. This time he got safely away and was welcomed by King Louis XIV of France.

Vacancy: monarch wanted

In January 1689, parliament met and declared the throne to be vacant. It then had to decide who would be monarch. The throne was offered to William and Mary jointly, but only if they accepted parliament's conditions. They agreed and the following month they were crowned king and queen.

At their coronation, they promised to rule according to the laws of parliament, which meant accepting the Bill of Rights, 1689.

Key term

Bill*: The draft of a proposed law.

The Bill of Rights, 1689

The bill* included some important points.

- The agreement of parliament was needed:
  - for an army to be kept in peacetime
  - for all taxes
  - before any law could be set aside.
- There had to be freedom of speech in parliament.
- No Catholic could become a monarch.

The long title of the bill was 'An Act Declaring the Rights and Liberties of the Subject and Settling the Succession of the Crown'. It was clear that parliament linked the freedoms of the British people with the succession.

Family problems – and another succession crisis

In 1689, parliament clearly thought that William and Mary would have children who would reign after them. However, Mary died in 1694 without leaving any children. Mary's sister, Anne, was due to inherit the throne when William died. She was married to Prince George of Denmark and had a lot of pregnancies, but only one child survived. He died, aged 11, in 1700. Parliament was now worried. If Anne had no more children, her heir would be her half-brother, James – the 'warming pan' baby – child of her father, James II's, second marriage and a Catholic. Although the Bill of Rights stated that no Catholic, or person married to a Catholic, could inherit the throne, MPs felt they had to make the position crystal clear: there was to be a Protestant succession.

In 1701, parliament passed the Act of Settlement. It stated that, if neither William nor Anne had any more children, the Crown would pass, on Anne's death, to the Protestant Sophia of Hanover and her successors. It was Sophia's son, George of Hanover, who became King George I in 1714.

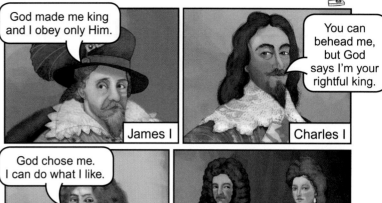

Figure 3.6: Was the Divine Right of Kings finished?

Your turn!

1   a   Protestants called the events of 1688 a 'Glorious Revolution'. Why do you think they did this?

   b   What do you think Catholics would have called the same events? Why?

2   How did the Bill of Rights try to make sure that no future monarch would behave like Charles I, Oliver Cromwell or James II?

3   Parliament wanted to make sure there was a Protestant succession. How did it do this?

4   Look at Figure 3.6. What words would you put in the last box? Was the Divine Right of Kings really finished?

Checkpoint

1   Name two things James II did that upset people.
2   Whose son was the 'warming pan' baby?
3   Give two reasons why William invaded England in 1688.
4   Who were the next three monarchs after James II?
5   Name one way in which parliament took control of the succession.

The changing power of parliament

- Learn about parliament in the reigns of George I and George II.
- Understand how general elections were organised.

The power of parliament changed a great deal in 1600–1760. In some periods, the Crown had more power; in others, parliament had more.

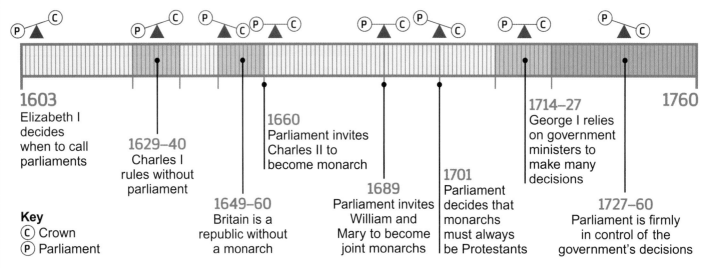

1603
Elizabeth I decides when to call parliaments

1629–40
Charles I rules without parliament

1660
Parliament invites Charles II to become monarch

1649–60
Britain is a republic without a monarch

1689
Parliament invites William and Mary to become joint monarchs

1701
Parliament decides that monarchs must always be Protestants

1714–27
George I relies on government ministers to make many decisions

1727–60
Parliament is firmly in control of the government's decisions

1760

Key
Ⓒ Crown
Ⓟ Parliament

Figure 3.7: The changing power of parliament.

In the 17th century, parliament was made up – and still is – of the House of Lords and the House of Commons. The Lords were there because they had been born into a noble family. Members of the Commons were there because they had been elected.

There were 558 MPs.

MPs were not paid, and so had to have private wealth.

No Catholic could become an MP.

The House of Lords could overrule any law passed by the House of Commons.

Only men could become MPs and only men could vote for MPs in general elections.

Only men with wealth or property could vote in general elections.

The king appointed government ministers. Most of them were already in the House of Lords.

The king had to give his approval to all laws passed by parliament.

Parliament decided how much money to give the king out of taxes.

Figure 3.8: The House of Commons during the reign of George II, 1727–60.

What were elections like in the 17th century?

The law said there had to be a general election at least every seven years. Elections were usually lively affairs. The polls were kept open for several days. This was so that everyone qualified to vote could come in from the surrounding countryside to do so. The candidates paid for the cost of transport and for the board and lodging of those they thought would be voting for them. A successful candidate usually had to pay for feasts and celebrations as well. Candidates had to be pretty rich!

The rules about who could vote varied from place to place. Only men could vote, and their right to vote was dependent on money or the ownership of property, or both. The vote was not secret. Voters would climb onto a platform, called the hustings, and shout out the name of the person for whom they were voting. A clerk would write this down and give them a certificate. They could use this to claim back expenses from the candidate who got their vote.

Source A: A picture painted by William Hogarth in 1755 called *An Election Entertainment*. Hogarth became famous for his paintings and drawings that criticised society. He often exaggerated people's expressions and actions in order to make a point.

Source B: A picture painted by William Hogarth in 1755 called *The Polling*.

Your turn!

 1 Look at Figure 3.8. How different is parliament today? Write down two things that are the same and two things that are different. Share your ideas with your class and put together a complete class list. If you are uncertain about parliament today, use the internet to check your ideas.

2 Work with a partner. One of you should choose a person from Source A and the other should choose a person from Source B. Write a conversation between the two of them about the election. (Hint: Are they taking it seriously? What's happening around them?)

3 Use Source A and Source B together. Work with a partner and make a list of the different ways in which people could cheat the voting system. What has changed in modern times to stop cheating?

Prime minister, patronage, power

Learning objectives

- Learn about the way in which Sir Robert Walpole became prime minister, and the importance of the job.
- Understand how the British form of government differed from that in France.
- Work out the balance of power between the British Crown and parliament.

Did you know?

The Cabinet got its name because in earlier reigns leading government ministers met in the monarch's private rooms, or cabinet.

Source C: A cartoon published in 1740.

Key terms

Gentry*: People of high social status, just below the nobles, and usually landowners.

Patronage*: The power to appoint people to jobs and positions. Sometimes this was in return for money or favours, or because they were relatives or friends.

How did Sir Robert Walpole become prime minister?

George I was 54 years old when he became king of Britain in 1714. He spoke very little English, didn't like England and spent as much time as he could back in Hanover, Germany. His son, who became George II in 1727, felt much the same. Because of this, they relied on a group of leading English nobles and gentry* in parliament to run the country. This group was called the Cabinet.

Someone had to run Cabinet meetings, convince MPs (and the House of Lords) that what the Cabinet wanted to do was right for the country, and meet with the king to persuade him to agree with what parliament wanted. Sir Robert Walpole, a Norfolk landowner and MP for King's Lynn, emerged as the person who could do this. He was the leading minister for 21 years (1721–42). His official title was 'First Lord of the Treasury' but he was sometimes called the prime minister. At first this was only a nickname, but it gradually became the official name for the head of government. Walpole became extremely powerful and very rich.

The very rude cartoon in Source A shows a person kissing Walpole's bottom. Another person is holding a petition in one hand and a hoop in the other. Round the hoop are written the words 'wealth', 'vanity', 'folly', 'luxury' and 'corruption'. The cartoon is criticising the way in which Walpole ran the country, which was by using patronage*.

George II was so grateful to Walpole for all his hard work that he gave 10 Downing Street in London to him as a present. Walpole refused to accept the house as a personal gift. Instead, he asked the king to make it the official home, and office, of all future First Lords of the Treasury. The king agreed, and Walpole moved in on 22 September 1735.

Over the Channel in France

In the 18th century, the government in France was different from that in Britain.

- Monarchs had supreme authority in France and their power was not restricted by written laws. A monarch, for example, could have someone arrested and thrown into prison just by signing a letter saying this had to be done.

- 'The Estates' (a sort of French parliament) were occasionally summoned by the monarch, but the assembly was dominated by the aristocracy and the clergy.

- The nobles and clergy had a huge number of privileges and paid very little in taxes, whereas the peasants were taxed heavily.

In 1789, France exploded in a bloody revolution. King Louis XVI was imprisoned and later executed. The balance of power was changed dramatically and violently in favour of the ruled.

By contrast, 18th-century Britain saw gradual change in the balance of power between the ruler and the ruled.

Source D: An engraving showing the execution of Louis XVI, by Georg Heinrich Sieveking, 1793.

Your turn!

1 In no more than 150 words, describe Robert Walpole's job in government.

2 Imagine a conversation between King George II and Louis XVI, the king of France. What hints would George have given him about how to govern his country?

Checkpoint

1 Name one thing that shows the Crown's power over parliament in the 18th century.

2 Name one thing that shows parliament's power over the Crown in the 18th century.

3 Who was the first British prime minister?

4 Name one difference between the government of Britain and the government of France in the 18th century.

Who ran the country: Crown or parliament?

- Robert Crane, a wealthy British landowner, was born in 1680. In 1740, he told his grandchildren about the changes he had seen in the way in which the country was run. Write down what you think he would have said.

- Draw a pair of scales and label them 1660. On the left-hand pan, write all the things that the monarch could do. On the right-hand pan, write all the things that parliament could do. The balance should be tilted in favour of the Crown. Now do the same for a pair of scales labelled 1760. Are the scales evenly balanced or tilted in one direction? Write a paragraph to explain what happened to change the balance of power between Crown and parliament.

How 'modern' was England by 1789?

The England of 1789 was very different from that of Elizabeth I or even Charles II. New ideas had taken hold and had had a profound effect on the way people viewed themselves and society. New discoveries and inventions were having an impact on medicine and industry. New wealth was being invested in art, architecture and landscaping. England, for some, was a lively, exciting place. But it was not like this for everyone. Most people still lived in the countryside and worked on the land, at the mercy of landlords and the weather. Crop failure would mean starvation. For them, life went on as it had done for their parents and their grandparents. For them, there was little change.

In this section you will:

- find out how much ideas had changed by 1789

- understand what impact the new ideas had on science, government and architecture

- compare Tudor monarchy and society with those of the Hanoverians.

Exciting ideas!

Learning objectives

- Learn how new ideas were put into practice.
- Understand that change happened to different people in different ways and at a different pace.

What do you think?

What decides the speed, or pace, at which change happens?

Figure 3.9: Discussing ideas in an 18th-century coffee house.

Let's follow through some of the things that were being discussed in the coffee houses at the time (see Figure 3.9). Remember that everything begins with an idea!

'… wonderful new houses…'

The old, Tudor thatched houses became unfashionable and some considered them cramped, dark and inconvenient. Downing Street is an example of the new terraces of houses that were built in the 18th century. They weren't built only in London. Towns such as Bath and Harrogate had similar sweeping terraces that were sometimes built around gardens and squares – and always for the rich. The move towards new, architect-designed houses spread into the countryside for those who could afford to live in style.

'… the heart is a pump…'

In 1628, William Harvey proved that the heart pumped blood round the human body. He proved this by experimenting on animals, sometimes when they were alive. Many doctors refused to accept Harvey's discovery, but those who repeated his experiments found he was right. By the 18th century, surgeons were able to perform operations more successfully by tying off arteries to stop the bleeding as they amputated limbs and cut out diseased tissue.

… drain water out of… mines…

Thomas Savery's first steam engine had problems. One of them was that using steam under pressure meant that the boiler joints often burst and frequently needed repairs. It was the partnership of Savery with Thomas Newcomen in 1702 that resulted in a reliable steam engine being developed. By 1789, steam engines were used to power factories and mills and were a vital part of the Industrial Revolution (see Chapter 6).

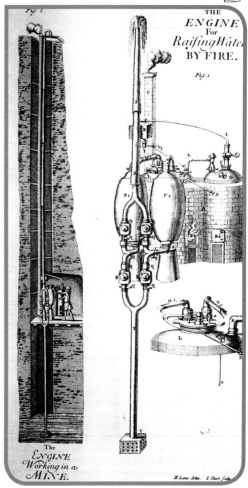

Source A: Thomas Savery's design for a pump that would 'lift water by fire'.

Source B: Reddish House, built in Wiltshire in the 18th century for Jeremiah Cray, a cloth merchant.

Your turn!

 1 Look at Figure 3.9. Which of the new ideas do you think were the most exciting? Why?

 2 Sometimes change happened slowly and sometimes quickly. What was needed for new inventions, discoveries and ideas to bring about a quick change? (Hint: Think about attitudes and money.)

Change and continuity questions

A different kind of monarchy and society?

Queen Elizabeth I, who reigned between 1558 and 1603, was a strong and successful monarch. Yet parliament met only 13 times during her reign of 45 years, and then averaged only about three months in each sitting. She had good advisers, chose her own ministers and made her own decisions. By 1789, all of this had changed. Or had it?

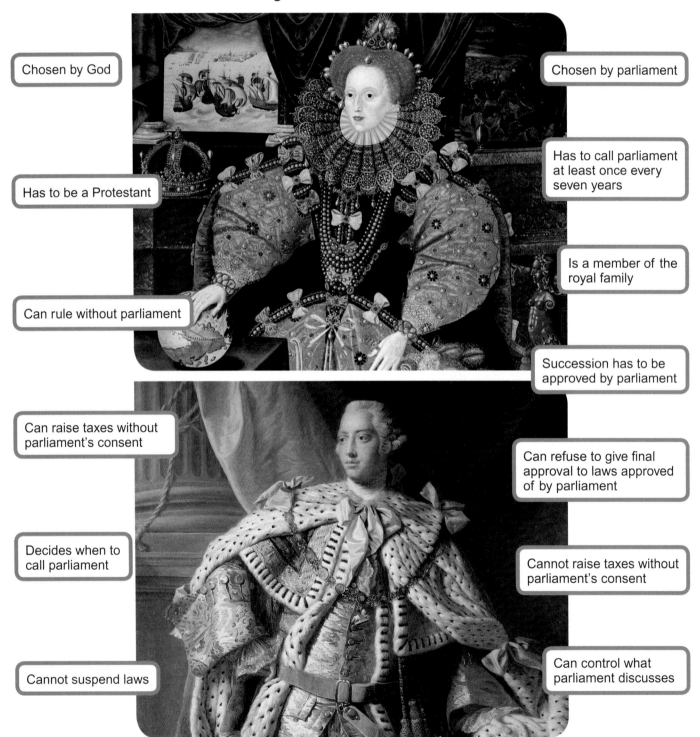

Chosen by God

Chosen by parliament

Has to be a Protestant

Has to call parliament at least once every seven years

Is a member of the royal family

Can rule without parliament

Succession has to be approved by parliament

Can raise taxes without parliament's consent

Can refuse to give final approval to laws approved of by parliament

Decides when to call parliament

Cannot raise taxes without parliament's consent

Cannot suspend laws

Can control what parliament discusses

Figure 3.10: What could Elizabeth I do compared with George III? You will need to decide to answer question 1a opposite.

Between the reigns of Elizabeth I and George III, though most people still made their living from the land, towns were starting to grow. People were beginning to move there to work in mills and factories, which did not exist in Elizabeth's time.

Whatever was happening in the country around them, ordinary people lived, died, ate, slept, worked, married, had children, worried and loved. They managed to have fun, too.

Source C: A contemporary painting of a wedding party in Bermondsey, London in 1594.

Source D: A contemporary painting by William Hogarth of a fair held in Southwark, London in 1724.

Checkpoint

1 Name two ideas that were new in the 18th century.
2 What did Harvey discover in the 17th century? Why wasn't his discovery used until the 18th century?
3 What could both George III and Elizabeth I do as monarchs? Name two things.
4 Name two things that George III couldn't do as a monarch that Elizabeth I could.

What have you learned?

In this section you have learned that:

- new ideas were not accepted immediately and they were not accepted by everyone

- changes happened at different speeds and did not affect everyone in the same way.

Your turn!

 1 Draw up a list of all the changes you can find in this chapter. Sort them into political, economic and social change. You could do this in a grid or concept map. Colour code the changes that happened quickly and those that happened slowly.

 2 Which changes would have affected the Andrews family, and which would have affected the Carpenter family? Write a paragraph to explain your thinking.

Quick Quiz

1 Give one reason why Charles II became king in 1660.

2 Who was Samuel Pepys?

3 What was the Great Plague?

4 What horrific event happened in London in 1666?

5 Who was put on the throne as a result of the Glorious Revolution?

6 Give two of Isaac Newton's discoveries.

7 What did Robert Hooke invent?

8 Who was Sir Robert Walpole?

9 Who could vote in general elections?

10 What part did women play in the government of 18th-century Britain?

Thinking about change

It is important to understand that there are different kinds of change: political change (government), economic change (trade, industry and money) and social change (religion, ways of living and working). Some of these changes happen at different speeds, and different kinds of change affect different people in different ways.

Fact file: the Andrews family

Robert Andrews and Frances Carter were married in 1748 and had nine children. They lived on a large estate, land given to them by both fathers. They were landed gentry. Their income came from managing their estate and from inheriting shipping and textile businesses.

Figure 3.11: Mr and Mrs Andrews painted by Thomas Gainsborough in 1750.

Fact file: the Carpenter family

Benjamin Carpenter and Lydia Newman married in 1740 and had nine children. They lived in a village and worked as labourers for a local farmer. It was a constant struggle to feed and clothe their family. Neither Benjamin nor Lydia could read or write.

Figure 3.12: Agricultural labourers like the Carpenter family in the 18th century.

Writing historically

Change and continuity questions

We are going to explore how to answer the question:
'The most important change to take place in Britain between 1660 and 1789 was that parliament had more control over choosing the monarch. Do you agree?'

Planning your answer

This is a big question and covers a lot of different aspects of change, so it is important to plan carefully. Your plan will need to cover three main areas: (i) what was important about the change, (ii) other events or discoveries in 1660–1789 that were important, and why, and (iii) the number of people affected by the events and discoveries you are considering, and how this affects their importance. You will then need to reach a conclusion about whether or not parliament having more control over choosing the monarch was the most important change at this time.

Writing your answer

Student 1

> Parliament inviting William and Mary to take over the throne from James II who was the rightful monarch was a very important change. This was because parliament was taking control. There were other important changes at this time, like rebuilding the city of London after the Great Fire and Isaac Newton's discovery of gravity.

The student has noted the importance of parliament inviting William and Mary to become monarchs but has said little about why it was important. Two other important changes have been identified, but nothing is said about why they were important. There is no conclusion, and nothing about the people that were affected by the changes.

Student 2

> Parliament inviting William and Mary to become joint monarchs instead of James II was an extremely important change as far as the government of the country was concerned, as parliament had taken control. This meant that MPs became important in running the country. There were other important changes, like the rebuilding of London, putting new ideas about architecture into action. This would have been seen by Londoners, but not by people living, for example, in the north of England. Another important change was the result of Isaac Newton using scientific method in his experiments. However, not many people at the time would have known about this or thought it was important.

The student has explained why parliament having more control over choosing the monarch was important, but needs to develop the importance of the changes brought about by Christopher Wren and Isaac Newton. There is no conclusion.

Parliament, by inviting William and Mary to become monarchs, was showing that governing the country was to be shared between the Crown and parliament…

Christopher Wren's designs influenced architects all over Europe…

All scientists after Isaac Newton used his scientific method in their experiments in order to make sure they were valid…

Student 3 – you!

Now use the opening sentences alongside to write your own answer to the question. Don't just say something was important but say why and to whom, and remember to write a conclusion.

What was it like to be involved in the slave trade?

In this enquiry we will be investigating different groups of people who were involved in the slave trade and the impact that it had on them. This section of the book will look at:

- Britain's role in the transatlantic slave trade

- West African kingdoms before the transatlantic slave trade and the impact of the slave trade on them

- how the trade triangle worked

- what life was like for the slaves.

What do you think?

Who do you think benefited from the slave trade and how did they benefit?

What part did Britain play in the transatlantic slave trade?

Learning objectives

- Understand the importance of the transatlantic slave trade* in Britain's growing wealth and power between the 16th and 19th centuries.
- Consider how historians can use different types of evidence when studying the transatlantic slave trade.

Key term

Transatlantic slave trade*: The forced movement of around 12 to 15 million Africans across the Atlantic Ocean to the Americas and the West Indies, where they were used as slaves. It occurred between the 16th and 19th centuries.

By the end of the 18th century, Britain dominated global trade. This domination brought with it great wealth for the country, making some people very rich, and transforming many British towns and cities. It was Britain's ports that changed the most, in particular Liverpool, Bristol and London.

Source A: A picture of Liverpool and the river Mersey made in about 1771. It shows how important trade was to Liverpool.

Sir Thomas Johnson (1664–1728)

- Known as 'the founder of modern Liverpool'.
- Imported sugar and tobacco into Britain.
- Established salt mines in Cheshire.
- Created Liverpool's wet dock, leading to its growth as a port.
- Knighted by Queen Anne in 1708.

Bryan Blundell (1675–1756)

- One of Liverpool's most successful merchants.
- Twice Mayor of Liverpool.
- Built a school for Liverpool's orphans, called The Blue Coat School.
- Gave one-tenth of all his earnings to support the poor.

Foster Cunliffe (1682–1758)

- From one of Liverpool's most influential families.
- Imported tobacco, sugar and rum into Britain.
- Had shares in 26 ships.
- Mayor of Liverpool three times.

Sir Hardman Earle (1792–1877)

- From a well-known merchant family.
- Imported raw cotton for the mills of Lancashire.
- Director of the Liverpool and Manchester Railway, one of Britain's first and most important railways.
- Knighted by Queen Victoria for his work.

Figure 4.1: Some of Liverpool's most famous and successful businessmen from the 17th to the 19th centuries.

The four men in Figure 4.1 all contributed to the development of the city of Liverpool, but they also have something else in common. They were all involved in a particular type of trade that made their families very wealthy, but destroyed the lives of countless others: the transatlantic slave trade.

There were hundreds of slave owners and merchants involved in the slave trade in Liverpool and thousands who were involved across Britain. It was not just the slave owners and traders themselves who benefited. The money they made was invested into Britain – in banking, industry, global trade and in the development of towns and cities. In short, the transatlantic slave trade helped to make Britain very rich and, some argue, is one of the reasons that it enjoys such relative wealth today.

Your turn!

1 Look at Source A. What can we learn from this painting about Liverpool in the 18th century? Refer to details from the picture and say what they imply about the city. For example, you could write: 'In Source A I can see… This implies that Liverpool was…'.

2 Look at Figure 4.1 and answer the following question. Who, aside from the four businessmen, benefited from the money that they made from the slave trade (directly and indirectly)? Identify at least five groups or types of people.

The scale of British involvement

It was not just Britain that profited from the slave trade. Portugal, Spain, the Netherlands, Denmark and France all traded slaves across the Atlantic. It was, however, Britain that became the dominant slave trading nation. Historians have calculated that British ships transported three and a quarter million Africans across the Atlantic between the 17th and 19th centuries. So, where did all these slaves end up?

The answer, as you can see in Figure 4.2, is the West Indies and the Americas. The slaves were taken to the British colonies* to work on plantations* that mostly grew sugar, tobacco and cotton. The produce of these plantations was then exported to Europe and sold for profit.

These statistics, however, hide something very important. They reveal nothing of the history of the slaves themselves: the history of suffering and tragedy that the transatlantic slave trade brought to the lives of real human beings. We will explore some of this history later in the chapter.

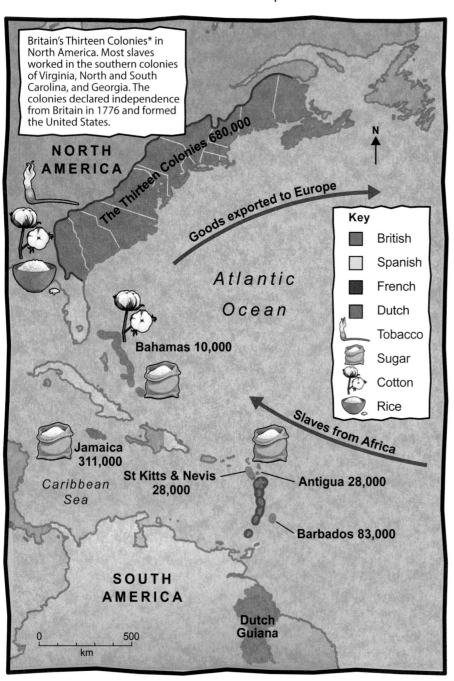

Britain's Thirteen Colonies* in North America. Most slaves worked in the southern colonies of Virginia, North and South Carolina, and Georgia. The colonies declared independence from Britain in 1776 and formed the United States.

NORTH AMERICA

The Thirteen Colonies 680,000

Goods exported to Europe

Atlantic Ocean

N

Key
- British
- Spanish
- French
- Dutch
- Tobacco
- Sugar
- Cotton
- Rice

Bahamas 10,000

Slaves from Africa

Jamaica 311,000

Caribbean Sea

St Kitts & Nevis 28,000

Antigua 28,000

Barbados 83,000

SOUTH AMERICA

Dutch Guiana

0 — 500 km

Figure 4.2: Slavery in Britain's American and West Indian colonies around the year 1750. The map shows the approximate total number of slaves imported into each colony, and the main crops that were grown in each area.

Key terms

The Thirteen Colonies*: The British colonies established in North America between 1607 and 1732.

Colony*: An area of land settled by and under the control of people from another country.

Plantation*: A large farm or estate where one main crop is grown.

How do we know?

'How do we know?' is an important question for a historian to ask. For example, how do we know how many Africans were taken as slaves? How do we know where they were taken? Essentially, what we are asking is: what evidence do we have? Figure 4.3 shows some of the different types of sources that historians use when studying slavery.

Anti-slavery campaign publications: from the 1790s, some people who opposed slavery began researching what conditions were like for slaves and publishing their findings. Some former slaves published accounts of their lives.

Business accounts: plantation owners and slave traders kept records of their finances and their property, including slaves.

Colonial office records: the governors of colonies kept records of things like imports, which at the time included slaves, and exports from their colonies, as well as reporting on slave rebellions.

How do we know?

Ships' log books: captains kept records of their cargoes, including slaves, as well as recording their origin and destination.

Journals and diaries: some slave traders and plantation owners kept diaries of their lives and experiences.

Newspapers: these sometimes contained adverts for the sale of slaves, details of auctions and information on runaway slaves.

Legal records: as slaves were considered to be property, their owners included them in things like wills and insurance records.

Figure 4.3: Some of the different types of sources that historians use when studying the transatlantic slave trade.

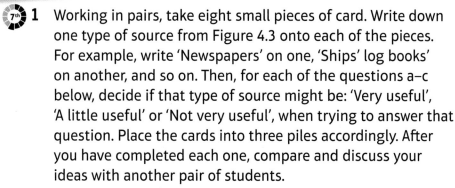

Artefacts: objects that have survived from the past, such as items used on plantations.

Following up a source

Source utility questions

Your turn!

1 Working in pairs, take eight small pieces of card. Write down one type of source from Figure 4.3 onto each of the pieces. For example, write 'Newspapers' on one, 'Ships' log books' on another, and so on. Then, for each of the questions a–c below, decide if that type of source might be: 'Very useful', 'A little useful' or 'Not very useful', when trying to answer that question. Place the cards into three piles accordingly. After you have completed each one, compare and discuss your ideas with another pair of students.

   a How many Africans were transported across the Atlantic to America?

   b What were conditions like on the ships in which the slaves were transported?

   c How did slaves try to resist their situation?

2 You may have noticed that few of the sources shown in Figure 4.3 comes from the slaves themselves. Why do you think this is? How might this affect our understanding of slavery? Discuss these questions as a class.

Checkpoint

1 What was the transatlantic slave trade?

2 Name two British cities that prospered due to the transatlantic slave trade.

3 What were the Thirteen Colonies?

4 What were the three most common products grown on the slave plantations in America and the West Indies?

What were 16th-century West African kingdoms like?

Did you know?

One of the biggest ever man-made structures was built in the Kingdom of Benin. The walls of Benin were interconnected earth mounds built to defend its towns and villages. They are believed to have been an amazing 16,000 kilometres in length, four times longer than the Great Wall of China! Sadly, hardly any of the structure still survives.

Before exploring how the transatlantic slave trade operated, and what conditions were like for slaves, it is important to understand what life was like in West African kingdoms before the transatlantic slave trade. The case studies below feature two of the most important kingdoms in West Africa that existed around the time that European traders first arrived in the 15th century.

Case Study 1: The Kingdom of Benin

The Kingdom of Benin was one of the most developed kingdoms in Africa, in what is now Nigeria. It lasted from the 15th to the 19th century. Early explorers' accounts of Benin City describe it as a very well organised city: clean, free from crime and with happy residents. It was ruled by a king, known as the Oba, but there was also an organised system of government, guilds and law courts. The kingdom became very wealthy due to trade. The area was known for its gold and bronze, and there were skilled metalworkers in Benin City. The people of Benin also traded ivory, cotton cloth and slaves with other Africans, Arabs and, later, with Europeans.

Source A: Benin City, 1686. An engraving showing the king of Benin with a procession of musicians and horsemen. The palace and city are in the background. The picture is from a book written by a Dutchman called Olfert Dapper, based on descriptions from other European travellers.

Source B: Adapted from a description of life in the Kingdom of Benin by Olaudah Equiano. Equiano was a slave who, after buying his freedom, went on to campaign against slavery. He wrote an autobiography detailing the story of his life, called *The Interesting Narrative* (1789).

We are a nation of dancers, musicians, and poets… Our manners are simple, our luxuries are few… our important women wear golden ornaments… Before we taste food we always wash our hands: indeed our cleanliness on all occasions is extreme… Our main luxury is in perfumes… [For] our buildings… each master of a family has a piece of ground, surrounded with a moat or fence, or enclosed with a wall made of red earth. Within this are his houses to accommodate his family and slaves… Our land is… rich and fruitful, and produces all kinds of vegetables in great abundance… Everyone contributes [to farming]… and as we are employed and busy, we have no beggars. The benefits of such a style of living are obvious… Indeed cheerfulness and affability [friendliness] are two of the leading characteristics of our nation.

Key term

Inference*: Something that can be learned from a source, which goes beyond the surface detail of what the source says, to what it suggests.

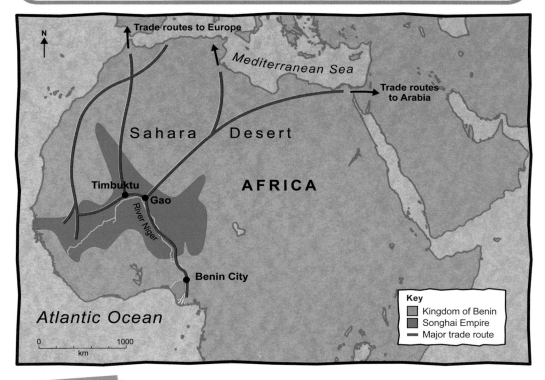

Figure 4.4: A map showing the locations of the Kingdom of Benin and the Songhai Empire c.1500. The map also shows major trade routes at that time.

Your turn!

 1 Look at Sources A and B. From this evidence, what inferences* can you make about the Kingdom of Benin? Aim to make three inferences and support them with specific details from the sources.

 2 Consider Source B. In his book, Olaudah Equiano says he was born in 1745 in the Kingdom of Benin. However, there is also evidence that he was actually born into slavery in South Carolina, America. Either way, he would have known many slaves who were born in Benin. If he was not born in Benin, does this mean that we should not trust what he says? Discuss this question with a partner and then share your thoughts with the rest of the class.

Case Study 2: The Songhai Empire

The Songhai Empire was centred on its capital city, Gao, in what is today the country of Mali. The main cities of the Songhai Empire, Gao and Timbuktu, were located on the River Niger, which provided water to farm their fertile land, as well as plentiful supplies of fish.

Source C: Adapted from a description of the city of Timbuktu, one of the most important cities in the Songhai Empire. It is taken from a book called *Descriptions of Africa* written by Leo Africanus in 1526. Leo Africanus grew up in Morocco. He travelled widely across northern and western Africa and recorded his observations.

The houses of Timbuktu are huts made of clay with thatched roofs. In the centre of the city is a temple built of stone and mortar… and there is a large palace where the king lives. The shops of the artisans, the merchants, and especially weavers of cotton cloth are very numerous. Fabrics are also imported from Europe to Timbuktu… The inhabitants are very rich… Grain and animals are abundant… The king has a rich treasure of coins and gold ingots [bars]. One of these ingots weighs 970 pounds [440 kilograms]. The royal court is magnificent and very well organized… The king has about 3,000 horsemen and [a huge number] of foot-soldiers… There are in Timbuktu numerous judges, teachers and priests, all appointed by the king. He greatly respects learning. Many hand-written books are sold. There is more profit made from selling books than from all other merchandise. The people of Timbuktu are of a peaceful nature. They have a custom of almost continuously walking about the city in the evening… playing musical instruments and dancing. The citizens have at their service many slaves, both men and women.

The River Niger was also a major trade route and boats would go to and from Benin City and the ocean beyond (see Figure 4.4). Gold, copper, ivory and slaves were transported along the river. Goods would then be transferred onto camels and taken across the Sahara Desert to North Africa and, eventually, Europe and Asia. In return, Songhai traders would receive salt (for preserving food), pottery, glass, silk, perfumes and spices. People also moved along these trade routes and Arabic, Italian and Jewish merchants could be found living within the Songhai Empire.

Culture flourished under Songhai rule. It was an Islamic empire and the rulers encouraged research and study. Timbuktu became a centre of religion and learning.

The impact of the transatlantic slave trade on Africa

Slavery and slave trading existed within Africa long before Europeans began buying African slaves. However, the transatlantic slave trade transformed slave trading.

When Europeans began trading with West African kingdoms, including both Benin and Songhai, they bought slaves from African rulers and traders. These were usually slaves that had been taken as captives during war or had been kidnapped. The captives would be marched to the coast before being imprisoned in wooden cages called barracoons, or in large stone forts built by European traders. When the ships arrived from Europe, their captains would give gifts and pay taxes to local African leaders, before exchanging their goods for the slaves.

Figure 4.5: The vicious cycle created in Africa.

As demand for slaves in the Americas grew, African slave traders had to become even more active and aggressive to capture enough slaves. Due to this, the scale and the violence of the slave trade increased. Furthermore, Europeans often traded guns in exchange for the African slaves, which meant that there were more guns in Africa. More guns meant more war. More war meant that more slaves were captured. A vicious cycle was created.

Key terms

Enslaved*: Made into a slave.

Legacy*: Something handed down from the past.

It was not just the lives of the millions of people who were enslaved* that were negatively affected. Those left behind in Africa were affected by famine as there were not enough farmers left. Entire communities disappeared as people fled away from the slave trading routes. Some historians argue that the present-day underdevelopment of certain regions of Africa is partly a legacy* of the slave trade.

Source D: A 19th-century engraving showing slaves in Africa being walked to the coast, where they would be sold to European traders. Those too weak to walk would be killed or left behind to die.

Your turn!

1   Imagine that you are a 16th-century travel writer like Leo Africanus. You are visiting the Songhai Empire for the first time in your life. Use the information on these pages, and your own further research online, to produce a journal of your travels in the empire. Include information on the people that you meet, the places you see, as well as your observations of what life is like in the Songhai Empire.

6th 2   Historians compare different sources of evidence in order to judge their trustworthiness. We call this cross-referencing. Compare Source B with Source C. Make a list of similarities between what they say and suggest about West African kingdoms.

7th 3   Do you think the similarities between Sources B and C make Equiano's account (Source B) more or less trustworthy?

Checkpoint

1   Why was the Kingdom of Benin so wealthy?
2   What goods did the Songhai Empire receive from North Africa, Europe and Arabia?
3   Who did European traders buy slaves from?
4   Give two ways in which the transatlantic slave trade negatively affected Africa.

The trade triangle and the horrors of the Middle Passage

Learning objectives

- Explain how the trade triangle operated.
- Know about conditions during the Middle Passage.
- Explore the difficulty of deciding who was responsible for the transatlantic slave trade.
- Consider how and why contemporary accounts of the Middle Passage vary.

Key term

Globalisation*:
The world becoming more interconnected.

The shipping of slaves from West Africa to the Americas was one part of what is known as the trade triangle. Figure 4.6 shows how this system operated.

As so often in history, things were actually more complex than they first appear. The slave trade was just one part of a much larger, complex system: a system of international trade and a part of the process of globalisation*.

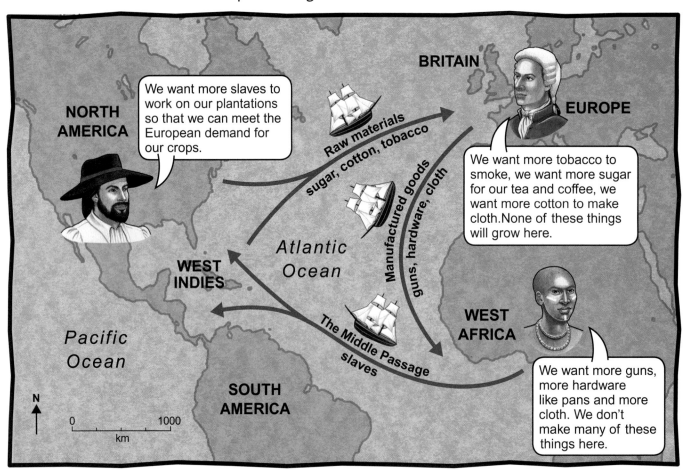

Figure 4.6: A map showing the operation of the transatlantic trade triangle. You can see what each region demanded and what was transported on each of the routes across the Atlantic.

Who was responsible for the transatlantic slave trade?

A. West African slave trader

 I capture people from neighbouring communities and then sell them to European traders.

B. European monarch

 I grant licences to allow my traders to sail to West Africa and buy slaves there.

C. Plantation owner in the West Indies

 I need slaves to grow sugar, in order to meet the demand in Europe.

D. Sailor working on a slave ship

 The conditions on the ships are terrible. Sailors as well as slaves die of disease.

E. West African leader

 The Europeans can trade with my people, as long as they give me goods and money.

F. Captain of a slave ship

 I sail between West Africa and the Americas. I am well paid for my work.

G. European banker

I've invested my money in a ship that is going to complete the trade triangle. If it is successful, I could earn a lot of money.

H. European factory owner

My factory produces guns and hardware, a lot of which are shipped to West Africa.

I. European textiles factory worker

 My job relies on cotton imported from the plantations. I'm paid badly, but without the cotton, I might not have a job at all.

Figure 4.7: Some of the people involved in the transatlantic slave trade.

Your turn!

In this activity, you are not looking for a 'correct' answer, but simply aiming to explore this complex issue.

1   Work in a pair or a group of three. Draw three concentric circles on a piece of A4 paper. Label the circle in the centre 'To a large extent', label the next ring 'Partly', the next 'A little' and outside of the circles 'Not at all'.

2   Read each of the descriptions of the people above and discuss in your group if they were to a large extent, partly, a little or not at all responsible for the transatlantic slave trade. Write the letter corresponding to that person onto your circles in the appropriate place. To do this, you should consider the following points: How directly was that person involved? Did they have a choice? Did they know the consequences? How much did they profit?

3   Join with another group and compare your answers. Discuss any differences of opinion.

4   Finally, discuss the following questions as a class.
    a   Is it possible to say that all of the nine people in Figure 4.7 are partly responsible?
    b   Could any of these people have stopped the slave trade if they had chosen to?
    c   What does this activity suggest about why it was so hard to stop the transatlantic slave trade, and why so many people were willing to defend the system?

The Middle Passage

It is estimated that, between the 16th and 19th centuries, 12 to 15 million Africans were shipped across the Atlantic, on a route known as the Middle Passage. We can learn from slave ship log books that 10 to 20 per cent of slaves died on the Middle Passage due to the horrendous conditions on the ships. In total, over two million died on the journey.

Before the late 18th century, few people in Europe, apart from sailors, would have had any idea how slaves were treated on the Middle Passage. That changed when abolitionists* began researching the conditions on the ships and publishing their findings. The image below was used on many posters produced by abolitionists, such as Thomas Clarkson. Clarkson interviewed people connected with the slave trade as part of his research.

Source A: An engraving produced around 1790 showing a slave ship called the *Brookes*. It was recorded that, on one journey, the *Brookes* transported 744 slaves. This was achieved by forcing the slaves to lie on their sides.

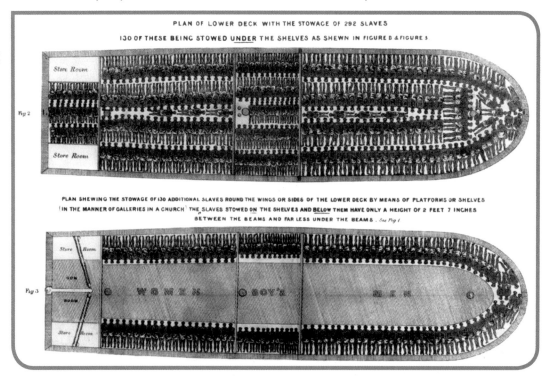

Source B: Adapted from a description by John Newton of conditions on the Middle Passage, written in 1788. Newton was an English vicar and abolitionist. In his younger life he was captain of a slave ship.

The slaves were laid in rows so that as little space as possible might be lost. The poor creatures were cramped and in irons [chains], usually on both hands and feet which makes it difficult for them to move without hurting themselves. When the weather allows, the slaves are brought on deck. Often the weather is not good so they are kept below deck, to breathe hot and polluted air. Depression quickly seizes their spirits. Fevers and flu often break out. Nearly half the slaves on board sometimes die, and the loss of a third of the slaves is not unusual.

Source C: Adapted from Olaudah Equiano's account of the Middle Passage, taken from his autobiography, *The Interesting Narrative* (1789). Equiano was a former slave who worked as a sailor on slave ships so would have known about the conditions.

I was soon put down under the decks and there I received such a stench in my nostrils as I had never experienced in my life. I became so sick and low that I was not able to eat, nor had I the least desire to taste anything. I now wished for death to relieve me.

... if I could have got over the nettings, I would have jumped over the side, but I could not as the crew used to watch us very closely when we were not chained down to the decks...

The heat of the climate – added to the number in the ship, which was so crowded that each had scarcely room to turn himself – almost suffocated us. This ... brought on a sickness among the slaves, of which many died... This wretched situation was made worse by the discomfort of the chains and the filth of the necessary tubs [toilets], into which the children often fell, and were almost suffocated. The shrieks of the women, and the groans of the dying, rendered the whole a scene of horror almost inconceivable.

Source D: Adapted from an account of how slaves were treated on the Middle Passage written by a Frenchman, John Barbot. Barbot was a slave trader and an explorer. He wrote a book called *Journey to the Congo River*, published in 1700.

In large ships five or six hundred slaves can be carried. Below deck in such ships is at least five and a half or six foot high [which is] more airy and convenient for such a considerable number of human creatures; and consequently far more healthy for them. The women are allowed to be up on the deck whenever they like, as are many of the men... few, or none, are kept in shackles [chains]... We allow them tobacco, and some coconuts... Towards the evening, the slaves entertain themselves as they choose, some conversing together, others dancing and singing.

Your turn!

1 What three inferences can we make from Source A about the Middle Passage?

2 In what ways do Sources B and C give a similar impression of conditions on the Middle Passage?

3 In what ways does Source D give a different impression from Sources A, B and C? Why do you think this is?

4 Do differences between the sources mean that one must be wrong or not telling the truth? If not, why else might there be differences between them?

Checkpoint

1 What goods were transported:
  a from Europe to West Africa
  b from West Africa to the Americas and the West Indies
  c from the Americas to Europe?

2 What is the voyage from West Africa to the Americas known as?

3 Approximately how many slaves were taken from Africa to the Americas?

4 Give three reasons why so many slaves died on the Middle Passage.

Slaves' lives in the Americas

Learning objectives

- Understand how slaves were bought and sold and what daily life was like for slaves on the plantations.
- Consider what was done to prevent slaves from running away.
- Consider how the selection of evidence can affect how we view the past.

Key terms

Legal rights*: Rights that a person has according to the laws of a country: for example, the right to be protected from harm, the right to an education, and so on.

Field slaves*: By far the largest percentage of slaves in the Americas, field slaves would work in the fields on the plantations. They were more commonly, but not always, men.

Domestic slaves*: Slaves who performed household jobs such as cooking and washing. These were usually female slaves. They would work in the homes of their owners.

To us in the 21st century, Source A is both shocking and tragic. Each and every one of the slaves listed were bought and sold as property, not as human beings. Just like objects, slaves had few – or no – legal rights*.

56 VERY CHOICE Cotton Plantation SLAVES, MECHANICS, SEAMSTRESSES, COOKS, &C.

By J. A. BEARD & MAY.   J. A. BEARD, Auctioneer.

WILL BE SOLD AT AUCTION,

ON MONDAY, JANUARY 29, 1855,

At 12 o'Clock, at Banks' Arcade,

WITHOUT RESERVE,

The following list of Choice and Valuable SLAVES, from the Plantation of Gen. W. BAILEY, Lake Providence, La., viz:

ONE FAMILY.
1.—BIG HENRY, aged about 21 years, a superior field hand, fine servant, and first rate cotton picker; and his wife—
2.—AMY, aged about 18, superior cotton picker and fine servant.
3.—LITTLE HENRY, aged about 16, slightly near-sighted, a superior cotton picker and fine servant.
ONE FAMILY.
4.—BOSTON, aged about 26 years, a complete ostler and field hand, and superior cotton picker, and an invaluable servant.
5.—LITTLE MILLY, his wife, aged about 19, a superior cotton picker, and a most valuable hand.
ONE FAMILY.
6.—STEPHEN, aged about 24 years, a fine ox driver and superior cotton picker, etc.
7.—BIG FANNY, aged about 24, his wife, a good seamstress, and superior cotton picker and field hand; his child—
8.—WIRT HENRY, aged about 20 months.
ONE FAMILY.
9.—CASWELL, ox driver, aged about 30, very slightly ruptured, a fine field hand, and an invaluable servant.
10.—AGGY, his wife, aged about 30, a superior cook, washer and ironer, a most valuable woman, and superior field hand and cotton picker.
11.—FAYETTE HENRY, her child, aged about 5 years.
12.—STANHOPE McLANHAN, aged about 2 years.
ONE FAMILY.
13.—BIG JIM, a rough carpenter, a superior field hand and cotton picker, aged about 25 or 26 years—invaluable.
14.—ANN RANDOLPH, his wife, aged about 22 years, can pick cotton with any negro, and is invaluable.
ONE FAMILY.
15.—GEORGE, aged about 26 years, plain but useful plantation smith, a fine driver, and one of the best cotton pickers and field hands in the State, without exception.
16.—LITTLE FANNY, his wife, aged about 23 years, a most valuable cotton picker and field hand.
17.—RODERICK DHU, her child, aged about 4 years. This man and wife can pick more cotton than any two hands in the State.
ONE FAMILY.

22.—DOLLY, his wife, aged about 21 years; can pick from 420 to 500 lbs. of cotton per day; a superior field hand, sews well.
23.—NELSON, aged about 28, slightly ruptured; a most valuable field hand and superior cotton picker; has never lost an hour's work from his rupture.
24.—JORDEN, aged about 19, a very valuable field hand, a fine cotton picker and ginner.
25.—ADDISON, aged about 18, an invaluable field hand and cotton picker, one of the best.
26.—SAM, aged about 18, a fine cotton picker, and as valuable a boy as can be found.
27.—WASHINGTON, aged about 15 or 16, a fine cotton picker and valuable boy.
28.—DICK, aged about 20, a fine cotton picker and superior gin hand.
29.—CHARLES, aged about 19, field hand, a good boy.
30.—JOHN, aged about 23 years, fine cotton picker and field hand.
ONE FAMILY.
31.—EDWARD, aged about 19, one amongst the best cotton pickers and field hands in the State.
32.—MARGARET, his wife, aged about 18, a valuable cotton picker; and her two children—
33 and 34.—JENNY LIND, aged 2 years, and Infant 3 mos.
35.—BIG WILLIAM, aged about 20, a fine cotton picker and good servant—a strong and valuable man.
36.—JIM HENRY, aged about 19 years, a fine field hand and cotton picker.
37.—HOYT, aged about 11 or 12 years, cotton picker, etc.
38.—WILLIAM NELSON, aged about 14 years, fine cotton picker, etc.
ONE FAMILY.
39.—JESSEE, aged about 20 years, fine field hand; can pick 500 lbs. cotton; invaluable boy.
40.—CAROLINE, his wife, aged 17 years, can pick as much as Jessee.
41.—AMANDA, aged about 18, fine field hand, etc.
42.—MARY PATE, aged about 18, field hand and cotton picker, etc.
43.—YELLOW MARY, aged about 18, a good seamstress, can pick 500 lbs. cotton per day.
44.—DINAH, aged about 45, a good field hand, strong and

Source A: Part of bill of sale for a slave auction in New Orleans, USA in 1855. Slavery was abolished in British colonies in 1833, but was not abolished in the USA until 1865.

Upon arriving in the Americas the slaves would be sold. Some would be sold directly from the ships to the buyers. Others would be sold at auction, to the highest bidder. Yet there were many slaves working in the Americas who were not born in Africa, but born in the Americas to other slaves. If a slave had a child, then that child would become the property of the mother's owner.

After sale, slaves would be taken to their respective jobs. As we can see from Source A, slaves performed a wide variety of jobs including some highly skilled jobs like blacksmithing. The vast majority of slaves, however, fell into two categories: field slaves* and domestic slaves*. Field slaves most commonly worked on plantations, where a large amount of labour was required.

The following pages give some idea of what life was like on these plantations.

Source B: An English wood engraving showing slaves being sold at auction in Virginia, America, 1861.

Your turn!

1 Make a list of legal rights to which you are entitled (see the 'Key terms' box). Now consider the fact that slaves had none of these rights. What dangers, difficulties and disadvantages would they face because of this?

2 Look carefully at Source A and discuss the following questions with a partner.
   a How many of the slaves do you think are field slaves, and how many are domestic slaves?
   b What do you notice about the ages of the slaves? Are they old or young? Why do you think this is?
   c None of the names listed are traditional African names. Why do you think this is? Who might have named them?
   d Which slaves do you think would have fetched the highest price at auction and why?

3 Look at Source B. What makes us think that this source was created by an abolitionist?

4 Consider Sources A and B. Which of the two do you think is more useful to a historian investigating how slaves were sold? Explain your answer.

Life on the plantation

Source C: A mid 18th-century engraving of a sugar plantation in Haiti, in the West Indies. Can you identify the slaves' houses, the owner's house, the sugar cane field and the sugar mill?

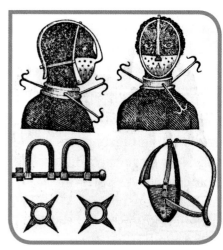

Source D: An image from a poster of 1807 showing some of the artefacts used to punish slaves, including a face mask, iron collar, leg shackles and spurs (to go around the ankles to prevent running away).

Source E: A painting called *Negroes Sunday-Market at Antigua* produced in 1806, showing a market on the West Indian island of Antigua. Slaves would often be given a small amount of land to farm in their spare time. They would sell any extra produce at markets like this one. Note that the word 'negroes', meaning 'black people', is today considered an offensive term.

Source F: Adapted from *An History of Jamaica*, written by an Englishman called Robert Renny who had visited plantations on the island, published in 1807.

The first gang [of slaves]... is called just before sunrise. The register is then called, and the names of absentees noted. After which they commence their labour and continue till 8 or 9 o'clock, when they breakfast on boiled yams and vegetables seasoned with salt and cayenne pepper. In the meantime, the absentees generally arrive, and are punished by a number of lashes [of the whip]. At sunset they return to their huts. Slaves usually work ten hours per day, excluding Sundays. In the harvest season the arrangement is different and slaves often work late in the mill and the boiling houses, frequently all night.

Source G: An engraving from 1596 showing African slaves working on a plantation in the West Indies. It shows the many processes involved in making sugar: cutting and carrying the cane, crushing it in a press, then boiling.

$50 REWARD.

Ranaway from the subscriber on
TUESDAY MORNING, 26th ULTIMO,

My negro boy calling himself Severn Black. The said negro is about 5 feet six inches in height, chesnut color, has a scar on his upper lip, downcast countenance when spoken to, blink-eyed, showing a great deal of white, long bushy hair, is about twenty years old, had on when he left a blue fustian Jacket, pantaloons of a greyish color, blue striped shirt, A BLACK SLOUCH HAT and shoes nearly worn out.

The above reward will be paid by me for the apprehension and delivery of the said negro in the County Jail at Princess Anne, Somerset county, Maryland.
April 1, 1861.   RICHARD E. SNELLING.
                            SOMERSET HERALD Print, Princess Anne, Md.

Source H: Despite the risk of punishment if caught, some slaves did run away from plantations. This advertisement was printed in a newspaper in Maryland, USA on 1 April 1861. It offers a reward for the return of a runaway slave, a boy called Severn Black.

Your turn!

6th 1 Imagine you are a researcher for a documentary film about the life of slaves. You are covering the short section on plantation life, but you are allowed to include just three pieces of evidence within it. Which three pieces of evidence from Sources C to H would you include? Write a justification for why you have chosen those three.

7th 2 Now compare your selections and justifications with a partner. How are theirs similar to or different from yours? Would their documentary portray plantation life differently from yours?

7th 3 How can a historian's choice of evidence affect how they portray the past? Discuss this question as a class.

Checkpoint

1 How were slaves sold upon arrival in the Americas?
2 What were slaves in the Americas most commonly used for?
3 What did domestic slaves do?
4 What forms of punishment were commonly used on plantations?
5 What was done to prevent slaves from running away?

What was it like to be involved in the slave trade?

Produce a concept map showing all the groups of people that you can think of who were involved in the slave trade. Next to each, write down how they benefited or suffered, drawing connections between those who benefited or suffered in similar ways. Try to be specific and use all your knowledge. For example, do not just write, 'Plantation owners became rich', but explain why: 'Plantation owners became rich by using slaves to grow sugar, which they exported to Europe'. For the slaves themselves, you should be able to give a large number of different ways in which they were affected.

What have you learned?

In this section you have learned:

- how to make inferences and how to cross-reference different sources.

Figure 4.8: What do you do when you have a lot of sources and they don't all agree?

Imagine there has been a fight in your school yard. A teacher has heard about the fight and wants to find out who was responsible. The teacher would not just ask one student for their view of what happened. He or she would ask a number of different students, and would then compare their stories to gain a fuller and more accurate view of what happened.

In history, we do the same thing with historical evidence. We try to gather multiple sources of evidence. We then compare these sources, identifying similarities and differences. We call this comparing process 'cross-referencing'.

You now need to re-read Sources B, C and D on pages 106–107, as you are going to cross-reference sources relating to the Middle Passage. When cross-referencing evidence, we can compare the overall impression that the sources give of an event, as well as the details. A table like the one below can be a useful tool to cross-reference different historical sources.

To be compared	Source B	Source C	Source D
The feelings of the slaves	'Depression quickly seizes their spirits'	He was 'so sick and low' he was 'not able to eat'	Slaves were 'dancing and singing', indicating they were happy
The space the slaves had	'…laid in rows so that as little space as possible might be lost'	Not mentioned	Below deck is 'six foot high'
Overall impression given			

Your turn!

Draw the table above and complete it using the information from Sources B, C and D on pages 106–107. Try to add an extra three rows to the table by considering other comparisons and contrasts, before completing the 'Overall impression' row.

When pieces of historical evidence give a different impression of the same event, we need to investigate why. To do this, we need to consider where the sources come from. Differences do not necessarily mean that some of the sources must be incorrect or not telling the truth. For example, Sources B, C and D are discussing the conditions on *different* ships. Perhaps conditions were worse on some ships than on others. Furthermore, Source D is from 1700, whereas B and C are from later. Perhaps conditions deteriorated over the century.

Writing historically

You are now going to write an answer to the question: 'Do Sources B, C and D give a similar impression of conditions on the Middle Passage?' The information on this page will help you to structure your answer.

Introduction

In your introduction, try to show that you have understood what the question is asking and briefly introduce the sources you are using. For example, you could begin with:

The Middle Passage was the journey from Africa to America that slaves were forced to make aboard the slave ships. Sources B, C and D are all pieces of evidence written by people who would have witnessed the conditions on this journey.

Paragraphs

Since the question asks about what is *similar*, it is logical to begin your answer by discussing the *similarities* between the sources. Try to support your inferences with details from the sources (use your table from page 112 to help with this). Read the two examples below; one is a good example and one is weaker. Which do you think is the strongest answer and why?

Student 1

Sources B and C are similar because they both mention that slaves were in chains. They both make the Middle Passage sound really bad and horrible. Source C even mentions children falling into the toilets, which is disgusting.

Student 2

Sources B and C both give a similar impression of how the Middle Passage affected slaves. Source B says that 'Depression quickly seizes their spirits' and Source C, written by a former slave, says that he was so 'sick and low' he was 'not able to eat' and that he would have killed himself if he could have done.

Now try to write your own paragraph about the similarities between the sources. Aim to make at least three comparisons (and don't forget to use details to support them).

Next try to write a paragraph identifying some of the *differences* between the sources. Follow the same technique: make a point and then support it with evidence from the sources, as shown below.

However, the sources disagree about whether the slaves were chained up. Source B says the slaves were 'cramped and in irons', and Source C mentions the 'discomfort of the chains'. However, Source D says that 'few, or none, are kept in shackles'.

Conclusion

Finally, write a short conclusion. Make sure you directly answer the question – think about whether the sources give a very similar, slightly similar, slightly different or very different view. For example:

Overall, Sources B and C give a very similar impression of the Middle Passage: that it was an awful and terrifying experience that killed many people. Source D, however, implies that the conditions were not so bad. This may be because Source D was written by a slave trader who might not want to reveal the true horrors aboard his ships.

Why was the slave trade abolished?

In this enquiry we will be investigating the factors that led to the abolition of the slave trade. This section of the book will look at:

- the debate surrounding the causes of the abolition of the slave trade

- the nature and impact of slave resistance and revolt

- the fate of the slaves and slavery after 1807.

What do you think?

Why do you think that, after almost three centuries, people turned against the slave trade?

The road to abolition

Learning objectives

- Understand the key events and factors that led to the Abolition of the Slave Trade Act in 1807.
- Recognise how historians' interpretations of the abolition* have changed over time.

Key terms

Abolition*: Banning or getting rid of something.

The Enlightenment*: New ways of thinking that emerged in the 18th century which emphasised reason and logic over tradition and superstition.

Your turn!

As you progress through the information on pages 114–116, make two lists:
- a list of all the methods and tactics used by the abolitionists. How many can you find?
- a list of all the people (individuals and groups) who were involved in the abolition movement. How many can you find?

For nearly 300 years, the British had been trading slaves, but in 1807 that came to an end. What caused this change? Why did people turn against a system that for so long they had either ignored or simply accepted?

During the Enlightenment, when some writers and philosophers began to question old traditions and ideas, the idea that people have a right to liberty and equality began to become more common. Some people used this idea to begin to challenge slavery. One such man was a lawyer by the name of Granville Sharp. In 1787, he established an organisation to campaign against the slave trade. The Abolition Committee, as it was known, was initially just a group of 12 men. Yet they were influential men and, very quickly, their campaign gained support.

Thomas Clarkson: educating the public

Thomas Clarkson was one of the first men on the Abolition Committee. He realised that their campaign needed the support of the public and, to get public support, he needed to educate people about the horrific realities of the slave trade.

Few British people at that time would have had any real idea of what it was like on the slave ships or the plantations. Clarkson interviewed over 20,000 people connected with the slave trade and recorded their stories. His findings were then made public with a huge propaganda campaign. Between 1787 and 1794, Clarkson travelled an incredible 35,000 miles around Britain, holding meetings and giving lectures. Many people were shocked and appalled by what they heard.

Black abolitionists

The Abolition Committee was keen for the voices of slaves to be heard. In 1787, it published the autobiography of Ottobah Cugoano. Cugoano was a former slave who had worked on plantations in the Caribbean, before eventually being brought to England where he gained his freedom. In 1789, another freed slave, called Olaudah Equiano, published his autobiography (see pages 101 and 107). These accounts were important as they helped the public to see slaves as real people, not property. The authors also proved what former slaves could achieve if given the chance of freedom.

William Wilberforce: the campaign in parliament

However, abolition could never have been achieved without the support of members of parliament, as they were the ones who could pass a law to abolish the slave trade. The abolitionists' representative in parliament was the MP William Wilberforce. Wilberforce was a powerful speaker and a skilful politician who worked to convince other MPs to join the abolition cause. For many years, he had the support of the prime minister, William Pitt.

Wilberforce was met by a lot of opposition within parliament. Some MPs were slave owners themselves and many profited from the trade triangle. Others feared that abolishing the slave trade would ruin Britain's economy. Yet Wilberforce was a very determined man. He introduced an abolition bill to parliament almost every year between 1790 and 1806, but they kept being defeated. MPs needed to be convinced that change had to happen.

Source A: An engraved picture of Olaudah Equiano, taken from his popular and widely read autobiography of 1789.

Source B: A painting from 1808, showing the House of Commons as it would have looked in William Wilberforce's day.

Key terms

Popular movement*: Where a large proportion of the general public support a cause.

Nonconformist*: A Protestant who does not follow the teachings of the Church of England. Examples are Quakers, Baptists and Methodists.

Petition*: A list of requests or demands signed by many people.

Boycott*: When people refuse to buy something as a protest.

The popular movement*: abolition becomes fashionable

Within a few years of the establishment of the Abolition Committee, there were numerous anti-slave trade societies across the country. Often these were formed by nonconformist* groups who used religious arguments to protest against the slave trade. Women's anti-slave trade societies also became common. These societies would encourage others to join their cause. Books, plays and poetry were written in favour of abolition. People proudly wore abolition medallions and brooches. The public mood had turned against the slave trade.

Members of the public put pressure on MPs to pass an abolition law. The most direct method was through petitions* that were sent to parliament. By 1792, parliament received over 500 different abolition petitions per year, containing thousands of names. Another way that the abolition campaigners put pressure on the government was through the use of a sugar boycott*. This added economic pressure to the increasing political pressure on MPs.

> **Source C:** Adapted from *Slavery: A Poem* by Hannah More. More was an abolitionist whose poems and writings against slavery were popular during the 1790s.
>
> See the dire victim torn from social life, the shrieking babe, the agonising wife! She, wretch forlorn, is dragged by hostile hands, to distant tyrants sold, in distant lands!
>
> Transmitted miseries, and successive chains, the sole sad heritage her child obtains!
>
> Ev'n this last wretched favour their foes deny, to weep together, or together die.

Your turn!

1   Consider your two lists from page 114. How do they help to explain why the abolition campaign was successful?

2   Working with a partner, draw a flow diagram to represent the events that led to the Abolition Act 1807. You might want to begin with 'Enlightened ideas', then link that to 'People challenge the slave trade', then 'Sharp forms Abolition Committee', and so on.

The final push

Public outcry against the slave trade was such that it was impossible for MPs to ignore it. Many MPs came around to the side of the abolitionists. Some probably did so to protect their reputations and positions; others because they genuinely believed that it was morally the right thing to do. Some also may have done so because they feared that, if they did not, the slaves on the British plantations might rebel as they had done in the French colony of Saint-Domingue (see page 120).

In 1807, Wilberforce once again introduced a bill to parliament to attempt to abolish the transatlantic slave trade. After a 10-hour debate, and at the end of a 20-year campaign, the bill finally passed. The British transatlantic slave trade was abolished.

Differing interpretations of abolition

Historians often have differing interpretations of the same event. For example, historians disagree about what the main reasons were for the abolition of the slave trade in 1807.

Before the 1930s, historians tended to suggest that slavery was abolished due to the actions of great British men, in particular William Wilberforce. They argued that Wilberforce and other British leaders realised that the slave trade was wrong and so led a moral campaign against it.

The slave trade was abolished due to the actions of great British leaders.

Historian A

Later historians questioned this view. A historian from Trinidad argued that the British parliament banned the slave trade because it was afraid that, if it did not, the slaves would revolt, as they had on the West Indian island of Saint-Domingue (see page 120).

The slave trade was abolished due to the actions of the slaves themselves. Parliament feared slave revolt.

Historian B

Another historian from Trinidad, argued that the main reason that the British parliament was willing to abolish the slave trade was because it was no longer profitable enough.

The slave trade was abolished as it was no longer making enough money.

Historian C

Many historians have since disagreed, arguing that the slave trade was still making a lot of money at the time it was abolished. Historians today still debate what the main reasons for abolition were, and they will no doubt continue to do so in the future (see Interpretation 1).

Your turn!

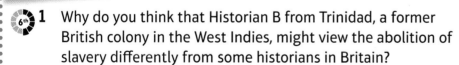
1 Why do you think that Historian B from Trinidad, a former British colony in the West Indies, might view the abolition of slavery differently from some historians in Britain?

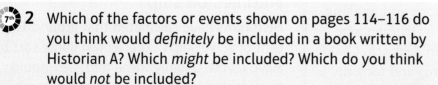
2 Which of the factors or events shown on pages 114–116 do you think would *definitely* be included in a book written by Historian A? Which *might* be included? Which do you think would *not* be included?

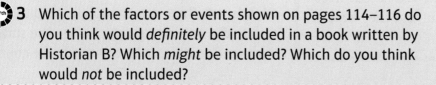
3 Which of the factors or events shown on pages 114–116 do you think would *definitely* be included in a book written by Historian B? Which *might* be included? Which do you think would *not* be included?

Interpretation 1:

From *A Short History of Slavery* by the historian James Walvin, published in 2007.

In the last quarter of the eighteenth century, the British slave trade thrived. In the 1780s alone, British (or British colonial) ships transported more than 300,000 Africans, though only 276,100 arrived. In the process, more than 1,000 slave ships cleared British and British colonial ports bound for the slave coasts of Africa.

Why interpretations differ

Checkpoint

1 In what year was the British slave trade banned?
2 What was the Enlightenment?
3 What was the name of the politician who campaigned in parliament for the slave trade to be banned?
4 Name five different methods used by the abolition campaign.
5 In what way did the slave revolts make abolition more likely?

117

Slave rebellion and resistance

Learning objectives

- Understand the different ways that slaves rebelled against their captivity.
- Explore some of the evidence connected with slave resistance.

Source A: An early 19th-century wood engraving showing slaves who had mutinied aboard a slave ship being thrown overboard.

Source B: Adapted from a letter by Captain George Scott describing a mutiny on his ship, *Little George*, in 1730. The slaves managed to take control of the ship and sail it back to Africa, where they escaped.

[We] sailed from the Coast of Guinea [West Africa], on 1st June 1730, having on board 96 slaves. On the 6th June at 4.30 in the morning, the male slaves got out of their irons and, making way through the deck, killed the watchmen who were all asleep. I heard noise upon deck (they were throwing the watchmen overboard) and took my pistol and fired. This made all the slaves that were loose run forwards and [capturing us] they kept us confined in the cabin.

Slaves were controlled through a system of fear and violence. Their masters – in Africa, on the slave ships and on the plantations – possessed guns and other weapons, making resistance very dangerous. The majority of slaves had no choice but to accept their circumstances. Yet, despite all the risks, there were many acts of resistance.

Slaves reacted against their captivity in various ways. There were revolts on ships, runaway slave communities and major slave rebellions. Yet there were undoubtedly also many thousands of small acts of resistance that are not recorded in the historical evidence, such as slaves pretending not to understand instructions, working intentionally slowly or inefficiently, or taking more food than allowed.

There was also cultural resistance. Through language, music and dance, slaves kept alive aspects of their African heritage, resisting attempts to destroy their culture. Music was also used to unite slave communities. Traditional drums could be used to send messages to slaves in other villages, and some songs, known as negro spirituals, contained secret, coded messages about freedom.

Mutinies on ship

Historians have calculated that around 10 per cent of slave ships experienced some sort of slave revolt. Usually these mutinies would be defeated by the crew, often with great bloodshed. There are, though, examples of successful mutinies on ship, when the slaves managed to defeat the crew and take control.

The Maroons

In some places, communities of runaway slaves developed, such as the Maroons of Jamaica. The Maroons were a group of former slaves who had escaped enslavement. They lived in the Blue Mountains of Jamaica, where they established their own towns and ways of life. The Maroons assisted other slaves in escaping and joining their community. In the early 18th century, they were led by a woman known as 'Nanny'. Historians know little about Nanny, but she has become a legendary figure in Jamaican folk tradition.

The Maroons caused such a problem for the British that, from the 1670s until 1740, soldiers were sent to try to defeat them. Eventually, the Maroons were imprisoned and then shipped to British colonies in Nova Scotia (Canada) and Sierra Leone (West Africa).

However, slaves continued to escape the plantations to go and live in the mountains. It has been estimated that 2500 slaves per year were escaping Jamaican plantations by the 1820s.

Interpretation 1: A Jamaican $500 bank note. It features an image of Nanny, the Maroons' leader.

Source C: An engraving of 1801 showing a treaty being agreed between Maroons and British officials.

Your turn!

 1   Historical evidence is sometimes limited in what it tells us about an event. Read Source B and then make two lists: one list of what the source does tell us about the mutiny on *Little George* – for example, it tells us there were 96 slaves on board – and one list of what it does not tell us – for example, it does not tell us what happened to the slaves after the mutiny. Overall, how useful is this source for studying that mutiny?

 2   Jamaica gained its independence (freedom) from British rule in 1962. Why do you think that the Jamaican government chose to put an image of Nanny on their currency? Consider what she might symbolise.

Source D: A coloured engraving of Toussaint Louverture made in England in 1805.

Source E: An announcement made by Toussaint Louverture on 29 August 1793. He was aiming to gain the support of the rebel slaves.

Brothers and friends, I am Toussaint Louverture. I have undertaken vengeance. I want Liberty and Equality to reign in St Domingue. I am working to make that happen. Unite yourselves to us, brothers and fight with us for the same cause.

Your very humble and obedient servant, Toussaint Louverture.

The Haitian Revolution (1791–1804)

In the 18th and early 19th centuries, there were slave uprisings on many West Indian islands, including Grenada, Jamaica, Antigua and Barbados. The most famous revolt was in the French colony of Saint-Domingue (modern-day Haiti). It is the most famous for one reason: it was successful.

From 1793 until 1802, the man who led the slave revolt was Toussaint Louverture. Louverture was a former slave who had been granted his freedom by his master. He was a highly organised and skilful military leader capable of turning untrained rebel slaves into a serious fighting force. He also inspired the slaves with his message of liberty and equality.

Louverture was imprisoned by the French in 1802, and died in captivity a year later. Despite this, the revolution continued and, in 1804, the self-liberated slaves defeated their colonial rulers and declared the country of Haiti as their own. The Haitian Revolution had shown the world that a slave revolt could be well organised, skilfully led and, most importantly, successful.

Slave revolts after 1807

Whilst the Abolition of the Slave Trade Act of 1807 was important in stopping the British trade in slaves, it was also limited in its aims. The 1807 Act also had a consequence that the abolitionists did not predict. Banning the trade meant that there were fewer slaves in the British colonies. This meant that the slaves in those colonies were forced to work even harder to make up for the loss. It also meant that slaves were moved around more, as plantation owners tried to use their labour more efficiently. This led to more slave families being split up. So the 1807 Act actually made the lives of the slaves on the plantations even worse. It is not surprising then that there was an increase in slave revolts between 1807 and 1833.

Of all British colonies, it was Jamaica that witnessed the largest slave revolts. There were significant revolts on the island in 1816 and 1823, but the revolt of 1831–32 was the most serious. More than 200 plantations in the north of the island were affected as 60,000 slaves seized large areas of land.

The slaves were led by a man called Samuel Sharpe, who had been born a slave in Jamaica in 1801. He was an educated and powerful speaker who used religious arguments to condemn slavery. He was also well aware of the abolition movement in Britain.

Sharpe encouraged a peaceful protest against slavery but events quickly escalated into a major revolt. British soldiers were called in to defeat the rebels. The rebellion lasted just 10 days, but caused extensive damage and claimed the lives of 14 slave masters and over 200 slaves. Sharpe was publicly hanged on 23 May 1832. Just before his death, he said: 'I would rather die upon yonder gallows than live in slavery'.

Interpretation 2: From *A Short History of Slavery* by the historian James Walvin, published in 2007.

… the slaves in the Caribbean were acutely aware of the debate in Britain. With planters and merchants, traders, sailors and visitors to the islands all discussing the ways slavery was being handled in London, and slaves' masters talking about the news from London, it was inevitable that West Indian slaves would hear about what was being discussed in Britain.

Source F: A painting from 1833 showing the destruction of the Roehampton Estate, a plantation estate in Jamaica, during the revolt of 1831–32.

Your turn!

1 Toussaint Louverture is a fascinating historical character. Conduct some research into his life. What can you find that is interesting or surprising?

2 Read Source E and answer the following questions:
 a Why do you think Louverture describes himself as a 'servant' to the slaves?
 b What evidence is there within the source that Louverture was familiar with the ideas of the Enlightenment (see page 78)?

3 Look at Source D. What impression is the artist trying to give of Toussaint Louverture? Explain your answer by referring to specific details within the image.

4 The artist who produced Source D was English. In 1805, Britain was at war with France. How might this help explain why the artist has drawn Louverture as he has done?

Checkpoint

1 Give three non-violent ways in which slaves showed resistance.
2 Where was the only successful slave rebellion?
3 Give two reasons why the number of slave revolts increased in the early 19th century.
4 Which British colony witnessed a major rebellion in 1831–32?

Slavery after 1807

Learning objectives

- Arrive at your own conclusion regarding the causes of abolition.
- Understand Britain's role in fighting slavery internationally.
- Consider some of the legacies of transatlantic slavery.

Did you know?

The 'Legacies of British Slave-ownership' website features an online archive that allows you to search for the names of slave-owning families who were compensated in 1833. You could search for your family name to discover if there are any slave owners in your family history. Alternatively, you could search for the area where you live to see how many slave owners lived near you (use the 'Maps' page).

Source A: An illustration from 1833 showing former slaves on the island of Barbados celebrating their freedom.

From 1807 to 1833

Although the British slave trade had been banned in 1807, there was still a fight to be fought: for the total abolition of slavery and the emancipation* of slaves within the British Empire.

From 1823, Thomas Clarkson led the abolition campaign. Slave resistance was increasing and the slave revolt of 1831–32 in Jamaica shocked people in Britain. Abolitionists protested against the brutal execution of so many 'rebel' slaves. Even those who supported slavery feared that the slaves would overthrow their masters if freedom was not granted.

All these factors came together to convince parliament that slavery needed to be abolished in the British Empire and, in 1833, the Slavery Abolition Act was passed, freeing around 800,000 slaves.

The fears of those who claimed that the freed slaves would rise up and kill their masters proved to be unfounded. Instead, emancipated slaves celebrated their freedom with parades, festivals and church services.

Some MPs, however, argued that the end of slavery would bankrupt slave owners and that this, in turn, would damage Britain's wealth and power. The decision was taken to compensate* all slave owners for their 'loss of property'. Over 46,000 claims were made and a total of £20 million was paid, equivalent to £16 billion today. No former slaves were ever compensated for their suffering and losses.

Poacher turned gamekeeper

The transatlantic slave trade did not end in 1807, despite the USA also banning the trade in 1808 (slavery was abolished completely in the USA in 1865). It is estimated that a further 1.7 million slaves were transported across the Atlantic after 1807, mostly from Angola to Brazil.

Britain – the country that had dominated and benefited most from the slave trade in the 18th century – began a campaign to stop other countries from trading in slaves. In 1815, at the Congress of Vienna, British officials convinced representatives from France, Spain and Portugal, amongst others, to abolish their slave trades. From 1807, Britain also used its navy to 'police' the oceans, capturing slave trading vessels and releasing the slaves. By 1865, it had freed around 150,000 slaves. The historian James Walvin noted that: 'the world's greatest poacher had become the world's most strident gamekeeper'.

By the 1870s, due to abolition campaigns, laws, treaties and international pressure, as well as a decline in the Caribbean sugar industry, the transatlantic slave trade was no more.

Source B: A photograph taken in 1868 aboard the British ship, the *HMS Daphne*. The Africans on board had been rescued from a slave ship trading out of Zanzibar in East Africa.

Key terms

Emancipation*: Freedom from slavery.

Compensate*: Give money to make up for the loss of something.

Your turn!

 1 Follow these steps to arrive at your own judgement about why slavery was abolished.

    a First, create three note cards with the following headings: 'Factor 1: The role of slaves and former slaves', 'Factor 2: The role of British abolitionist leaders' and 'Factor 3: The popular movement'.

    b Next, gather information from pages 114–123 that could be used to support each of those factors. For example, on the Factor 1 card, you might write 'On Haiti, slaves successfully rebelled. This scared the British parliament'.

    c Once your cards are complete, work with a partner to try to identify and write down connections between the factors. For example, you might say, 'It was abolitionist leaders (Factor 2) that created petitions in the first place, but it was the public that signed them (Factor 3)'.

2 Finally, write a one-paragraph conclusion about which of the factors you believe to have been most important in causing the abolition of slavery and why.

The legacy of the transatlantic slave trade

The transatlantic slave trade was one of the biggest movements of people in history. Today, there are many societies in the Caribbean and the Americas that largely consist of people of African descent. What was the legacy of the slave trade for the former slaves themselves?

The lives of emancipated slaves did not suddenly improve after abolition. Some remained working on the same plantations, being paid very low wages and charged high rents for poor quality houses. Other former slaves used their freedom to move to new places, to start new lives for their families, but they were starting from scratch. Few owned many possessions or had received any education, and poverty remained a problem.

Source C: An engraving from 1865 showing a village in Virginia inhabited by freed slaves.

Racism

Another significant legacy of the slave trade was racism. Supporters of slavery, and those who tried to defend the system for their own gain, did so by claiming that black people were inferior to white people, saying that they were stupid, lazy and that slavery was good for them. These ideas spread during the 18th and 19th centuries and it became common for people of European descent to consider themselves superior to people of African descent. Even today, as wrong and as horrible as these ideas are, they still have not gone away.

The fight for equality

Racism and economic inequality between black and white people were significant legacies of slavery, but there were many others. Black people often had little political power, limited legal rights and little access to education. Freedom from slavery was a major success, but it was also the start of a new battle: the fight for equal rights. It is a fight which continued throughout the 19th and 20th centuries, and continues to this day.

Source D: A civil rights march in 1963. The campaigners, led here by Martin Luther King, are demanding the rights to vote, to equal employment and to equal education.

The end of slavery?

Slavery did not begin with the transatlantic slave trade, and nor did it end when that trade was abolished. Many forms of slavery continued and still continue. Today, slavery is illegal all over the world, yet because something is illegal that does not mean that it stops.

> **Modern slavery in the United Kingdom**
> - It is believed that there are 13,000 slaves in the UK today.
> - Most, but not all, come from other countries.
> - They are tricked into moving to the UK with the promise of a good job.
> - When they arrive, their passports are kept from them by their 'masters'.
> - They are often forced to work on farms, in factories or at car washes.
> - They are given little or no pay and forced to live in bad accommodation.
> - Violence and threats are used to stop them from escaping.

Although slavery continues, the importance of the abolition of slavery in the British Empire should not be ignored. It granted freedom to hundreds of thousands of people, it changed the way people thought about slavery itself and it paved the way for many other campaigns against slavery.

Your turn!

1 Read the information on 'Modern slavery in the United Kingdom'. What similarities and differences are there between transatlantic slavery and modern slavery in Britain?

2 Discuss the following as a class: Before the abolition campaign in Britain, many people simply ignored or just accepted slavery. Do you think we as a society simply ignore or accept modern slavery? If so, why?

Checkpoint

1 In what year was slavery abolished in the British Empire?
2 In total, how much compensation did the British government pay to slave owners?
3 What is a legacy?
4 Give two examples of legacies of the transatlantic slave trade.
5 Give two examples of ways in which life was hard for former slaves after emancipation.
6 Does the transatlantic slave trade still continue today?
7 Does slavery still exist today?

Why was the slave trade abolished?

Look ahead to Source A on page 128. It shows one interpretation of the reasons for abolition: that William Wilberforce was the main cause of abolition. Design and draw your own 'engraving' to represent what you think the main causes of abolition were. You should accompany your image with a written justification of why you have chosen that design.

The big history of slavery

- To understand how the transatlantic slave trade fits into the wider history of slavery.

Transatlantic slavery in context

The history of transatlantic slavery is one part of a much wider history of slavery. It is a history that spans almost all cultures, religions and nationalities. Whilst slavery is a common feature of the past (and present), the nature of slavery differs between different time periods and between different places.

Early slavery – around 5000 years ago
Slavery did not just suddenly start but developed gradually in the earliest civilisations. It probably began with small numbers of people being captured in war with neighbouring communities, and then being forced to work. There is evidence of slavery in Ancient Sumer (in modern-day Iraq).

Slavery in medieval Europe – around 1000 years ago
In the medieval period, the scale of slavery declined. However, slaves could still be found in almost all parts of Europe, working mostly as farmers. It has been estimated that in Anglo-Saxon England around ten per cent of the population were slaves. At this time, it was the Vikings who controlled the slave trade in Western Europe. They raided coastal areas and captured slaves from Britain and Ireland, among other places.

Before slavery – 10,000 years ago
For much of human history, people lived as family groups of hunter-gatherers. These groups did not have slavery as it was not necessary or practical for their way of life.

Ancient slavery – around 2000 years ago
As civilisations grew larger, so did the scale of slavery. All ancient civilisations had slavery, from Egypt to Greece to China. It is estimated that there were over 10 million slaves in the Roman Empire. Most slaves were captured during wars and could be traded over long distances. Skilled slaves could be doctors, teachers or entertainers, though most would be domestic servants or labour for farms and mines. Laws were introduced to control the ownership of slaves and slavery became a part of everyday life.

Interpretation 1: A 19th-century coloured engraving depicting a slave market in Ancient Rome.

Source A: A coloured engraving from 1884 showing a slave market in Egypt, part of the Arabic slave trade.

Slavery becomes globalised – around 500 years ago
As trade networks grew, so did slave trading. Slavery became globalised as Asian, African, Arab and European trade networks connected. Europeans extended slave trading to the Americas, with the transatlantic slave trade. The scale of slavery was at its greatest height, with mass trading occurring over vast distances. As well as the transatlantic slave trade, from the 7th to the 20th centuries, Arab traders traded slaves from East Africa. As many as 14 million Africans were taken to the Middle East and India.

Slavery in decline? – from 200 years ago
From the late 18th century, several countries began to ban their own slave trades and fight against slavery. In 1947, the United Nations declared that everyone has a right to freedom and in 1981 Mauritania in (West Africa) became the last country in the world to ban slavery. Keeping slaves is now a criminal activity. Yet trade in people (trafficking) continues illegally. Today, we often think of modern slavery as exploitative work (like low paid 'sweatshop' work) and this exists on a large scale. It is believed there are over 45 million modern slaves globally.

Figure 4.9: Timeline showing the changes to slavery.

Change and continuity questions

Your turn!

1   Work in a group of three. Each choose one of the following three examples of slavery: slavery in the Roman Empire, the Viking slave trade or the Arabic slave trade. Conduct further research as listed below.

   a   Consider: the size and scale of slavery, how slaves were obtained, what roles slaves played in society, what types of people tended to be slaves and how slaves were treated.

   b   Next, compare your example with transatlantic slavery. What are the similarities and differences?

   c   Finally, discuss your findings with the rest of your group.

2   Decide whether each of the following statements are true or false. For each, give examples from Figure 4.8 to support your answer.

   a   Slavery has always existed.

   b   Europeans have never been used as slaves.

   c   Many different countries, cultures and religions have enslaved people.

   d   Slavery still exists today.

   e   Slavery today is the same as in the past.

What have you learned?

Source analysis questions

In this section you have learned:

- that there are different interpretations of the reasons why the slave trade was abolished in 1807.

Source A: An engraving designed in Britain in 1808 to celebrate the abolition of the slave trade. The woman in the middle of the image is Britannia, who symbolises Britain. The woman holding the scales represents justice. The bust on the right is of the abolitionist William Wilberforce.

Source A was designed with the purpose of celebrating the achievements of the British abolition campaign. It was intended to make people feel proud of their country and what had been achieved, at a time when many British people were very patriotic*. Britain was growing in wealth and power, and people were brought up to believe that Britain was the best and most important country in the world. It was also a time when artists and writers tended to focus on the actions of important leaders, rather than the actions of ordinary people.

Key term

Patriotic*: To be very loyal and devoted to your own country.

Quick Quiz

1 Where did British ships transport slaves from and to during the transatlantic slave trade?

2 Approximately how many slaves in total were transported during the transatlantic slave trade?

3 What types of work were most common for slaves in the Americas?

4 Name two people involved in the campaign for the abolition of slavery, and state what their roles were.

5 In what year was the British transatlantic slave trade abolished?

6 In what year was slavery abolished in the British Empire?

Your turn!

1 Study Source A. For what purpose was this source made?

2 What does the artist believe to be the main cause or causes of the abolition of the slave trade? (Look back at pages 114–123 if you need to revise the causes of abolition)

3 Why do you think the artist has shown light shining down onto Britannia and William Wilberforce?

4 How do we know that this image was created by a patriotic person?

5 Which cause or causes of the abolition of the slave trade are not included in the source?

Writing historically

Source analysis questions

You are now going to write an answer to the question: 'Study Source A. How does it portray the causes of the abolition of the slave trade and why does it portray them in this way?' The information on this page will help you to structure your answer.

Identification

Begin by answering the 'How?' aspect of the question by identifying what the source suggests and how it does this. Use details from the image to support your answer. You could use the sentence starters below to help you.

'The engraving in Source A indicates that the abolition of the slave trade was mostly due to…

It implies this as it shows…'

Considering purpose

Next consider the 'why?' aspect of the question by identifying why the source presents the view it does. Begin by considering the **purpose** of the source. What can we see in the source that shows us that the artist is celebrating the achievements of British abolitionists?

Amongst other things you may want to consider:

- the bust (Who does the bust represent? What types of people have busts made of them?)
- the light (Where does it shine and why?)
- the central figures (Who do they represent? How has the artist portrayed them?).

Again, use details from the source to support your points.

The purpose of the engraving is to celebrate the abolition of the slave trade, so it is likely it was made for abolitionists. Wilberforce was a leading abolitionist. It portrays him as a hero by including a bust of him in the image. Light is shining down onto the bust, almost as if God is shining down on Wilberforce in thanks for what he did.

Considering context

Next consider the **context** of the time when the source was made. Try to explain why the image gives the view that it does, by looking at **when** and **where** it was made. The text next to the source will help. You might begin:

'The reason that the engraving gives all the credit for abolition to Britain and Wilberforce is because…'

Conclusion

Finally, write a short summary to complete your answer.

'Overall, Source A suggests that abolition of the slave trade was due to… It suggests this because…'

Now combine the points above to write your own answer to the question: 'Study Source A. How does it portray the causes of the abolition of the slave trade and why does it portray them in this way?'

How did the British Empire develop?

In this enquiry we will be investigating how the British Empire developed in the 17th and 18th centuries, and the reasons for this development. This section of the book will look at:

- the origins of the British Empire and early British colonies in North America

- the development of the British Empire in the Caribbean and trade in the Atlantic

- the British Empire's gains and losses in the 18th century.

What do you think?

How does a country build an empire?

The origins of the British Empire

Learning objectives

- Understand where and when the British Empire existed.
- Understand how Britain's early colonies in North America were established.
- Identify the reasons for British expansion in the Americas.

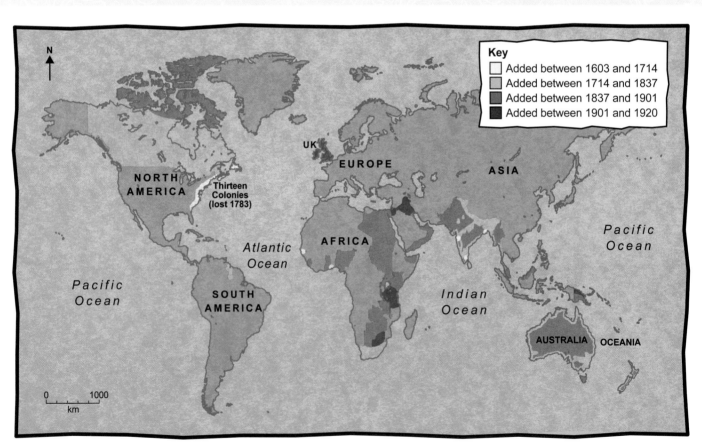

Figure 5.1: A map showing the development of the British Empire.

More than one-quarter of all countries in today's world were once ruled by Britain as part of one of the largest empires* that the world has ever seen. It was an empire that lasted for centuries and, whilst little of it still exists, its legacy lives on.

The British Empire did not exist in the medieval period but England was, at times, a part of other empires.

- After the Norman Conquest of 1066, England became a part of the Norman empire that included parts of France and, later, territory in and around the Mediterranean Sea.

- Under the Angevin kings of England (1154–1216), English monarchs also ruled parts of France. Most of this land was lost at the end of the Hundred Years' War (1337–1453).

These medieval empires were very small in comparison with the European empires that began to grow during the 16th century.

Following Columbus's explorations of the Americas after 1492, many other European explorers travelled to the Americas. Spanish explorers led the way and, by the mid-16th century, Spain controlled a large territory in the Americas. This empire was making Spain very rich as it imported huge quantities of gold and silver from South America.

English monarchs saw the wealth that Spain was gaining and wanted to imitate its success, so they began sending their own ships to the Americas. During the reign of Elizabeth I, the famous captain and explorer Sir Francis Drake claimed territory for England on the Pacific coast of America, but no colony was established. Another explorer, Sir Walter Raleigh, established a colony on the Atlantic coast of America in an area he named Virginia, after Elizabeth I, the 'Virgin Queen'. In many ways, these voyages were the beginnings of the British Empire.

Key term

New World*: A name given to the Americas during the colonisation by Europeans in the 16th century.

Figure 5.2: The thought processes of Queen Elizabeth I.

Your turn!

1 Look at Figure 5.1. Use an atlas to name the modern countries that were once partly or wholly ruled by the British. List as many as you can.

2 Historians refer to parts of history in different ways, including centuries, dates or periods. Figure 5.1 shows territory added to the British Empire in the Stuart (1603–1714), Georgian (1714–1837), Victorian (1837–1901) and Edwardian/modern (1901–1910) time periods. Use the information shown on the map to answer the following questions.

   a During which period were Britain's colonies in North America mostly founded?

   b Name three places that were added to the British Empire during the Georgian period.

   c During which period did the British Empire greatly expand in Africa?

   d Overall, during which period did the British Empire expand the most?

Key term

Joint-stock company*:
A company where a group of investors share the cost and the profits of their business between them.

Early English colonies in America

The first successful English colony in America was Jamestown, named after King James I. It was founded in 1607 by members of the Virginia Company, an English joint-stock company* set up to establish settlements in America. The colonists discovered that a particular crop that was known and used by the natives grew very well there. That crop was tobacco. Over time, plantations developed. By 1621, Virginia was exporting 160,000 kilograms of tobacco per year to Britain.

Interpretation 1:
Mid 20th-century drawing of James Fort in Jamestown, the first permanent English colony in Virginia.

England's second colony in America was established in 1620. The colonists' ship, the *Mayflower*, was aiming for Virginia but was blown off course. The colonists landed in an area that became known as New England and established a colony, which they named Plymouth. The coast of New England offered an abundance of good fishing. By the 1680s, hundreds of thousands of barrels of dried cod were being sent from New England to Britain. As more British people came to see the potential wealth that America offered, more companies were set up, more ships were chartered and more colonists made the journey across the Atlantic.

- By 1700, over 700,000 people had emigrated from Britain and more colonies were founded.

- Between 1607 and 1732, 13 colonies were established by the British on the North American Atlantic coast.

The colonists included some people who had no choice about whether or not to go to America. The first African slaves were brought to Jamestown in 1619 to work on Virginia's tobacco plantations. In addition, about 50,000 convicts were sent from Britain to America and forced to work on cotton plantations.

The Virginia Company

The Virginia Company financed the founding of the American colonies. It paid for the ships and the resources needed to establish the colonies.

> With the permission of the monarch, we can import tobacco, fish, furs and timber from America and sell at a great profit.

King James I

King James I established a royal monopoly on the tobacco trade, meaning that the Virginia Company was the only English company that could trade tobacco.

> Tax from the tobacco trade is proving to be very profitable. I shall encourage more ships to head to the New World.

Indentured labourers

Around two-thirds of British colonists in America were indentured labourers – volunteers who signed up to move to America. If they worked for a fixed amount of time, they would then be given their own land.

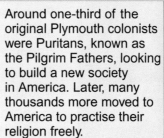

> There simply aren't enough jobs here in England. We'll starve! What are we going to do?

> I've seen an advert from the Virginia Company. If we work for free on the plantations in Virginia for five years, then they will give us land of our own.

The Pilgrim Fathers

Around one-third of the original Plymouth colonists were Puritans, known as the Pilgrim Fathers, looking to build a new society in America. Later, many thousands more moved to America to practise their religion freely.

> In England we are not allowed to practise our Puritan faith. If we do, we are punished. We must go to the New World where we can worship freely.

Figure 5.3: Some of the people involved in British colonisation in North America, and their motivations.

Your turn!

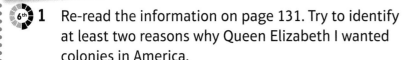

1 Re-read the information on page 131. Try to identify at least two reasons why Queen Elizabeth I wanted colonies in America.

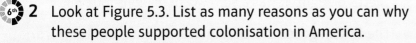

2 Look at Figure 5.3. List as many reasons as you can why these people supported colonisation in America.

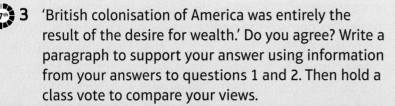

3 'British colonisation of America was entirely the result of the desire for wealth.' Do you agree? Write a paragraph to support your answer using information from your answers to questions 1 and 2. Then hold a class vote to compare your views.

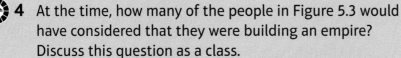

4 At the time, how many of the people in Figure 5.3 would have considered that they were building an empire? Discuss this question as a class.

Checkpoint

1 Which European country ruled the largest American empire in the 16th century?

2 During whose reign were the first attempts to establish an English colony in America?

3 Where was the first successful English colony in America and when was it founded?

4 List three things that the early British colonies in America exported to Britain.

Extending and controlling the Empire

Source A: Sir Henry Morgan in an English engraving from 1704, by an unknown artist.

A pirate of the Caribbean

When Henry Morgan was born in around 1635, no one could have predicted that he would become one of the wealthiest and most powerful pirates in the Caribbean. Morgan is thought to have been born in Wales to a farming family. At some point, he joined a ship bound for Barbados in the Caribbean.

Penniless, Morgan sought work on the pirate ships. He became one of around 1500 pirates on the island of Jamaica, a British colony at that time. Yet it was the Spanish, not the British, who controlled much of the Caribbean. Their treasure ships would pass through carrying gold and silver from their mines in South America back to Spain. Both the British government and British pirates wanted a share of these riches so they used Jamaica as a base from which to seize Spanish ships and attack Spanish settlements.

Morgan prospered as a pirate, earning enough money to buy a share in a ship and enough popularity to be elected captain. In 1663, Morgan and his crew joined the largest pirate fleet ever seen, with a total of 14 ships and 1400 men. King Charles II of England had ordered the Royal Navy* to try to reduce Spanish power in the Caribbean but the Royal Navy did not have enough ships, so pirate ships like Morgan's were recruited. The huge fleet successfully attacked the Spanish town of Campeche in Mexico and plundered* 150,000 Spanish dollars, known as 'pieces of eight'. It was a sum worth millions today.

The British governor* of Jamaica, Sir Thomas Modyford, encouraged attacks on Spanish ships and settlements. As well as damaging Spanish power, piracy made Modyford and other British officials rich, as they took a share of the pirates' plunder. Modyford gave Morgan a licence to attack the Spanish, making him a privateer*. Morgan went on to lead many daring attacks on Spanish ships and settlements. He also gained a reputation for brutality. There are accounts of his men torturing and abusing prisoners. Despite this, many British people considered him a hero.

Did you know?

Henry Morgan's legend lives on in an alcoholic drink! Captain Morgan rum, one of the best-selling brands of rum in the UK, is named after him.

From piracy to politics

Morgan's raids made him very wealthy, allowing him to buy 4000 acres of land in Jamaica. By the 1670s, Jamaica was rapidly changing and many sugar plantations were being established. Morgan followed the trend and started growing sugar cane. He had gone from chasing Spanish gold to growing 'white gold'. 'White gold' was the nickname given to sugar in the 17th century, due to its value. Sugar became the British Empire's most profitable trade and made many people, such as Morgan, a lot of money.

In 1674, King Charles II knighted Morgan for his services against the Spanish. Sir Henry Morgan was one of the wealthiest and most important men in Jamaica. He became the chief justice (the most senior judge) and was, for a time, governor of the whole island.

Source B: Henry Morgan's attack on Puerto Principe (Spanish Cuba) in 1664. Morgan is in the middle with his sword raised. Engraving from *The Buccaneers of America*, written in 1678 by a Frenchman called Alexandre Exquemelin, a privateer who knew Morgan.

Key terms

Royal Navy*: The official naval fighting force of Britain.

Plunder*: To steal goods by force.

Governor*: Most British colonies had a governor who was responsible for ruling on behalf of the monarchy. As they were so far from London, they had a lot of power and independence.

Privateer*: A naval captain who has permission from their government (in the form of a document called a 'letter of marque') to attack and rob the ships of another country.

Your turn!

1 Make a series of notes recording what Henry Morgan's story reveals about the British Empire. Consider the following.

 a Why the British were first interested in establishing colonies in the Caribbean.

 b Why the British government initially allowed and encouraged piracy.

 c How the nature and purpose of the Caribbean colonies changed over time.

 d How people gained power in British colonies.

 2 a To what extent does Source A give a similar impression of Henry Morgan to Source B?

 b Why might they differ?

Controlling trade in the Atlantic

The trade in tobacco and sugar continued to grow rapidly in the late 17th and early 18th centuries. Demand in Europe increased as smoking became fashionable and sugar became a fashionable luxury item. Other trades also developed in the northern Atlantic.

In the 16th century, British traders had ventured into newly discovered areas of what is now Canada. In the area around Hudson's Bay (named after the English explorer Henry Hudson) they found an abundance of furs and timber. They established trading factories* and began exporting back to Britain.

A large and profitable empire meant that Britain needed a much bigger navy to protect colonies and control trade. In 1650, the Royal Navy had just 72 ships. By 1700, that number had more than doubled to 166, making it the most powerful navy of any European country.

Source C: An English map of North America and the Caribbean from around 1650.

In addition, laws were introduced to ensure that some of the profits from trade made it back to the government in London. British monarchs awarded monopolies to particular companies in return for the payment of high tariffs*.

Table 5.1: Large companies that were awarded monopolies.

Date	Company	What it traded	Where it traded
1622	Virginia Company	Tobacco	East Coast of North America
1660	Royal African Company	Slaves	West Africa
1670	Hudson's Bay Company	Furs	Canada

In the mid 17th century, a series of Navigation Acts were also introduced. These laws said that British colonies were allowed to trade only with England. Colonists were supposed to buy goods only from England and sell their produce only to English traders. The ships of the Royal Navy would 'police' the oceans, ensuring, as best as they could, that the laws were upheld.

Monopolies and the Navigation Acts proved unpopular with many traders and colonists, as they limited who they could trade with. They also led to an increasing number of smugglers*, as people tried to avoid the laws. Despite this, these new laws did help to increase the British monarchy's control over the British Empire and ensured that the British made greater profit from trade within the Empire.

Key terms

Trading factory*: A building or settlement where people could meet to carry out trade.

Tariff*: A tax paid on goods that are imported.

Smuggler*: Someone who trades goods illegally.

The rise and fall of piracy

Smuggling and piracy reached a peak in the early 18th century. Pirates, once useful allies of the British Empire, instead became a serious problem as they disrupted trade. During what is known as the Golden Age of Piracy (c.1690–c.1720), the Caribbean pirates became so powerful that they even took control of Nassau, a British colony in the Bahamas.

Blackbeard was an important pirate leader. He was hunted down by the Royal Navy and, in 1718, he was killed in battle. Whereas pirates like Morgan had once been rewarded and even knighted, by the 18th century they were being hunted and killed. The British Royal Navy retook control of Nassau in 1718, after which piracy declined in the Caribbean. Without a base for pirates to harbour their ships and sell their goods, piracy became a much more difficult and dangerous job, and fewer sailors were willing to take the risk. By the middle of the 18th century, the Golden Age of Piracy was over. Instead, the Royal Navy ruled the waves.

Source D: Edward Thatch, more commonly known as Blackbeard, is one of the most famous pirates from the Golden Age of Piracy. He placed lit fuses in his hair and beard to make himself appear more terrifying to his victims. The image is taken from a book called *A History of the Pirates*, published in 1736.

Did you know?

Pirates had many rules on their ships. One rule was that no women were allowed to work as crew. That did not stop all women, though, as some dressed up as men to gain work on the ships! Two women who did just that were Mary Read and Anne Bonny. They went on to become two of the most famous pirates of the Golden Age.

Your turn!

 1 Study Source C and answer the following questions.
  a Which areas shown were most developed at the time? How do you know?
  b Why do you think that central North America and the north-west of America are left blank?
  c Can you identify any inaccuracies on the map? Why do you think these mistakes were made?

2 Can you think of any other questions that a historian might use Source C to answer?

Checkpoint

1 What is a privateer?
2 Why did the British government have to rely on privateers to attack its enemies?
3 What is a monopoly?
4 Why were monopolies and Navigation Acts unpopular with some traders?

Eighteenth-century gains and losses

Learning objectives

- Understand where and why the British Empire expanded during the 18th century.
- Consider the consequences of the Seven Years War for the British Empire.
- Understand why the 13 American colonies fought for their independence.

The growth of the British Empire did not go unchallenged by other countries. In the 17th century, the Dutch dominated global trade, especially the highly profitable spice trade in south-east Asia.

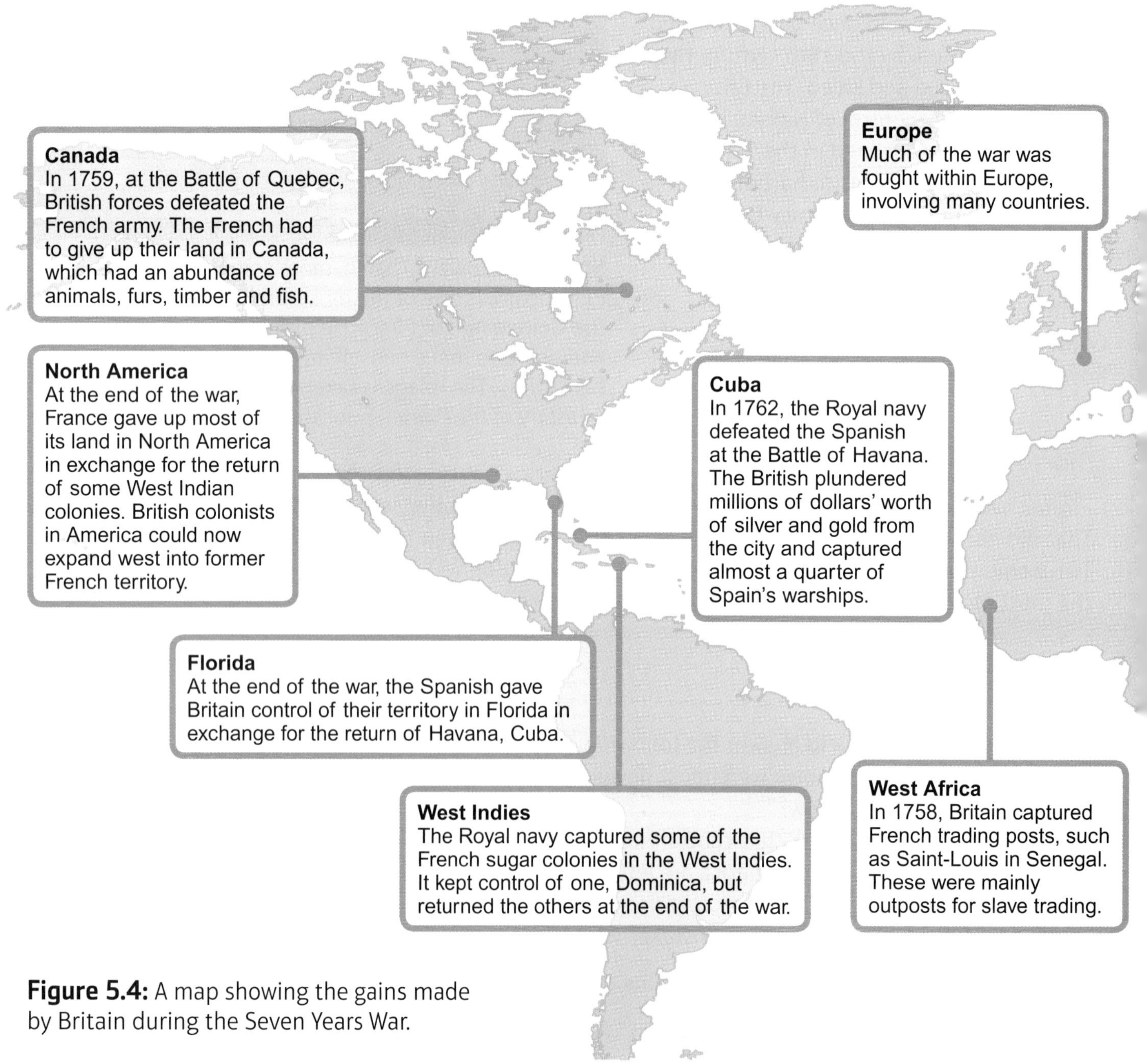

Canada
In 1759, at the Battle of Quebec, British forces defeated the French army. The French had to give up their land in Canada, which had an abundance of animals, furs, timber and fish.

Europe
Much of the war was fought within Europe, involving many countries.

North America
At the end of the war, France gave up most of its land in North America in exchange for the return of some West Indian colonies. British colonists in America could now expand west into former French territory.

Cuba
In 1762, the Royal navy defeated the Spanish at the Battle of Havana. The British plundered millions of dollars' worth of silver and gold from the city and captured almost a quarter of Spain's warships.

Florida
At the end of the war, the Spanish gave Britain control of their territory in Florida in exchange for the return of Havana, Cuba.

West Indies
The Royal navy captured some of the French sugar colonies in the West Indies. It kept control of one, Dominica, but returned the others at the end of the war.

West Africa
In 1758, Britain captured French trading posts, such as Saint-Louis in Senegal. These were mainly outposts for slave trading.

Figure 5.4: A map showing the gains made by Britain during the Seven Years War.

Between 1652 and 1674, Britain fought three wars against the Dutch. This conflict came to an end in 1688 with the Glorious Revolution (see page 84), when the Dutch leader, William of Orange, became King William III of England. The Dutch and British became allies and worked together to defeat the French and Spanish in the War of the Spanish Succession (1701–14).

The Seven Years War (1756–1763)

Peace did not last long between the European powers. By 1756, England found itself at war against the Spanish and the French. This was the largest war of the 18th century. It stretched across the globe, claimed around one million lives and, ultimately, resulted in a significant expansion of the British Empire.

Your turn!

 1 Study Figure 5.4 carefully and answer the following questions on the consequences of the Seven Years War.

  a What territory did the British Empire gain as a result of the war?

  b What trade goods did the British gain greater access to?

  c What other benefits did the war bring for Britain?

 2 Use your answers from question 1 to write a paragraph answering the following question: 'Why was the Seven Years War important for the British Empire?' In your answer, make statements and then support them with specific details.

N

Philippines
In 1762, the Royal navy captured the city of Manila, Spain's most important colony in the East. Manila was later returned to Spain for a ransom of two million dollars.

India
In 1757, in Bengal the British overthrew the Indian leader, who was an ally of the French. Britain then controlled Bengal's trade, including cheap cloth and silk. Britain also captured the important French colony of Pondicherry. It was later returned, but French power in India was destroyed forever.

0   1000
km

Today, tea is Britain's national drink and many people associate tea with Britishness, yet the tea plant does not grow in Britain – it is Asian. It was not until the 18th century that tea became popular in Britain, when it was imported from China, via India, in large quantities. Today, tea is also grown in India and Sri Lanka, often on plantations first established by the British.

Economic developments

The British Empire grew due to many different factors. We have seen how military success led to the expansion of the British Empire, but there were also economic factors involved in the growth of the Empire.

In the 17th and 18th centuries, trading companies established trading factories in West Africa and India. For example, the East India Company, a joint-stock company that had been established in 1600, founded trading factories in southern India, allowing it to trade in textiles, spices and tea. These were initially small trading settlements which, unlike the colonies in North America, did not become home to many British settlers. The trade they generated, however, was very important for Britain.

As Figure 5.5 shows, economic and military factors in the growth of the Empire were interconnected.

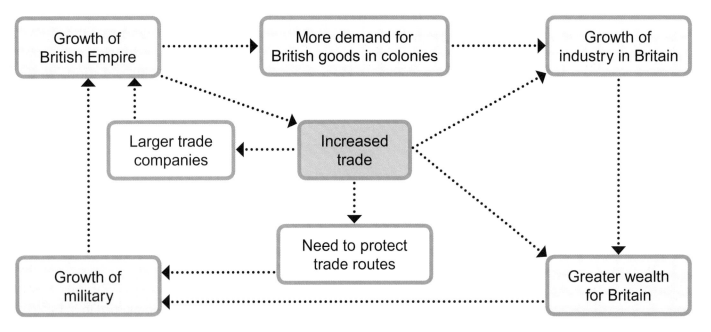

Figure 5.5: The cycle of factors that were partly responsible for the expansion of the British Empire.

Causation questions

Your turn!

1 Using Figure 5.5 to help you, explain how military factors involved in the expansion of the British Empire (such as the growth of the Royal Navy) were connected to economic factors (such as the growth of Britain's trade).

2 Turn Figure 5.5 into a written paragraph by explaining how one thing led to the next. Begin and end your paragraph with the 'Growth of British Empire' point. You will need to think carefully about the order in which to explain the points. Use connecting statements such as 'this led to', 'as a result of', 'because of', 'due to' and 'as a consequence of'.

Loss of the 13 colonies

While the British Empire did make significant gains in the 17th and 18th centuries, it did not enjoy continuous victory.

The Seven Years War cost Britain a huge amount of money, so the British government began introducing new taxes in the American colonies. The colonists felt they should not pay taxes that were being spent thousands of miles away in Britain. Although many colonists had British ancestors, most had never been to Britain and saw themselves as American rather than British. The Americans began protests against British rule. By 1775, there was open conflict between British and American forces.

The 13 American colonies joined together to form the United States of America and declared themselves independent from British rule. Britain responded with force, leading to the American War of Independence. With French assistance, the Americans succeeded in defeating the British and, in 1783, the United States of America won independence. The loss of the 13 valuable colonies was a major blow to the British Empire. British traders and politicians started to turn their attention to the east instead: to India, the subject of the next enquiry.

Source A: An engraving by Paul Revere showing British soldiers firing on their colonial subjects in Boston, New England in 1770. Events like this contributed to hatred of British rule.

Your turn!

Work in groups to create your own 'Empire builders' board game. Draw a board with a grid of ten by ten squares. Next, add 'bonuses' to certain squares that allow a player to move their counter forward if they land on that square. For the bonus squares, consider events and factors that caused the growth of the Empire, for example, 'You establish a trade outpost in India and begin trading spices. Move forward two squares.' Then add 'penalties' to some other squares. For the penalty squares, consider events and factors that could cause the decline of an empire, for example, 'Your colony in the West Indies is badly hit by disease. Move back two squares.' Include eight bonus squares and eight penalty squares. Finally, decorate your game appropriately and play.

Checkpoint

1. Who were Britain's two main enemies during the Seven Years War?
2. Name two territories that the British Empire gained due to the Seven Years War.
3. Give two causes of the American War of Independence (1775–83).
4. What did the 13 American colonies join together to become?
5. In what year did the 13 colonies officially gain independence?

How did the British Empire develop?

Plan and produce a presentation to show how and why the British Empire developed between the start of the 17th century and the end of the 18th century. Cover the early colonies in America (pages 132–33), colonies in the West Indies (pages 134–35) and the impact of the Seven Years War (pages 138–39). Attempt to explain why the Empire developed as it did in different places.

What have you learned?

In this section you have learned:

- how the British Empire developed over time.

Figure 5.6 gives a chronology of the development of the British Empire in certain regions.

		The British Empire in...		
Century	Period	North America	The Caribbean	India
16th	Tudor until 1603	1502 First English voyage to America. 1580s Explorers claim territory for England in North America. 1583 Newfoundland colony established.	1590s English explorers search for gold.	
17th	Stuart 1603–1714	1607 Jamestown colony established. 1670 Hudson's Bay Company formed. By 1682, 12 of the 13 colonies established.	1625 Barbados becomes the first English colony in the West Indies. 1655 English forces capture Jamaica from the Spanish.	1600 East India Company (EIC) formed. 1615 First EIC trade outpost established in India.
18th	Georgian 1714–1837	1732 Georgia, the last of the 13 colonies established. 1759 English capture Quebec from the French. 1775 American War of Independence begins. 1783 The United States (13 colonies) gain independence.	1756–1763 Britain captures a number of Caribbean islands from the French. Most are returned at the end of the Seven Years War, but Dominica was kept.	1757 The EIC takes control of Bengal.
19th	Victorian 1837–1901		1802 English capture more Caribbean colonies during Napoleonic Wars. 1862 Belize, in Central America, becomes part of the Empire.	1818 The EIC defeats the Marathas, taking their land. 1858 The British government takes control of India from the EIC.
	Edwardian 1901–1910			
20th	Modern 1910 onwards	1982 After a gradual process of separation, Canada gains full independence from Britain.	1960s–1970s Most islands gain their independence. A few remain British Overseas Territories*.	1947 India and Pakistan gain independence.

Figure 5.6: The development of the British Empire.

Key term

British Overseas Territory*: The name given to the parts of the British Empire that remain ruled by Britain to this day.

Writing historically

Historians use a range of different chronological terms when writing about the past.

Using centuries, periods and dates

- Sometimes we refer to centuries (for example, the 20th century).
- Sometimes we refer to periods based upon the monarch(s) of that time (for example, Tudor or Victorian).
- Sometimes we refer to periods based upon the characteristics of that time (for example, the Industrial Revolution).
- Sometimes we simply use dates.

Making terms more precise

Often historians will use the terms 'early', 'mid' and 'late' to make their comments more precise. For example, you might say something happening in the early Tudor period or that a change occurred in the mid 18th century.

Selecting the correct term

Deciding on the correct chronological term to use can be difficult. Some might not be precise enough. They might refer to a long period of time, when the actual event was only short. Others might be too precise. They might refer to a short period of time, when the actual event was much longer.

Your turn!

Use Figure 5.6 to answer the following questions.

1 During which century were most of the 13 colonies of America established?
2 During which period did English sailors first explore America and the Caribbean?
3 During which century did the English first establish colonies in the Caribbean?

Your turn!

Look up the dates for the events below and answer the questions using the terms 'early', 'mid' or 'late' followed by the name of a period or century (decide which is most appropriate). You might be able to give more than one answer.

1 When did Jamaica become a British colony?
2 When did Britain capture more Caribbean colonies due to the Napoleonic Wars?
3 When did India gain its independence from British rule?

Your turn!

Working with a partner, decide if the chronological terms used in the following statements are too precise, too broad or well chosen. If you decide that the term used isn't well chosen, rewrite the sentence using a better term. Remember that you can use the terms 'early', 'mid' and 'late' as well as the names of centuries and periods.

1 The 13 British colonies of America gained their independence in the Georgian period.
2 British traders began establishing trading factories in Hudson's Bay (Canada) in the 17th century.
3 Many Caribbean colonies of the British Empire gained their independence in the mid 20th century.
4 The British Empire in India began in the 17th century.

Who benefited from the British Empire?

In this enquiry we will be investigating the impact of the British Empire, focusing in particular on India. This section of the book will look at:

- how and why Britain came to rule the Indian subcontinent

- who gained and who lost out due to British rule in India

- different historians' views of the impact of British rule in India

- responses to the Empire: the Indian Rebellion of 1857, the Zulu and Boer Wars.

British expansion in India

What do you think?

Who do you think would have benefited from the British Empire? Who do you think might have suffered due to it?

 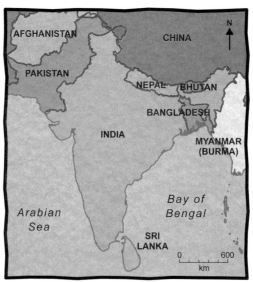

Figure 5.7: The Indian subcontinent (a) in 1789 and (b) in 2017.

Historically, the term 'India' was used to describe the area of land between the Himalayan mountain range and the Indian Ocean. Today, this area includes the independent countries of India, Pakistan, Bangladesh and Sri Lanka. In this enquiry, when we refer to 'India' we are referring to the territory covered by all these modern-day states.

The Mughal Empire

Like most countries, India has been ruled by different groups of people at different times in its past. One of the most significant empires to rule India was the Mughal Empire which, at its height, ruled four million square kilometres of land, including almost all of modern India.

The Mughals were Muslim rulers who invaded India from Afghanistan in the early 1500s. The wars of conquest were bloody and brutal, in which countless people were killed and enslaved.

Over time, Mughal power grew and, with it, a strong culture. Art, architecture, poetry and literature flourished. Beautiful mosques and palaces were built, as well as huge and imposing forts.

The Mughal Empire was extremely wealthy. It had efficient taxation and a highly developed banking system. Mughal rulers were keen to encourage trade with outsiders. During the 17th century, small numbers of European traders, mainly Dutch, French and British, began to arrive, keen to get their hands on Indian spices and textiles.

Source A: The Taj Mahal in Agra, India is often said to be the most beautiful building in the world. It was built in the 1640s by the Mughal emperor Shah Jahan to house the tomb of his favourite wife.

Decline of the Mughal Empire

Some Mughal emperors, such as Akbar the Great (1556–1605), allowed Hindus, Sikhs and Buddhists to practise their faiths freely. However, Emperor Aurangzeb (1618–1707) destroyed Hindu temples and placed extra taxes on non-Muslims. These actions caused revolt and the empire became less stable. In 1739, the emperor of Persia (modern-day Iran), Nader Shah, took advantage of the weakness of the Mughal Empire and invaded. His armies caused destruction across India, including the capital city of Delhi. The Mughals never recovered, and India became divided into regions at war with one another.

Your turn!

1 Go online and type 'Mughal architecture', 'Mughal design', and/or 'Mughal art' into an image search. What similarities and styles do you notice? Make a list of the features you can identify, and then try to draw your own Mughal design (note that Islamic art does not include images of people or animals).

2 Find details from pages 144–145 to support the following statements.
  • There were goods produced in India that were highly valued by the British.
  • In the 18th century, the Mughal Empire was losing power and becoming vulnerable.

Source B: A painting from the 16th-century Mughal *Book of Akbar*, showing Akbar seated above his subjects, who are presenting to him prisoners captured in battle. The walls of his palace are studded with precious stones and metals.

Empire-builders

From the middle of the 18th century, British power in India grew enormously. Yet this expansion was not led by the British government, but by the East India Company. It was the employees and armies of the East India Company that conquered India for Britain. Here we look at some of the individuals, all employed by the Company, who played a role in this expansion.

Robert Clive (1725–74)

Who was he? Clive was the East India Company's military commander-in-chief in India. He spent years in India fighting the French and rival Indian princes for control.

How did he expand British rule in India? During the Seven Years War (see page 139), Clive formed an alliance with a powerful Indian called Mir Jafar and defeated the Nawab* of Bengal's army at the Battle of Plassey (June 1757). Jafar became the ruler of Bengal, but he owed his position to the Company and so was little more than a puppet ruler*. In 1763, when the second puppet ruler of Bengal, Mir Qasim, refused to do what the East India Company instructed, the British overthrew him. The Company gained control of Bengal (see map on page 144), one of India's largest and wealthiest territories.

Source C: A painting by Francis Hayman in 1757 showing Robert Clive and Mir Jafar congratulating each other after the Battle of Plassey.

Key terms

Nawab*: An Indian prince or ruler.

Puppet ruler*: An official ruler who has little political power because they are controlled by someone else.

Governor-general*: The chief representative of the British in India.

Garrison*: A base for soldiers.

Lord Richard Wellesley (1760–1842)

Who was he? Wellesley was the governor-general* of India from 1798 to 1805. By this time, the East India Company had around 100,000 soldiers in India.

How did he expand British rule in India? Wellesley was determined to increase British power in India. He sent British forces to defeat the two most powerful empires remaining in India, the Mysores and the Marathas. The British were victorious.

Wellesley was also famous for the deals that he made with Indian princes. He promised the princes that they could keep their official titles and be paid large pensions, as long as they allowed a British garrison* within their territory, and allowed the British to claim the wealth and taxes from their land.

Source D: An Indian painting from around 1830 showing a British official of the East India Company riding in the procession of an Indian prince.

James Ramsay, Earl of Dalhousie (1812–60)

Who was he? Dalhousie was the East India Company's governor-general in India from 1848 to 1856. By this time, large parts of India were under British influence and control.

How did he expand British rule in India? Dalhousie developed an idea known as the 'doctrine of lapse'. This idea meant that, if an Indian ruler died and had no male heir, their land would become Company territory. The Indian nobles had little choice but to accept this, as British power was so strong by that time. Dalhousie also oversaw more wars of conquest, such as against the Sikhs in the Punjab.

Your turn!

 1 Make a list of all the different methods that the three empire-builders described above used to increase British power and influence in India.

 2 Using your list, answer the following question: 'British expansion in India was achieved through military action.' Do you agree? Try to make arguments for and against the statement, before giving your overall judgement.

Checkpoint

1 Which empire ruled much of India when the British East India Company first arrived?
2 Name two types of goods that the British wanted from India.
3 What was the first region of India to come under British control?
4 What is a puppet ruler?
5 What was the doctrine of lapse?

The impact of British rule in India

Learning objectives

- Explore some of the benefits and drawbacks of British rule in India.
- Understand and assess different interpretations of the impact of British rule.

Trade and industry

India became the most important part of the British Empire for trade. Around a quarter of all British exports were sent to India. Britain had initially imported textiles from India but, by the 19th century, Britain had destroyed India's textile industry by insisting that India's raw cotton was exported to Britain, processed there and then exported back to India as fabric. As well as cotton, Britain also imported coal, metals and precious stones from India.

In the 19th century, the British built over 24,000 miles of railway track in India to increase trade. This led to the development of certain industries, especially mining. Whilst industry provided jobs for local Indians, their wages were low and they had to endure very poor working conditions.

Permission to establish business and to trade was mostly given to British-owned companies. Indian-owned companies were taxed at a higher rate so it was very hard for Indians to compete. This meant that much of the wealth from trade and industry in India went to Britain.

Agriculture

The British invested money in Indian agriculture by building dams and providing irrigation*. By the end of British rule in 1947, the amount of land usable for farming was eight times greater than at the beginning. Despite this, India had to start importing food from other countries. Cash crops* were grown, especially cotton and tea, as a result of the demand from British companies. So, whilst more land was in use, it was not producing food for the local population. This meant that, when harvests were poor, many Indians would starve. Between 1770 and 1900, 25 million Indians are estimated to have died from famine.

Source A: A British cartoon from 1877, the year of a great famine in India, entitled *Disputed Empire*. It shows Queen Victoria unable to stop Death from taking the starving Indians.

Governing India

Under British rule, no Indian had the right to vote and few contributed to the governing of their own country. Though some Indian princes maintained their positions and wealth, it was the East India Company that ruled much of India (until 1858, when the British government took direct control of India). British officials oversaw law and order, collected taxes, and controlled trade and industry. A large number of Indians did work for the British, but they tended to be in more junior jobs.

Law and order

The British needed a large army to control India and so they employed many Indians as soldiers, known as 'sepoys'. However, these soldiers were not just used in India. They were sent to fight for the British Empire all around the world. In the First World War, 1.3 million Indian soldiers fought for Britain. Over 70,000 were killed.

Some historians accuse the British of increasing cultural divisions in Indian society. The British favoured higher castes* when it came to jobs in the army and the government. This meant that favoured castes became wealthier than other castes, increasing the divide between them.

Language and culture

English became the official language used in government. Whilst this made ruling simpler (as there were many different local languages), it meant that many Indians were excluded as they did not speak English.

During the early years of British rule in India, there was a lot of mixing of British and Indian cultures. Some East India Company employees married local Indian women. However, as time went on, and as Britain became wealthier and India poorer, many British people began to see themselves as superior. They viewed Indian culture as inferior and imported their own culture. They built houses in the European style and schools modelled on British ones. They also introduced European sports such as cricket, which has gone on to become one of the most popular sports in India.

Key terms

Irrigation*: Supplying water to dry areas of land so that they can be farmed.

Cash crop*: Crop grown and sold for profit rather than grown as food for local people.

Caste*: Class of person within Hindu society.

Source B: A late 18th-century coloured engraving of Calcutta. The British built European-style buildings in many Indian cities. Here we can see the courthouse and the offices of the East India Company.

Your turn!

 1 Draw a table with two rows, one for India and one for Britain, and two columns, one for benefits and one for drawbacks. Use the information from these pages to complete the table as a summary of the impact of British rule on India.

 2 Considering your table as a whole, who do you think benefited the most from British rule? Who do you think suffered the most?

Analysing
interpretations

Interpretations of British rule in India

Interpretations of the British Empire have changed over time. Interpretation 1 was written at a time when the British Empire was at its largest.

Figure 5.8: The cover of *The Wonder Book of Empire*.

> **Interpretation 1:** Adapted from *The Wonder Book of Empire*, a book aimed at young people that was published in Britain in the 1920s.
>
> We are all proud to belong to the British Empire. Are we proud enough? This book has been prepared in the belief that we are not and that if people knew more of each other and more of our glorious heritage then they would be prouder, and more ready to support an Empire that makes for the freedom and happiness of so many millions of the human race.
>
> In India, the British have welded scattered people into one, and filled them with such devotion that large numbers have gladly laid down their lives for the Empire. The people of India recognise that the British are honestly trying to benefit the Indian races and to raise the country to glory amongst all nations of the world.

Since the British Empire ended, there has been great debate about whether it was a good thing or a bad thing. Below are two more recent interpretations of British rule in India.

> **Interpretation 2:** Adapted from *Raj: The Making and Unmaking of British India*, written by the historian Lawrence James in 1997.
>
> British rule [gave new life to] India. It is the most perfect example of what Britain took as its duty to humanity as a whole. The British dreamed of a world transformed by reason and learning. In India they achieved this by spreading education and scientific knowledge.

> **Interpretation 3:** Adapted from *Inglorious Empire: What the British did to India*, written by the historian Shashi Tharoor in 2017.
>
> British rule in India meant economic exploitation [taking advantage of] and the ruin of millions of people, the demolition of successful industries, the denial of the rights of Indians, the removal of local governments, the transformation of lifestyles that had flourished for centuries, and the complete destruction of the most precious possession of the colonised [the Indians]: their identities and their self-respect.

The British helped India to develop. They introduced railways and the telegraph, as well as building dams and providing irrigation.

The British only introduced such things to India for their own benefit. More railways meant more profit for British businesses, more usable farm land meant more cotton for Britain.

But the British spread education, science and learning. They built many schools and excellent universities, such as Calcutta University.

If the British did such a good job of bringing education to India, then why could only 16 per cent of Indians read and write at the time British rule ended in India?

By being a part of the British Empire, India was opened up to world trade.

But India was open to world trade before the British even arrived. The Mughal Empire had controlled far more trade than Britain did.

Figure 5.9: Some of the arguments and counter-arguments that historians make when debating the impact of British rule in India.

Why interpretations differ

Your turn!

 1 Read Interpretation 1 and answer the following questions.
   a What can we learn from this extract about why *The Wonder Book of Empire* was written?
   b In what way do you think that the purpose of the book has affected what the author says about the British in India?

 2 Read Interpretations 2 and 3. For each interpretation, select three pieces of information from pages 148 and 149 that the historian might use to support their interpretation.

3 Read the different arguments in Figure 5.9.
   a Can you think of any more arguments that either side might make?
   b Which of the two sides do you find more convincing? Explain your thinking.

Did you know?

In a 2014 survey of British people, 59 per cent felt that the British Empire was 'something to be proud of', compared with 19 per cent who felt 'ashamed' of it. What do you think about the British Empire in India?

Checkpoint

1 Which industry did the British destroy in India?
2 Give two examples of things that the British constructed in India that were beneficial to the country.
3 Give one example of an aspect of British culture that spread to India.
4 Give three examples of the negative effects of British rule in India.

Resistance to the British Empire

Learning objectives

- Explain the causes of the Indian Rebellion of 1857.
- Identify some of the consequences of the Rebellion.
- Briefly consider the causes of the Zulu and Boer Wars.

Did you know?

Gun cartridges in 1857 consisted of a bullet and a measure of gunpowder wrapped in a greased paper cartridge. Soldier had to bite off the top of the cartridge before pouring the powder into the gun. Hindus and Muslims have rules about consuming certain animals, so having to bite into a cartridge greased with animal fat was unacceptable.

Key terms

Mutiny*: A revolt by the military. The Indian Rebellion is often known as the Indian Mutiny, but some historians say that it is wrong to call it a mutiny as it was not just a military revolt. Sometimes the Rebellion is described as being India's First War of Independence, as it can be viewed as an attempt to overthrow British rule.

Annexed*: Territory taken over without the owner's permission.

The Indian Rebellion of 1857

By the 1850s, the East India Company ruled nearly two million square kilometres of Indian land and 250 million Indian people. A large number of Indians were employed as soldiers. For every nine sepoys there was just one British-born soldier. For a long time, many British officers had feared what might happen if the sepoys decided to turn against them. In 1857, their fears became a reality as numerous sepoy regiments mutinied*, killing their officers and fellow soldiers. As Indian civilians joined the sepoys in their revolt, the mutiny turned into a full-scale rebellion. The Indian Rebellion of 1857–58 proved to be one of the bloodiest chapters in the history of British rule in India.

Source A: A contemporary illustration of the Indian Rebellion by an unknown Indian artist. Note that some of the soldiers on both sides are wearing the same uniforms.

Sepoys were treated unequally compared with British soldiers, which made them angry.

Figure 5.10: The causes of the Indian Rebellion of 1857.

Your turn!

6th Study Figure 5.10 and identify the following: an economic cause of the Indian Rebellion, a religious cause and a political cause.

Missionary*: A person sent on a religious mission, often to convert other people to Christianity.

Raj*: An Indian word meaning 'ruler'. It is often used to describe the period from 1858 to 1947 when the British government ruled India.

Source B: A cartoon in an English newspaper of 1857. The woman represents 'Justice'.

The Rebellion spreads

Violent mutinies were reported in over 80 garrison towns across large parts of India. Initially, the rebels targeted powerful British officials such as military officers, tax collectors and judges, but this changed as the rebel sepoys were joined by Indian civilians. Many Indians had been angered by attempts by British missionaries* to convert them to Christianity. In Agra and many other places, peasants destroyed churches and murdered anyone who was Christian. Across India, hundreds of British men, women and children were massacred. Many sepoys, however, remained loyal to the British and fought for them, and many were killed in the process.

In Delhi, the last Mughal emperor, Bahadur Shah Zafar, became the leader of the Rebellion. Before 1857, he had been little more than a puppet ruler. He issued a proclamation against British rule, accusing the British of destroying Indian businesses, taxing too highly and taking away the dignity of the Indian people.

Consequences

British forces fought back against the rebels. In September 1857, they stormed the city of Delhi and managed to defeat Bahadur Shah Zafar and the rebel armies there. Rebellions elsewhere in India took many months to defeat. The British then took revenge on the Indian rebels. Some prisoners were blown up with cannon, whilst others were hanged from trees lining roads, in order to send a warning to others. Just as the rebels had murdered innocent British people, the British forces murdered innocent Indians (though probably many more than the rebels had killed). Some people in Britain supported these brutal actions. Others felt that the British soldiers had gone too far.

The Indian Rebellion caused such shock and outrage in Britain that the government decided that the East India Company could no longer be trusted to rule India. In 1858, parliament passed the Government of India Act. This meant that India was to be directly ruled by the British government and the era of the British Raj* began.

Other resistance to the British Empire

The Indian Rebellion of 1857 was not the only conflict fought in resistance to the British Empire.

The Zulu War

In 1879, the British wanted to extend their empire into land in southern Africa controlled by the Zulus, and to use the Zulu people as labour in their diamond mines. The resulting war initially went well for the Zulus as they defeated the British at the Battle of Isandlwana. However, the defeat shocked the British government and they sent a larger army to fight against the Zulus. After six months, the Zulus were defeated and Britain took control of their territory.

The Boer War

In 1899, war again broke out in southern Africa. This time, the British fought the Boers, who were South Africans of Dutch descent. The Boers ruled their own territory, an independent area called the South African Republic. Their land was rich with gold and possessed the largest gold-mining complex in the world. The British wanted to expand their power into Boer territory and this led to conflict.

Although British forces hugely outnumbered the Boers, the war was hard fought. In 1900, in an attempt to break the resistance of the Boers, the British commander, Lord Kitchener, adopted a 'scorched earth' policy. This meant destroying all the food, animals and farms so the Boers would starve. Boers were also rounded up, including civilian men, women and children, and put into concentration camps where conditions were so poor that thousands died of disease. The Boer War lasted three years, and claimed nearly 100,000 lives, before the Boers were eventually defeated.

Source C: Fighting during the Boer War.

Your turn!

 1 Study Source B. Do you think that the artist who drew this source agreed with what the British did in revenge for the Indian Rebellion or opposed it? Explain your answer using the source.

 2 Conduct further research into the causes of the Boer War (1899–1902). What are the similarities with the causes of the Indian Rebellion? What are the differences?

Checkpoint

1 What were sepoys?
2 In what year was the Indian Rebellion?
3 Give one economic, one religious and one political cause of the Indian Rebellion.
4 Name one other rebellion or war against British rule.

Who benefited from the British Empire?

In a group, divide the following roles between you: an Indian prince, a sepoy, a British governor-general of India, an Indian peasant, a British-born soldier working for the East India Company, a British businessman working in India.

For the role you have chosen, consider ways in which the British rule in India (from 1800 to 1857) might have benefited you or made your life worse.

Hold a discussion. Acting in-role, tell the others in the group what you think of British rule and listen to their perspectives. Where do you agree and where do you disagree?

What have you learned?

Causation questions

In this section you have learned:

- that an event, like the Indian Rebellion of 1857, can have many different causes.

As with so many events in history, the causes of the Indian Rebellion are complicated. Causes rarely work in a linear order. It is not like dominoes where one thing causes another, which causes another, which causes another, and so on. Instead, causes form complex webs, as we can see in Figure 5.11, with different causes occurring at the same time.

Key

☐ Long-term causes

☐ Short-term causes

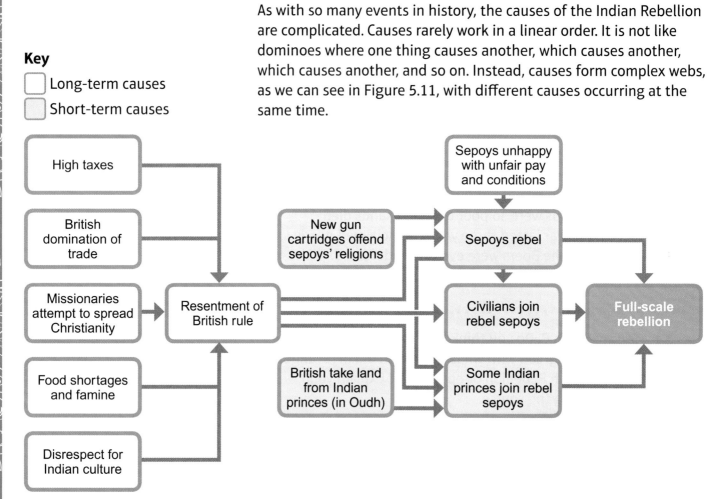

Figure 5.11: A flow diagram showing the factors leading to the Indian Rebellion of 1857.

Quick Quiz

1 Which empire ruled much of India prior to the arrival of the British?

2 Give one reason why British traders were first interested in trading with India.

3 Who was the East India Company general whose victory at the Battle of Plassey gave the British control of Bengal?

4 Name two methods used by the British to extend their control in India.

5 Give two ways in which Britain benefited from ruling India.

6 Give one way in which India benefited from British rule.

7 Give two drawbacks of British rule for India.

8 What was the British Raj?

Writing historically

It is part of a historian's job to explain how causes are connected. Below we will consider how you might answer the question: 'Explain why some Indians rose up against British rule in 1857–58.'

First, though, let us take a look at what not to do! Read the following sample student answer.

Student 1

There were many causes of the Indian Rebellion of 1857. The British were charging the Indians high taxes. There were missionaries in India trying to convert the population. The British also took land from Indian princes and this upset them. The Indian sepoys rebelled when the British tried to make them use gun cartridges that had animal fat on them. This offended their religion and so they started a rebellion.

The answer does show knowledge by identifying some of the causes of the Indian Rebellion. However, the problem is that it does not organise the different causes into any particular order, nor does it explain the connections between the causes. It reads like a list rather than an explanation.

Linking causes

There are many words and phrases that historians use to show links between causes. Some are listed below.

- for this reason
- owing to this
- therefore

- as a result of
- this led to
- due to

- consequently
- so
- because of

Now read the short paragraph below from another student answer.

Student 2

There was a lot of resentment against British rule in India. This was partly the result of the way the British governed India. Indians were given little say in or control over how their country was ruled and some Indians wanted control of their country back. This resentment became much stronger as a result of the British annexing the province of Oudh in 1856. Consequently, many Indian civilians supported the sepoys when they rebelled.

Your turn!

1 Copy out the second student answer and underline all the linking words and phrases that are used to show connections between different causes of the Rebellion.

2 Now attempt to write three short paragraphs of your own in answer to the question, using the sentence starters below. Within each paragraph, try to explain connections using linking words and phrases. Look at Figure 5.11 to help you identify some connections.
   a *British rule in India had caused economic problems…*
   b *Some Indians were angry about British rule because they felt that the British did not respect Indian culture…*
   c *Lack of respect for Indian culture also affected morale amongst the sepoys. It was for this reason that the sepoys…*

3 Finally, add a short concluding paragraph, identifying what you believe to have been the main cause of the Indian Rebellion and justifying your choice.

What was the Industrial Revolution?

Enormous, exciting changes happened in Britain between c.1750 and c.1850. In 1750, Britain was a largely agricultural country with a small population. A century later, steam-powered factories, foundries and mills were producing a huge range of manufactured goods, from cotton cloth to iron girders. The growing canal and rail networks supplied them with raw materials and took away the finished goods to sell in Britain and overseas. This was the Industrial Revolution, and it happened first in Britain. British manufactured goods dominated world trade, making Britain the richest and most powerful nation in the world. But not everyone prospered, and not everyone agreed with the changes.

This section of the book will look at:

- the importance of agriculture for the Industrial Revolution

- the connections between transport, industry and the growth of towns

- the reasons why people protested against the changes.

Farming, fences and food

Learning objectives

- Learn about the changes that happened in agriculture.
- Understand the connection between agriculture and industry.

What do you think?

Who loses out when a country becomes industrialised?

Source A: *The Durham Ox*, a painting produced in 1802 of a shorthorn bull bred by Charles Colling of Ketton Hall, County Durham. The animal weighed over 1700 kg and was exhibited at agricultural fairs around the country.

From about 1740 onwards, the population of Britain rose steadily. This was mainly because there were no major epidemics, like the plague, which resulted in a fall in the number of deaths. Therefore, there were more people to have babies and so the population grew. This growing population needed feeding, so farmers had to produce more food. There were a lot of different ideas about how this could be done, which led to a variety of changes to farming. Historians call these changes the 'Agricultural Revolution'.

Selective breeding

In open fields animals mated randomly. From the mid 18th century, farmers started choosing the animals they wanted to use for breeding.

By selecting the best animals, new breeds were developed for their wool or milk or meat, for example New Leicester sheep and Durham shorthorn beef cattle.

Enclosing the fields

Until the 18th century, most villages were surrounded by huge, unfenced fields. The fields were divided into strips, with villagers cultivating various particular strips in each field. Most villages had common land that any villagers could use for grazing their animals, and wasteland that was poor quality and could be used by anyone. Common land and wasteland were particularly useful for poorer villagers that couldn't afford to rent strips from the landowner.

Farming improvements, like selective breeding, wouldn't work where different people cultivated different strips of land in the same open fields. Landowners began creating smaller, fenced or hedged fields from open fields and common land.

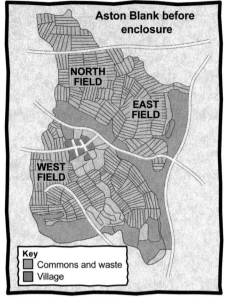
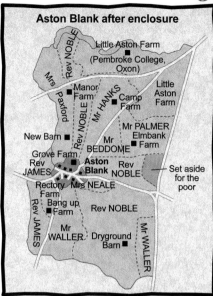

Figure 6.1: The enclosure of fields at Aston Blank, Gloucestershire, in 1752.

> **Source B:** From *General View of the Agriculture of the County of Lincoln*, written by Arthur Young in 1813.
>
> The open field farmers had been against enclosure but are now converted. The value of sheep's wool has gone up and the price of mutton has more than doubled. There are fewer cows but the land now produces more corn and is worth more. The poor are better employed. On the whole, the measure has been positive.

> **Source C:** From the diaries of Lord Torrington, 1782. He toured England, finding out about agriculture. This is what one woman told him.
>
> Enclosure of the common land was a bad job and ruined all us poor people. Before it we had our garden, our bees, our share of a flock of sheep, and the feeding of our geese. And could cut turf for fuel. Now that is gone! My cottage, along with many others, is pulled down and it is difficult for us poor to find a home.

Your turn!

1   Look at Source A. How useful is this source as evidence of what agriculture was like at that time?

2   **a**   Look at Figure 6.1. Write down as many changes as you can find between Aston Blank before and after enclosure.

   b   In what ways would (i) the landowners and (ii) the poor have been affected by enclosure?

3   **a**   Read Sources B and C. How do they differ about the impact of enclosure on poor villagers?

   b   Does Source C gives us reliable evidence about the impact of enclosure on the poor? What questions would a historian have to ask before accepting its evidence as being reliable?

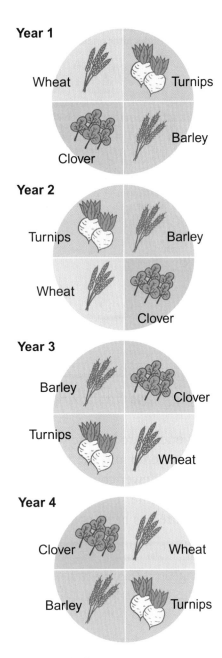

Year 1

Wheat | Turnips
Clover | Barley

Year 2

Turnips | Barley
Wheat | Clover

Year 3

Barley | Clover
Turnips | Wheat

Year 4

Clover | Wheat
Barley | Turnips

Figure 6.2: The Norfolk Crop Rotation system.

Crop rotation

Once the land was enclosed, farmers began to introduce new farming methods that would produce better crops. The traditional method was to grow crops on a field for two years and then leave it empty, or fallow, for a third year while the soil recovered. After enclosure, instead of leaving a field lying fallow, farmers began experimenting with growing root vegetables and clover to put nutrients back into the soil. In this way, more food was produced. The most common system of crop rotation was developed in Norfolk. Each crop drew different nutrients from the soil so they could be grown one after the other. Cows and sheep grazed on clover and their manure fertilised the soil.

Previously, farmers had to kill most cows as winter approached because there was nothing to feed them on. However, turnips and clover were excellent winter fodder for cows and so farmers could keep their herds through the winter months and there were more to breed from in the spring.

Farm machinery

Enclosure meant that farmers could try out new farm machinery. One of the first inventions was Jethro Tull's horse-drawn seed drill. This machinery made regular holes in the soil and planted seeds in them before covering them up again. This was much more efficient than the old method of broadcast sowing – throwing handfuls of seed onto the soil. As steam power became available, a variety of new farm machinery was introduced, including steam tractors.

All these changes in farming meant that fewer people were needed to work on the land. They moved to the towns and cities to work in the mills and factories. Because the land was producing more food than ever before, there was enough to feed people in the towns who weren't growing their own food.

Source D: A 19th-century steam-powered threshing machine. Threshing (separating the grain from the stalks) used to be done by hand. Here, the steam engine powers the threshing machine by turning a belt and the grain falls into sacks.

The effects of the Agricultural Revolution

The changes in agriculture affected different people in different ways, and not all of them were happy about it.

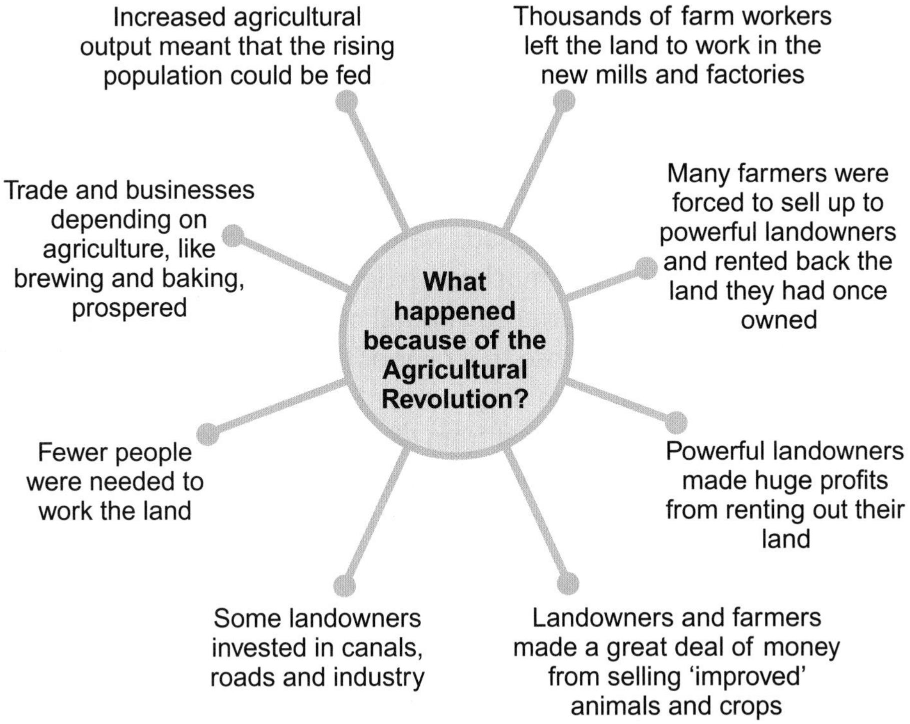

Increased agricultural output meant that the rising population could be fed

Thousands of farm workers left the land to work in the new mills and factories

Trade and businesses depending on agriculture, like brewing and baking, prospered

What happened because of the Agricultural Revolution?

Many farmers were forced to sell up to powerful landowners and rented back the land they had once owned

Fewer people were needed to work the land

Powerful landowners made huge profits from renting out their land

Some landowners invested in canals, roads and industry

Landowners and farmers made a great deal of money from selling 'improved' animals and crops

Figure 6.3: The consequences of the Agricultural Revolution.

Source E: From the *Illustrated London News*, August 1857.

The steam traction-engine with 3 double ploughs ploughed about 8 acres in one day of 10 hours at a cost for labour and coal of £1 12s. The work performed by 6 single ploughs with 18 horses in the same time would only be 4 acres at a cost of about £2 11s.

Did you know?

In the years 1830–32, rural workers in the south and east of England rose up in protest against their low wages and poor living conditions. They burned haystacks, tore down fences and smashed threshing machines. They sent warning letters to landowners, signing them 'Captain Swing', and so the riots were known later as the 'Swing Riots'. The landowners, many of whom were MPs, were worried by what seemed an organised revolt. The rioters were punished harshly: 19 men were hanged, 644 were imprisoned and 505 were sent to Australia.

Your turn!

 1 Imagine you are a wealthy landowner. What would you say to villagers to explain the benefits of enclosure? How would you answer them when they asked, 'What about us?'

2 Would you have been a Swing rioter? Work with a partner and create a conversation between a farm labourer joining the rioters and one who was leaving to look for work in the towns.

 3 'The information in Source E proves that the lives of farm workers will become easier.' Write three to four sentences to explain whether or not you agree.

Checkpoint

1 How did enclosure help farmers produce more food?
2 Why did farming improvements make some people rich?
3 Why did enclosing common land result in problems?
4 Why did increased food production lead to people leaving the countryside for the towns?

161

Canals, coal and cotton

- Learn about the connections between improved transport and developing industry.
- Understand how historians use sources to find out about the Industrial Revolution.

Why was efficient transport important?

Before the mid 1700s, most goods were transported around Britain by sea or by river. This was much more dependable than using roads, which were often badly surfaced and full of potholes. However, not every merchant worked close to a river or the sea. Canals were one answer. The first canal to be dug was the Sankey Cut. It was opened in 1757 for barges to carry coal from Lancashire mines to Liverpool. The idea quickly caught on, and by 1790 a network of canals linked Hull, Leeds, Liverpool, Bristol, Manchester, Birmingham and London.

By 1830, about 40,000 people were working on the canal system. However, by the 1850s, canals had been overtaken by a new form of transport – the railways. Soon a network of railways covered the country. Railways were important, not just because they carried goods quickly and cheaply, but because building and running railways created a demand for coal and iron and created thousands of new jobs.

Source A: A lock* on the Regents Canal, London, painted in 1827. The men carrying rods were working out the weight of the loads in the barges so that they could charge the correct toll*.

Source B: Joseph Priestley, writing at the time, commented on the advantages the Grand Junction Canal brought to London. The canal was finished in 1805. It linked several smaller canals.

The advantages which London gains from this grand undertaking are vast. Goods from Manchester, Stourbridge, Birmingham and Wolverhampton: cheese, salt, lime, stone, timber, corn, paper and bricks are carried along the canal to London. While in return, groceries, tallow, cotton, tin, manure and raw materials for manufacturing districts are constantly carried along it.

Key terms

Lock*: When canals had to cross hilly land, locks were dug in sections at different levels. They enabled barges to move from one level of water to another.

Toll*: A fee charged for using a stretch of canal or a lock, relating to the weight of goods carried. Tolls were also charged on some roads.

How did factories help towns to grow?

Before 1700, no one had seen a factory. Spinning and weaving were done at home. As the population increased and the demand for cloth grew, machines were invented that could spin thread and weave cloth quickly. However, these machines couldn't fit into small cottages and so factories were built. The first factories were built beside fast-flowing rivers, where water turned huge wheels to drive the machinery. Then, the invention of steam engines to drive machines changed everything. Factories could then be built in towns, where there were people to work the machinery as well as canals, and later railways, to bring in raw materials and take away the finished goods. As the factories prospered, more and more people moved into the towns to find work, and so towns and cities grew.

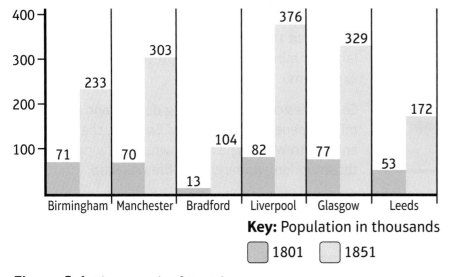

Key: Population in thousands
☐ 1801 ☐ 1851

Figure 6.4: The growth of British towns, 1801–51.

Source D: A picture of the Bowling Iron Works, Bradford, West Yorkshire, drawn in 1861.

Source C: From a report written about the city of Manchester in 1840 by John Robertson, a surgeon.

New cottages, huddled together, row behind row, may be seen springing up in many parts, but especially in the township of Manchester, where the land is higher in price for cottage sites than in other townships. A cottage may be badly drained, the streets may be full of pits, brim-full of stagnant water and dead dogs and cats, but the authorities cannot interfere.

Your turn!

1 Look at Source A. What does it tell you about canals in the early 19th century?

2 How do Sources A and B together help explain the importance of canals in the Industrial Revolution?

3 Look at Figure 6.4. Work out the percentage growth of each town. Which town grew the most between 1801 and 1851? Suggest two reasons why this was.

4 How reliable is the evidence given in Sources C and D about conditions in industrial towns?

Mining and machinery

After about 1750 there was a growing demand for coal. Steam engines that powered machinery, railway engines and the furnaces in iron foundries all needed coal. Landowners were very happy to invest money in developing new and deeper mines, as there were huge profits to be made. But there were also huge problems, and two important inventions solved them.

- **Flooding**

   Steam-powered pumps solved the problem of flooding. By 1775, there were 400 steam-driven pumps on coalfields and more coming into operation every year.

- **Gas explosions**

Gases seeping out of the coal caused explosions when they came into contact with the miners' lit candles. In 1815, Humphry Davy invented a safety lamp for miners to use that prevented these explosions.

Coal mines could then be dug deeper, and more mines opened in the north of England, the Midlands and South Wales. The mine owners grew rich, but for those working underground life was hard.

Source E: A woman in a mine, pulling a trolley, after a 19th-century English wood engraving.

Coal was needed for the new, steam-powered machinery. At the start of the Industrial Revolution, most of this new machinery was developed for the textile industry. By 1850, cotton cloth was Britain's biggest export and most of it was produced in the mills of Lancashire – and also in Manchester. The port of Liverpool thrived, importing cotton from the USA and exporting cotton goods. A lot of people, such as mill owners, became extremely rich.

However, all this was done at a cost. Mill workers – men, women and children, often whole families – spent long hours doing repetitive work in hot, noisy and unsafe conditions, where wages were low and discipline harsh.

Source F: A contemporary illustration of the inside of a cotton mill in 1835. The machines were connected by belts to a steam engine that produced the power to make them work.

Luddites!

Not everyone benefited from the Industrial Revolution. Thousands of people who worked on the canals were thrown out of work by the coming of the railways. The men and women who spun thread and wove cloth by hand suffered terribly.

Table 6.1: The wages of a handloom weaver in Bolton, Lancashire, 1797–1830.

1797	1800	1805	1810	1816	1820	1824	1830
30s	25s	25s	19s	12s	9s	8s 6d	5s 6d

Hundreds of workers took out their anger on the machines. They met in secret, swore oaths of loyalty to each other, collected weapons and plotted and planned. When they were ready, gangs of men broke into mills and factories at night and smashed the machines they thought were taking away their livelihood. Often they left a note signed 'Ned Ludd', which is why they are called Luddites. Luddites were active in Nottinghamshire, Yorkshire and Lancashire from about 1811. The authorities were frightened that the Luddites were spearheading a revolution similar to the one that occurred in France in 1789. Parliament passed a law saying that anyone found guilty of breaking machinery could be hanged. There was a mass trial in York in 1813, after which 17 Luddites were hanged.

> **Did you know?**
>
> In 1818, Mary Shelley wrote a novel called *Frankenstein* about a scientist who used modern technology to create a living, breathing monster. Many people believed that eventually technology would be able to do this in real life, and were afraid.

> **Checkpoint**
>
> 1 How did farmers producing more food help the growth of towns?
> 2 What did the Swing rioters do?
> 3 How did canals help industry to grow? Give two reasons.
> 4 State two ways in which the railways helped industry to grow.
> 5 How were steam engines used (a) in mines and (b) in cotton mills?
> 6 Why did Luddites smash up machinery?

Your turn!

 1 What can you learn from Source E about working conditions in mines at that time?

 2 Look at Source F. Make a list of the things it tells you about working in that particular cotton mill. Now make a list of the things it doesn't tell you about working in that mill. Use the two lists to explain whether or not the picture provides useful evidence of what it was like to work in a cotton spinning mill.

 3 How far does Table 6.1 explain the actions of the Luddites?

What was the Industrial Revolution?

- Draw a concept map to show how all the changes after about 1750 combined to bring about a revolution in British industry.

- You have been asked to explain the Industrial Revolution to pupils in your local primary school. Use the concept map you have drawn to create a storyboard, using no more than nine images.

Would you have survived the Industrial Revolution?

Children worked in mines and factories, brickworks and iron foundries. They worked long hours in appalling conditions and discipline was harsh. Their families lived in overcrowded houses where disease and crime flourished. To survive, children would have had to be tough, determined and lucky.

In this section, you will learn about:

- children's working conditions in factories and mines
- diseases and crime experienced by children living in the poorest parts of towns
- how and why attitudes toward children changed.

How hard was children's work?

Learning objectives

- Learn about the work children did in mills and mines during the Industrial Revolution.
- Understand how attitudes to children changed in the 19th century.

What do you think?

Why were people so keen to employ children?

Source A: A picture of working children from a novel published in 1840 called *Life and Adventures of Michael Armstrong: The Factory Boy* by Frances Trollope. She had visited mills in Bradford and Manchester so that she could make her story accurate.

Working in mills

Before the Industrial Revolution, children worked in the fields and workshops with their parents. When parents began working in mills and factories, their children worked with them there too. Mill owners liked employing children because they didn't have to be paid as much as adults, and they were small enough to crawl under machinery to clear away fluff and repair broken threads. Children often worked 12 hours a day with dangerous machinery and might be punished for the slightest mistake.

Source B: In 1833, Leonard Horner was appointed by the government to enquire into the employment of children in factories. Here he describes what happened to a girl in a textile factory.

She was caught by her apron, which wrapped around the shaft. She was whirled around and repeatedly forced between the shaft and the engine. Her right leg was found some distance away.

Source C: From *The Philosophy of Manufactures*, written by Andrew Ure, a scientist, in 1835.

I have visited many factories, entering the spinning rooms unexpectedly and at different time of the day, and I never saw a single instance of corporal punishment being inflicted on a child. They seemed always to be cheerful and alert, taking pleasure in the work they were doing.

Working in mines

Mine owners employed children for exactly the same reasons as mill owners. Children were cheap to employ and small enough to get into places where adults couldn't fit. But the work they did was grim and dangerous, and the children worked underground for as many as 12 hours a day. A Royal Commission was set up to investigate working conditions in mines. Commissioners visited coalfields and interviewed hundreds of men, women and children. Their report was published in 1842. Sources D and E come from this report.

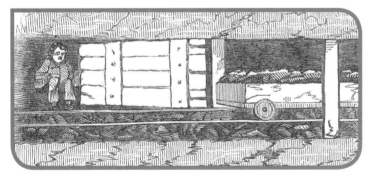

Source E: A boy trapper at work. His job was to open and close wooden trap doors whenever a coal tub had to get through.

Source F: Lord Londonderry explains why he believes the way in which the commissioners collected evidence was wrong. He owned a lot of coal mines.

The way in which commissioners collected evidence by talking to artful boys and ignorant young girls – and putting answers into their mouths – was most unfair. The report was designed to excite people's feelings, not help them form a reasoned judgement.

Did you know?

Parliament passed some important Acts related to children's work.

1833 – No child under the age of 9 could work in a factory.

1842 – No girl could work underground, and neither could any boy under 10 years old.

1847 – Children could not work for longer than 10 hours a day in a factory.

Source D: Part of what Patience Kershaw (aged 17) told the commissioners.

I push tubs of coal. I push them for a mile or more underground and back. They weigh three hundredweight [153 kg] and I push eleven a day. The coal diggers that I work for beat me with their hands if I am not quick enough. I am the only girl in the pit. There are about twenty boys and fifteen men. All the men are naked. I would rather work in the mill than in the coal pit.

Your turn!

 1 What can you learn from Source A about children's experience of mill work? It was drawn to illustrate a story. Does this mean it is of no use as evidence of children's mill work?

   2 **a** What different impressions do Sources B, C and D give of the way working children were treated?

 b What questions would a historian have to ask before accepting each of the sources as reliable evidence of the way working children were treated?

3 Read Source F. How convincing do you find Lord Londonderry's argument?

What happened to orphans and abandoned children?

There were many more orphans and abandoned children in the large industrial cities than there had been before the Industrial Revolution. This was because most people looking for new beginnings in the growing towns were young. They married and had many children. Then, too often, disaster struck. Industrial accidents and diseases killed hundreds of adults, leaving their children destitute. Extreme poverty drove some parents to leave their children in workhouses or abandon them on the steps of churches. Some children in the busy, crowded cities simply got lost and couldn't be found.

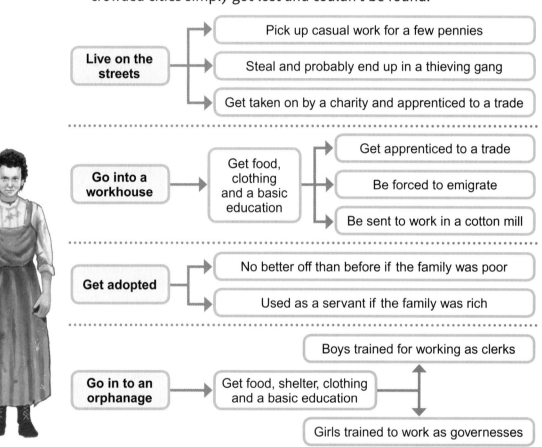

Figure 6.5: What would happen to you if, during the Industrial Revolution, your parents couldn't look after you?

There were problems with all of the options shown in Figure 6.5. Workhouses were often grim places where discipline was harsh; orphanages were often overcrowded and dirty; adoption only worked if the family treated the adopted child well. Living on the streets was as dangerous in the 19th century as it is now. However, most children didn't have a choice: they went where they were put, or they ran away.

However, not all workhouses were places of horror. In some, special care was taken of children to make sure they could get a job and wouldn't return to the workhouse as adults. Not all factory owners were cruel. Samuel Greg, for example, who owned Quarry Bank Mill in Cheshire, took on workhouse children as apprentices* and they were well looked after in a separate house.

Key term

Apprentice*: A person who agrees to work for an employer for a fixed period while learning a trade.

Changing attitudes

One way to change people's views is by writing stories that make them think about a situation in a different way. Two authors who did that were Charles Dickens and Charles Kingsley. Both wrote stories that were published first in weekly parts, making their readers keen for the next exciting instalment.

Oliver Twist by Charles Dickens, published in 1837–39

Oliver Twist is an illegitimate child whose mother dies giving birth to him in a workhouse. Oliver lives in the workhouse until he is about ten. He is cruelly treated and runs away to London. There, he joins a gang of child pickpockets. Eventually his mother's family, who are rich, find him and bring him home, where he lives a comfortable and happy life.

The Water Babies by Charles Kingsley, published in 1863

Tom works for a sweep, and climbs inside chimneys to clear out the soot. He is badly treated, runs away and drowns in a river. He turns into a 'water baby', where he has adventures and learns how to lead a good life. He turns back into a human being and becomes a great man of science, planning railways and designing steam engines.

By making a child the main character, both authors hoped to appeal to their middle-class* readers' consciences.

Source G: An original illustration from *Oliver Twist*. Here, Oliver joins a gang of pickpockets.

Source H: An illustration from *The Water Babies*. Tom is taught by Mrs Beasyouwouldbedoneby

Key term

Middle class*: The social group between the upper and working classes.

Your turn!

1 Work in groups of four. Each of you should take one of the four options open to orphaned and abandoned children (Figure 6.5). Make an argument for your option being the best. You could act this out.

2 In not more than 150 words, explain how Dickens and Kingsley hoped to change people's attitudes.

Checkpoint

1 Why did mill owners like to employ children? Give two reasons.
2 Name two types of work children did in the mines.
3 Give two ways in which abandoned children could be looked after.
4 How might novels change people's attitudes to working children?
5 In Source D (page 167), Patience Kershaw says she would sooner work in a mill than a mine. Explain whether or not you would agree with her.

169

Dirt and disease

Learning objectives

- Understand how poor living conditions led to disease.
- Find out what medical care was available for poor people.
- Know about the work of John Snow in discovering how cholera spread.

Houses built so close together that not much air or light can get in

Poor building materials meant most houses were damp

People got their water from a pump, which was usually supplied by the nearest river

Everyone used the same toilet, the contents of which ended up in a river

Many families were crowded into one room

The central drain emptied into the nearest river

There was no regular rubbish collection

Figure 6.6: Thousands of poor people lived in buildings like this in the middle of cities.

What was it like to live in a town if you were poor?

Thousands of people lived in houses crammed together in narrow streets around the factories and mills where they worked. Many houses were built around courtyards accessible through a narrow passage from the street, so little air or sunlight reached the rooms. Rents were low but living was unhealthy.

Source A: From a report written about Manchester by Dr James Kay-Shuttleworth in 1832. He worked as a doctor amongst the poor people in the city.

Frequently, two or more families are crowded into one small house and often one family lived in a damp cellar where twelve or sixteen persons were crowded. Children are ill-fed, dirty, ill-clothed, exposed to cold and neglect; in a consequence more than half of the children die before their fifth birthday.

What diseases did people catch?

Poor living conditions meant that diseases spread quickly. People caught tuberculosis (TB), typhoid, cholera, measles, whooping cough, influenza and scarlet fever. All of these were killer diseases, and they spread quickly in the overcrowded slums* of Britain's cities.

How did people get better?

In the 19th century, there was no National Health Service. If you needed a doctor, you had to pay for one. Some doctors, like Dr Kay-Shuttleworth (Source A), chose to work amongst poor working-class people. Their fees were low, but even so were too high for many people to be able to afford them. An alternative to a qualified doctor was to visit a 'quack' doctor*, who would sell patent medicines* that (falsely) guaranteed to cure just about everything. The very poorest people just waited and hoped they would recover.

IN THE SEASON AND OUT OF THE SEASON

TAKE

BEECHAM'S PILLS.

Source B: An advertisement for a patent medicine. The pills contained ginger, aloes (a bitter juice) and soap.

Key terms

Slums*: Overcrowded and filthy houses lived in by very poor people.

Quack doctor*: Someone who pretends to have medical skills.

Patent medicine*: Cheap medicine that does little to cure disease.

Source C: A picture called *The Doctor*, painted in 1891 by Sir Luke Fildes.

Your turn!

1 Look at Figure 6.6.
   a Make a list of all the things you can see that would encourage the spread of disease. Now turn your list into a concept map that shows how they are all linked.
   b If you could do one thing to improve the situation in cities, what would it be, and why?

2 How useful is Source A to a historian investigating living conditions in Britain's industrial cities?

3 Look at Source B. Manufacturing Beecham's Pills made Thomas Beecham a rich man. Does this mean the pills worked?

4 Look carefully at Source C. Paintings like this are called narrative paintings because they tell a story. Write the story that this picture tells, using all the information on pages 170–171. (Hint: who are the adults and the child? What has happened to the child? Why has the doctor been called?)

Cholera

REGISTRATION DISTRICT					*West London*			
1849. DEATH in the Sub-district of *West London* in the *City of London*.								
Columns :— 1	2	3	4	5	6	7	8	9
No.	When and where died	Name and surname	Sex	Age	Occupation	Cause of death	Signature, description, and residence of informant	When registered	Signature of registrar
100	*Eighteenth June 1849 106 Shoe Lane St. Brides*	*Maria Woolf*	*Female*	*32 years.*	*Wife of George Woolf Accountant.*	*Diarrhoea 8 days Cholera 4 days Premature Labour 32 hours Exaustion Certified.*	*G. Woolf Present at the Death 106 Shoe Lane London.*	*Nineteenth June 1849*	*William Nason Registrar*

Source D: The death certificate of Maria Woolf from 1849.

Why did Maria Woolf die?

Maria Woolf lived with her husband George and their five-year-old son Joseph in Shoe Lane in the City of London. The inhabitants of Shoe Lane drew their water from the Fleet Brook. This was the same brook into which household and human waste was tipped. In June 1849, Maria, who was seven months pregnant with her second child, was taken ill with cholera and died eight days later.

Maria died in a cholera epidemic that hit Britain in 1848–49, killing 62,000 people. Cholera outbreaks were frequent: one in 1831–32 had killed 32,000 people. The problem was that, in the 1840s, no one knew how cholera spread. Most people believed that disease was caused by 'bad air'. This miasma theory* had been held for hundreds of years.

Enter John Snow

John Snow was a man with an idea, which was that cholera was a disease carried in water. In 1853, when a third cholera epidemic hit Britain, Snow was working as a doctor in London treating hundreds of cholera victims. To test his idea, he plotted the locations of all the cholera deaths in Soho on a map.

Key term

Miasma theory*: The idea that disease is caused by bad air, called miasma.

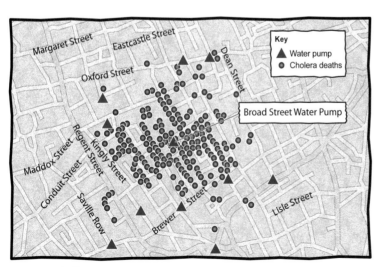

Figure 6.7: Cholera deaths in Soho, London, in 1854.

It was clear to John Snow that the cholera deaths were connected to the water from the Broad Street pump – so he simply took the handle off the pump so that no one could use it. Cholera deaths in Soho fell dramatically.

John Snow found other evidence that helped prove his theory.

- Seven workmen, who lived outside the area, drank water from the Broad Street pump, caught cholera and died.

- Seventy workers in a local brewery drank beer instead of water and none caught cholera.

- A widow who used to live in Soho had a bottle of water from the Broad Street pump delivered to her every day. She died from cholera. None of her neighbours, who drank different water, caught cholera.

Source E: Part of the report from the Committee for Scientific Enquiry into the Recent Cholera Epidemic, 1855.

If the Broad Street pump did actually become a source of disease, we believe this may simply be because its impure waters have become part of the atmospheric infection in the district.

- The 535 people in the local workhouse used a different water pump. Only five of them caught cholera and died.

Very few people working in medicine agreed with John Snow that cholera was a disease carried in water. They clung to the miasma theory and used it to explain Snow's findings.

Two important things happened that changed people's minds.

- A larger enquiry was carried out in south London in 1856 with the same results: people using water that contained sewage caught cholera.

- In the 1860s, Louis Pasteur's experiments discovered germs, and scientists made the connection between germs and disease. This is called the germ theory of disease.

Finally, in 1870, it was officially accepted that John Snow had been right: cholera was a disease carried in water.

Source F: A cartoon in the magazine *Fun*, published in 1866.

Your turn!

 1 Look at Source D. Write down all the information it gives you, and the inferences you can make from it. What use would it be to a historian trying to find out about the cholera epidemic of 1848–49?

 2 Look at Figure 6.7. Does this provide definite proof that the Broad Street pump was the problem? Now look at the other evidence collected by John Snow about cholera in Soho. Explain which piece of evidence, of all that he collected, you find the most reliable as evidence that cholera was spread in water.

3 Imagine you are John Snow's assistant. Design a poster warning people in Soho about the problem with the water. Make it as striking as you can!

 4 Look at Source F. How useful is it to a historian investigating cholera epidemics?

 5 Why did it take so long for people to accept that John Snow was right?

Checkpoint

1 What were the dates of the three cholera epidemics in Britain?
2 What was John Snow's theory about the spread of disease?
3 Why did John Snow take away the handle of the water pump in Broad Street, Soho?
4 What is the miasma theory and why did it hold up change?
5 What is the germ theory and why is it important?

Why was there so much crime in the cities?

Learning objectives

- Understand why the growth of cities led to an increase in crime.
- Learn about the establishment of a police force.
- Find out how novels made forensic science interesting and popular.

Source A: St Giles rookery, London, drawn in 1850.

Source B: From a letter published in the *Morning Chronicle* in 1851.

Where standpipes or public taps are erected, the charge by the water company is about 10 shillings a year for every house that wants to use them. Of all the petty thefts that occur in Manchester, the most common are thefts of water from taps and pumps.

Key term

Vagrancy*: Wandering and begging because a person is homeless.

Men, women and children committed crimes whether they lived in villages, towns or cities. However, city living made crime much easier. A criminal could disappear in a crowd. There were more places for criminals to hide from those who were looking for them, and more places for gangs of criminals to meet unseen and plan their activities. There were also many more possible victims.

Rookeries

Rookeries were those parts of cities where housing was poorest and hardened criminals lived. Narrow streets and alleyways, cellars, lodging houses and pubs provided secret meeting places and hideouts. In London, the largest rookery was in St Giles. There were also large rookeries across the country, in Liverpool, Leeds, Bristol, Birmingham and Manchester.

What kinds of crime took place?

About 75 per cent of crimes involved theft, mainly street robbery and burglary. The crowded streets of industrial cities, especially when events like public hangings drew huge crowds, provided excellent opportunities for pickpockets. Thefts of meat and bread from the growing number of shops were common, too. The new middle-class housing for mill overlookers, bankers and factory managers was attractive to burglars. There was also a fair amount of vagrancy*, drunkenness and prostitution.

However, not all criminals were poor. The huge numbers of new businesses led to an increase in fraud and many people were tricked out of money they invested in new enterprises.

Who caught the criminals?

Before the Industrial Revolution, there were several different ways of catching criminals (see Figure 6.8). By 1829, London's population had grown to 1.5 million and crime was increasing. Clearly, old methods of catching criminals were not sufficient. Something had to be done.

The Metropolitan Police Act 1829

In 1829, parliament passed the Metropolitan Police Act and 3200 police constables were recruited to work in London. London was divided into 17 divisions, each with four inspectors and 144 constables. They were all under the control of two commissioners based in Scotland Yard, who reported directly to the Home Secretary, Robert Peel.

Constables Appointed by villagers for a year at a time

Bow Street Runners Paid by the government to track down offenders identified by magistrates

Thief-takers Tracked down criminals and claimed rewards

Watchmen Patrolled the streets in towns and cities

Figure 6.8: Methods of catching criminals before the Industrial Revolution.

Timeline

1829 Metropolitan Police Force set up in London

1835 Towns and cities allowed to set up their own police forces

1839 Counties allowed to set up their own police forces

1842 The Metropolitan Police Force set up the first detective force

1856 Compulsory requirement for all cities and counties to set up police forces

1884 39,000 police in Britain

Did you know?

Police were nicknamed 'bobbies' or 'peelers' after Sir Robert Peel. Peel was Home Secretary in the government that introduced the 1829 Metropolitan Police Act.

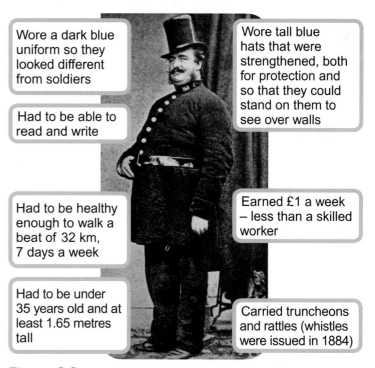

Wore a dark blue uniform so they looked different from soldiers

Wore tall blue hats that were strengthened, both for protection and so that they could stand on them to see over walls

Had to be able to read and write

Had to be healthy enough to walk a beat of 32 km, 7 days a week

Earned £1 a week – less than a skilled worker

Had to be under 35 years old and at least 1.65 metres tall

Carried truncheons and rattles (whistles were issued in 1884)

Figure 6.9: Tom Smith, one of the first London policemen.

Your turn!

1 In what ways did rookeries:
   a help and hinder criminals
   b help and hinder the police?

2 Make a list of the ways in which the Metropolitan Police Force of 1829 was different from the system of constables and watchmen. Explain which you think was the most important difference.

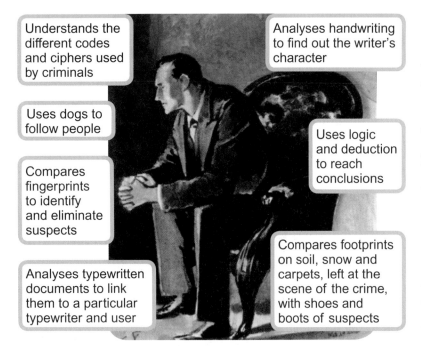

Understands the different codes and ciphers used by criminals

Analyses handwriting to find out the writer's character

Uses dogs to follow people

Uses logic and deduction to reach conclusions

Compares fingerprints to identify and eliminate suspects

Compares footprints on soil, snow and carpets, left at the scene of the crime, with shoes and boots of suspects

Analyses typewritten documents to link them to a particular typewriter and user

Figure 6.10: Some of the methods used by Sherlock Holmes.

Fact, fiction and forensic science

Detective novels and short stories were very popular towards the end of the 19th century. Many people loved reading thrilling stories about crime and criminals.

Sherlock Holmes

Sherlock Holmes was a fictional detective invented by the author Arthur Conan Doyle, writing between 1887 and 1927. Sherlock Holmes solved crimes using reason and logic, and was always at least one step ahead of the police. He used forensic methods years before they were officially adopted by the police.

How did the police use forensic science?

In 1842, the Metropolitan Police established the 'Detective Branch'. Detectives were to investigate crimes rather than keep order on the streets, which was the work of ordinary 'bobbies'. This was reorganised in 1878 as the Criminal Investigation Department (CID), where the police wore plain clothes and were clearly different from the uniformed police.

Developments in science and technology meant that the CID was able to use and develop forensic science in tracking down criminals.

- **Body temperature** In 1829, tests were developed that linked body temperature to the time of death.

- **Poisons** In 1836, James Marsh developed a test (later called the Marsh test) that identified the presence of arsenic* in a body. Up until then, arsenic had been thought of as the perfect poison because it was untraceable.

- **Bullet matching** From 1835, it was possible to match tiny flaws in bullets to the gun barrels from which they had been fired.

- **Blood** Tests to identify the presence of blood at crime scenes were used by the police from about 1850. In 1901, different blood groups were discovered, so crime scene blood could be used to help narrow down the list of suspects.

- **Photography** From the 1850s, criminals began to be photographed, and in 1867 the first photographs of a crime scene were taken.

- **Fingerprints** In 1892, Francis Galton identified fingerprint patterns. In 1902, the police began to fingerprint suspects.

Key term

Arsenic*: A white powder that has no taste or smell. It could easily be put in food or drink. It builds up in a body and eventually causes multiple organ failure.

Sarah Dazley: caught by forensic science

In 1838, a girl named Sarah married her boyfriend Simeon Mead. Two years later they had a baby called Jonah. Jonah died suddenly and, in October 1840, Simeon died unexpectedly as well. Sudden deaths were common in Victorian England. In 1841, Sarah married again. Her new husband, William Dazley, suddenly became very ill, with severe stomach pains and vomiting. The local doctor prescribed pills and William began to recover. Then Sarah took over making the pills. William deteriorated and died in October 1842. Was Sarah a murderer, or just unlucky?

Suspicion fell on Sarah and she was arrested. William's body was dug up, as was the body of Sarah's first husband Simeon and their son, Jonah. Arsenic was found in the bodies of Jonah and William, but Simeon's body was too decomposed for the test to work. Sarah was tried for the murder of William and publicly hanged at Bedford Gaol. Thousands of people came to watch her die.

Did you know?

In France, arsenic was called 'poudre de succession' (succession powder) because people would often use it to kill relatives in order to inherit their money.

Your turn!

 1 Look at the ways in which detectives used forensic science. Put them in order of importance, and explain your thinking.

 2 Write a Victorian detective story! You could begin like this: *It is 1900. The body of a stranger is lying in Mr and Mrs Dawson's kitchen, with a bloodstained carving knife beside them. Time to call the police. …* Use as much information from page 176 as you can in your story to make it authentic. Use Sherlock Holmes's methods as well as those of the regular police force. You could even call in Sherlock himself!

Checkpoint

1 Before the Industrial Revolution, who were the constables and what did they do?
2 What did the Bow Street Runners do?
3 What were rookeries?
4 In cities during the Industrial Revolution, what were the most common crimes?
5 Give two changes to policing brought in by the Metropolitan Police Act 1829.
6 Name two important developments in forensic science that helped the police catch criminals.

Would you have survived the Industrial Revolution?

Whether or not you would have survived the Industrial Revolution depended a great deal on luck. You are going to design a snakes and ladders board game that reflects this.

Draw a grid that is eight squares by eight squares and number each square, with the bottom right square being 1 and the top-left square being 64. Label the last square 'I survived!' Add some slithery snakes that will take you back down the grid and some ladders that take you up towards survival. Using all the information in this chapter, write on different squares events that may take you up or down. For example, 'Apprenticed to a mill owner' would take you up a ladder, but 'Caught cholera' might take you slithering back to the very beginning. Now play the game!

In this section, you have learned about:

- the ways in which developments in agriculture and transport led to industrial development and the growth of towns

- the working lives of children in industrial Britain

- how the growth of towns led to an increase in crime and the development of policing.

Nature
The picture is an illustration from a story about the adventures of a factory boy.

Purpose
The story was written to tell people about working conditions in factories, particularly the conditions in which children worked.

Origin
It was written in 1840 when there were hundreds of factories in Britain that employed children. The author visited mills in Bradford and Manchester.

Key detail
Two boys, crying and wearing ragged clothes.

Figure 6.11: A picture of working children from a novel published in 1840 called *Life and Adventures of Michael Armstrong: The Factory Boy* by Frances Trollope. She had visited mills in Bradford and Manchester so that she could make her story accurate.

In this section, you have looked at a lot of different sources and have used them to provide evidence about the Industrial Revolution. We are now going to look again at one of those sources, but in greater detail. There are three basic questions that historians ask of all sources.

- What is the **nature** of the source? For example, it could be a cartoon, a photograph, a painting or a speech.

- What is the **origin** of the source? It is useful to know when, and by whom, the source was produced.

- What is the **purpose** of the source? This asks for the reason why it was produced. For example, for the purpose of giving information or trying to persuade.

Look at Figure 6.11, which shows Source A from page 166.

Your turn!

1 Look at the boxes labelled 'Nature', 'Origin' and 'Purpose' in Figure 6.11. For each one, write a sentence saying why this would make you extra careful when using the source.

2 Look at the key details in the source. One has been picked out for you. List the others you can find.

Writing historically

We are going to look at the ways in which historians use the detail in a source to trigger further questions that would lead to a deeper understanding of the historical period they are studying.

Students' answers

A group of students are answering the question 'How would you follow up Source A on page 166 to find out more about mills and factories in the 1840s?'

They have been asked to begin their answers in the same way:

The key detail in the source that I would follow up is the drawing of the two boys who are crying and wearing ragged clothes. The question I would ask is…

The following are the questions the students asked about this key detail.

Student 1

Why are the boys crying?

The student has forgotten the **nature** of the source. It is a story. Reading the story would tell you why the boys were crying, but this wouldn't tell you much about mills and factories in the 1840s. A better question would ask whether children were badly treated.

Student 2

Why have the boys been drawn wearing ragged clothes?

The student understands that the source is a drawing of an imaginary situation, but hasn't focused the question sharply enough on the 'big' question. A better question would ask about wages paid to children in factories and mills in the 1840s.

Student 3

What point is the artist making by showing these boys looking ragged and crying?

The student understands the **purpose** of the source: it was written to tell people about conditions in mills and factories. But the question doesn't lead to a deeper understanding of the actual conditions in mills and factories. A better question would ask why writing emotional stories about the plight of children was necessary.

Student 4

Were real children treated like this in mills and factories in the 1840s?

The student understands the **origin** of the source: it was based on what the author had actually seen. It is a good question because it leads on to the next step, which would be to check the way these boys were drawn against evidence of the treatment of real children in real factories.

Writing your own answer

Look back at the list of key details you drew up in answer to question 2 on page 178.

Complete the following two sentences for each of the key details you have chosen.

The key detail in the source I would follow up is…

The question I would ask is…

Think about the comments above on the questions asked by the four students, and use those as hints to help you to write the best questions you can. Remember to focus on finding out more about mills and factories in the 1840s.

Did the Industrial Revolution bring progress and improvement?

The Industrial Revolution changed the lives of millions of people. It led to thousands living out their lives in poverty and desperation. For thousands of others, however, the Industrial Revolution opened up a wonderful world of new opportunities, where living was comfortable and there was time for fun and entertainment.

This section of the book will look at:

- the ways in which the Industrial Revolution led to better living conditions

- how Victorian people had fun

- the reasons why change affected different people in different ways.

Production and prosperity

What do you think?

Does change always lead to improvement?

Learning objectives

- Know about the Great Exhibition of 1851.
- Learn about the ways in which some people led comfortable lives.
- Understand how the Industrial Revolution led to prosperity for some people.

Did you know?

Some inventions did not catch on. One of the exhibits was George Merryweather's Tempest Prognosticator, which was supposed to predict thunderstorms. It was a device holding 12 glass bottles containing leeches. When they detected a change in the atmosphere, the leeches tried to climb out of the bottles. In doing this they triggered bells that rang to warn people of an approaching thunderstorm.

The Great Exhibition, 1851

During Queen Victoria's reign (1837–1901), British trade and industry grew and prospered. By the middle of the 19th century, Britain was known as the 'workshop of the world'. Prince Albert, Queen Victoria's husband, had the idea of holding a great exhibition to show how proud the Victorians were of their industrial and technological achievements. It was believed that British superiority would be obvious when British products were displayed alongside those from other countries.

Source A: The Crystal Palace in Hyde Park, London, which was designed by Sir Joseph Paxton for the Great Exhibition of 1851.

The exhibits

Half of the exhibition space was allocated to exhibits from Britain and the British Empire, and the other half to exhibits from 'foreign' countries. Exhibits came in from all over the world. There were more than 14,000 items altogether, ranging from steam locomotives to stuffed animals, jewellery to agricultural machinery, weapons to china tea sets.

The visitors

Visitors, both rich and poor, poured in to see the Great Exhibition. Special excursion trains with cheap fares were run to the venue. Different days had different entry fees: the most anyone could pay was £1 and the least was one shilling. Rich people paid for their workers and servants to attend. Altogether, six million people visited the Great Exhibition.

The Industrial Revolution changed the lives of thousands of people for the better. The Great Exhibition showed everyone just how prosperous Britain, and the British people, had become.

Source B: Inside the Great Exhibition, 1851.

Clean and healthy
Clean water pumped to the kitchen and bathroom helps the family stay free of diseases like cholera and typhoid.

Good food
The railways bring fresh fish, fruit and vegetables to inland towns and cities.

Keeping in touch
The railways bring national newspapers on the day they are printed.

Enough money
Mr Robinson earns enough to make life comfortable and safe for his family.

Crime free
A new house and gas street lighting reduce the chance of burglary and muggings.

Education
The boys go to one of the new grammar schools and the girls will go to a grammar school opening soon.

Figure 6.12: The prosperous Robinson family in 1870. You'll meet them again in the next enquiry.

Your turn!

1   Design a poster to encourage people to visit the Great Exhibition.

2   a   Read all the advantages enjoyed by the Robinson family, shown in Figure 6.12. Which do you think was the most important? Why?

    b   Look back at the drawing of the tenement building on page 170. List all the differences you can find between family life there and the Robinson's family life. Write a paragraph to explain the differences.

Reading, writing and arithmetic: the way forward for the poor

In 1861, there were three and a half million children in Britain. Fewer than half of them went to school regularly and, of those who did, only one in ten could read, write and do simple sums. Most schools were run by the Church. These schools were scattered throughout the country, and going to school was not compulsory. All this changed in 1870.

In 1870, parliament passed an Education Act, which said that every district had to have enough good schools for all young children aged 5–10 years old. They were called elementary schools. The government had done this for two main reasons:

- In 1867, a Reform Act doubled the number of men who could vote in general elections from one million to two million. The government needed new voters to be able to read the policies of the different political parties and understand for which party they were voting.

- The Industrial Revolution had created a lot of jobs that required young people to be able to read, write and do arithmetic. For example, to make machine tools people needed to understand numbers and to work in a shop people needed to read.

Timeline

1867
Parliamentary Reform Act meant that two in seven men could vote

1870
Education Act set up Board schools where there were not enough other schools

1880
Education made compulsory for all children up to the age of 10

1884
Parliamentary Reform Act meant that two in three men could vote

1891
Education for children up to the age of 10 was free

1899
Education made compulsory and free for all children up to the age of 12

Source C: From a speech made by W. E. Forster in the House of Commons, 17 February 1870.

Our industrial prosperity depends on elementary education. It is no use trying to give technical teaching to our workers without elementary education. If we leave our working people unskilled for any longer, even though they have physical strength, we will not be able to compete in world markets. Parliament has decided that England will have a government elected by the people. I will not wait until the people are educated before I trust them with political power. Now that we have given them political power we must not wait any longer to give them education.

Source D: Women typists in an office, 1889.

Having fun

Whether they are rich, poor or middle class, people have always found ways of having fun. Sometimes, though, it was difficult for anyone except the very rich to find the time to do so.

However, this changed gradually. Although Sunday had always been a day off, from 1850 textile workers were given a half-day off work on Saturdays, and this spread to workers in other industries. In 1871, the government introduced Bank Holidays (Christmas, Easter, Whitsun and the last Monday in August) when no one went to work. There was more time to have fun, which led to more organised leisure activities. For example, in 1863 the Football Association was formed and soon everyone was playing to the same rules and entering national competitions. After 1876, when a 'safety' bicycle* was invented, men and women all over the country joined cycling clubs.

Source E: The Royal Victorian Coffee Palace and Music Hall, London, 1881. Music halls were very popular. Shows were full of singing and dancing. Some of the songs were very rude, some were funny and some were serious. Most music halls had bars where people could eat and drink.

Source F: Victorian children at the seaside. The new railways made seaside holidays popular.

Key term

Safety bicycle*: A bicycle with a comfortable saddle that looks a bit like a modern bike. Women could ride it and be thought respectable.

Your turn!

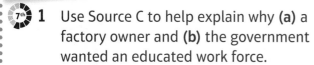 **1** Use Source C to help explain why **(a)** a factory owner and **(b)** the government wanted an educated work force.

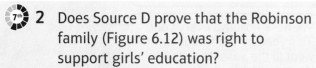 **2** Does Source D prove that the Robinson family (Figure 6.12) was right to support girls' education?

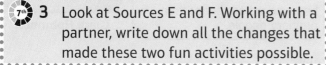 **3** Look at Sources E and F. Working with a partner, write down all the changes that made these two fun activities possible.

Checkpoint

1 Where and when was the Great Exhibition held?

2 Why was the Great Exhibition held? Give two reasons.

3 What did the 1870 Education Act set up?

4 What is the connection between the 1867 Parliamentary Reform Act and the 1870 Education Act?

Two families: change and continuity

Change can be exciting, opening up new opportunities for work and leisure. On the other hand, change can be depressing, leading to poverty and terrible working and living conditions. How change affected a family depended very much on where they lived, the work they were doing and how confident they were about taking risks. Risk-taking could involve moving to another part of the country or investing money in new enterprises.

The Robinson family

We are now going to return to the imaginary Robinson family, and to a conversation they might well have had about the changes that had happened in their lives.

James Robinson

> The biggest change in my life came in 1832, when parliament said I could vote because I owned enough property. As a manufacturer, I could have a say in how the country was run.

> My father always said it was the canal that made the difference to the family pottery business, but I think it was the railway.

> I'm worried about talk of extending the vote to working men. There'll be trouble in the factory if they think they are equal to the bosses.

> I think I made the biggest change to our family pottery factory when I invested in steam power.

Charles Robinson

Margaret Robinson

> All this talk of voting makes me cross. Women have never had the vote and it doesn't look as if they ever will.

> This house has been our home since we were married in 1850. We can now afford to employ a servant to do all the hard work around the house. This gives me time to go to my ladies' group that supports poor people when they can't work any more.

> I want to go to a grammar school like my brother Robert, but I can't because I'm a girl. Girls have never been able to go to schools like that.

> We have holidays every year. This year, for the first time, we went to the seaside by train. We travelled First Class because we are better than ordinary people.

Clara Robinson

Figure 6.13: Change and continuity in the Robinson family.

The Carpenter family

The Carpenter family, like the Robinsons, experienced change and continuity in their lives, but in very different ways.

Joseph Carpenter

> I never went to school. I didn't need to read and write. My parents didn't see the point of it.

> My work on the land never changed, although I worked for different farmers. It was sowing and reaping, milking cows and shearing sheep, year in, year out.

Samuel Carpenter

> Well, I sometimes went to school but the family needed the money I could earn on the land, even when I was a child.

> I worked on the land like my dad, but then the farmer bought one of those awful threshing machines and he didn't need me any more. I pick up a bit of work here and there, but I can see I'm heading for the workhouse when I'm old.

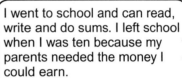

Eliza Carpenter

> I worked for the same farmer as Samuel, but in the dairy making butter and cheese. I can read and write a bit. The steam threshing machines didn't affect me, but Sam lost his job because of them.

> We could never afford a doctor. Two of my children died when they were babies and I nearly died giving birth to Martha. I'm determined she'll have a better life than mine.

Martha Carpenter

> I went to school and can read, write and do sums. I left school when I was ten because my parents needed the money I could earn.

> At the moment I'm working in the fields, but as soon as I'm old enough I'm off to London to work as a maid in a big house. One of my cousins has done that, and she's looking out for a place for me.

Figure 6.14: Change and continuity in the Carpenter family.

Change and continuity questions

Your turn!

1 Work in groups of four and look at the points made by the Robinson family in Figure 6.13. Each member of the group should take on the role of one of the Robinson family. Add some more comments, bringing in as much detail about change and continuity as you can.

2 Read through the experiences of the Carpenter family in Figure 6.14. Put yourself in Martha's shoes. How would she explain to her family why she was planning to leave the countryside?

3 Draw a table with three columns and nine rows. Head the columns 'People', 'Change' and 'Continuity'. In the 'People' column, write the names of the four Robinson people and the four Carpenter people, one on each row.

a Read each person's life experiences. Each time you spot a change, put a tick in the 'Change' column; each time you spot some continuity, put a tick in the 'Continuity' column. The ticks must be in different colours: red for a political change or continuity, green for an economic one and yellow for a social one.

b Write a paragraph to explain which person in the Robinson family, and which in the Carpenter family, has seen the most change.

Source A: The painting *Work* by Ford Madox Brown, completed in 1865.

Source B: A cartoon published in the magazine *Punch* in 1850. Here, 'Mr Punch' is showing a very different kind of exhibition to contrast with the Great Exhibition.

The speed of change

The Industrial Revolution brought rapid change to Britain. In the 100 years between 1750 and 1850, Britain was transformed from being a mainly agricultural country to being the 'workshop of the world'. For some people, the pace of change was too much. For example:

- a hand-loom stocking knitter in Nottingham could not readily adapt to factory work

- agricultural workers in Norfolk did not have the skills necessary for working as clerks.

Rail links to London and other cities meant nothing to people who couldn't, or wouldn't, adapt and they sank into poverty. Even some of those who tried to adapt found themselves exploited. Yet, for millions of people, in the right place and at the right time, the Industrial Revolution presented awesome opportunities.

In 1865, Ford Madox Brown finished a painting he called *Work* (see Source A). He said it showed 'the dignity of the British labourer'. The Victorians loved it.

Not everyone would have agreed with Ford Madox Brown. In 1850, the year before the Great Exhibition, the satirical magazine *Punch* published a cartoon *Specimens From Mr Punch's Industrial Exhibition*, (see Source B).

Source C: A picture called *The Dinner Hour, Wigan*, painted by Eyre Crowe in 1874.

Interpretation 1: From *The Victorian World Picture* by David Newsome, published in 1997.

To the British living at the time, it seemed as if the world they knew had vanished almost overnight. It was the suddenness of the changes that dominated their thoughts and writings. The coming of the railways showed that the whole process of life had been speeded up beyond what anyone could imagine. Not only were things getting faster, they were getting bigger, too. The buildings needed for the factory workers were awe-inspiringly massive. They seemed to prove that the industrial towns were expanding at an alarming and uncontrollable rate.

Your turn!

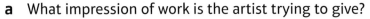

 1 Look at Source A.
   a What impression of work is the artist trying to give?
   b How far is the painting useful evidence of what labouring work was like in Victorian times?
   c How far is the painting reliable evidence of what Victorians liked to think about labouring work?

 2 Look at Source B.
   a What is the message of the cartoon?
   b How could a historian use the cartoon as evidence of the ways in which workers were treated in Victorian Britain?

3 Look at Source C. Imagine the women are chatting as they take a break from working in the factory you can see in the background. They are talking about the changes they have seen in their lives and have been told about by their parents.
   Are they pleased with the changes that have happened, or are they wishing they had lived in the old days? Work in pairs. Imagine, write up and act out their conversation.

Checkpoint

1 Give one example of political change during the 19th century.
2 Give two examples of social change during the 19th century.
3 Give three examples of economic change during the 19th century.
4 Give two examples of continuity during the time of the Industrial Revolution.
5 Did change always lead to improvement? Give one example of where it did, and one example of where it did not.

Did the Industrial Revolution bring progress and improvement?

- You have been asked to put together a virtual exhibition showing the progress brought about by the Industrial Revolution. You are limited to five exhibits. Remember that this is a virtual exhibition, so you can choose very large exhibits. Write a card to go with each exhibit, explaining why it has been chosen. Then use IT to set up your virtual exhibition.

- Read Interpretation 1. What sources would you use to check that the author's interpretation is correct?

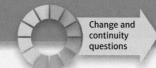
In this section you have learned that:

* the Industrial Revolution led to better living conditions and wider opportunities for many people

* different kinds of events worked together to bring about big developments.

Little and large

Really huge developments, like the growth of towns and cities and the wider opportunities for work and leisure, came about from a combination of much smaller events. Some of the smaller events didn't make much difference by themselves, but combined with other small events they led to really big developments.

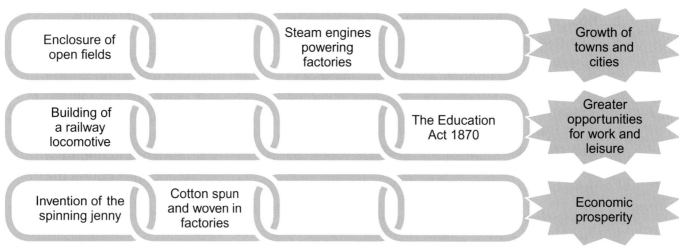

Figure 6.15: Chains of events.

Your turn!

1. **a** Look at the three chains in Figure 6.15. Some of the links have been filled in and others have been left blank. Look back through this chapter and fill in the missing links. You can do this either by drawing the chains on paper and filling in the gaps or by noting down what should go in the empty links.

   b Add dates to all the links in the chains.

2. The words 'pace' (speed) and 'extent' (amount; size; spread) are used by historians when describing change. Write a sentence or two about each of the chains, using the words 'pace' and 'extent' to describe them accurately.

Quick Quiz

1. Give two advantages of enclosing open fields.
2. Why were the first mills built beside rivers?
3. Give one reason why the use of canals declined.
4. Give two ways in which steam engines changed factories.
5. What was a Luddite?
6. How did the 1847 Factory Act affect children?
7. What did John Snow discover in 1854?
8. Why was the Great Exhibition (1851) held?
9. Give two ways in which railways helped improve the lives of people in Britain.
10. Why was the 1870 Education Act important? Give one reason.

Writing historically

Change and continuity questions

We are going to explore how to answer the question: 'The railways were the main reason why people's lives changed during the Industrial Revolution'. How far do you agree?

Planning your answer

It is important that you don't just work chronologically through the years of the Industrial Revolution, saying what brought about changes to people's lives and then picking out the one you believe was the most important. Start with the railways and the changes they brought. Then move on to other events, for example, the move to towns and the growth of factories. Remember, too, that historians refer to the pace and extent of change (page 188) and different types of change (page 187) and you should try to do this, too, where it is appropriate.

Writing your answer

Two students have drawn up their plans and written their answers below.

Student 1

The railways changed people's lives because they meant that poor people could have seaside holidays and rich people could eat fresh fish if they lived inland. It all happened pretty quickly because railways didn't really get going until the 1840s. Enclosure of the open fields meant that people used to working on the land moved into towns. This happened more slowly, and not all over the country.

The student has written about two of the changes brought about by the railways, but there were plenty more that affected people – increased job opportunities, for example. One further reason for change has been identified, but this needs development and detail. The student has shown some understanding about the extent and pace of change. There is no conclusion.

Student 2

Most people's lives changed dramatically during the Industrial Revolution and there were many reasons for this. Railways were an important reason. They brought about economic change to people's lives by creating new jobs as porters and engine drivers, for example, and social change by letting people travel to visit relatives and have holidays away from home, which they couldn't do before. But the pace of these changes was quick. Slower changes to people's lives happened because of the Agricultural Revolution, which threw many people off the land. These agricultural workers had to learn new skills and their lives changed when they took on factory work. All this happened gradually as towns grew slowly. Political events that changed people's lives were slow to come but had a quick effect. For example, Factory Acts and Reform Acts.

The student has explained why the railways were important in bringing about change to people's lives and has good understanding about the pace and type of change. However, although other reasons have been identified as bringing changes to people's lives, the changes need developing more. There is no conclusion.

Student 3 – you!

Now try to write a better answer than Student 2. Remember to give the same amount of detail for each of the reasons you choose. Stay focused on the changes to people's lives – and remember to write a conclusion, saying how far you agree that railways were the main reason people's lives changed.

Murder mystery: Why was Jack the Ripper never caught?

Some historical mysteries are never solved. One of these mysteries concerned a series of murders in Whitechapel, London, in 1888. The victims were all prostitutes and the serial killer was nicknamed 'Jack the Ripper' by the press because of the nature of his killings. Despite an enormous police investigation, Jack the Ripper was never caught.

A serial killer in Whitechapel!

What do you think?

What drives someone to kill, and kill and kill again?

Learning objectives

- Understand the evidence provided by the sources concerning Jack the Ripper.
- Evaluate the evidence.
- Use the context and the evidence to reach a conclusion.

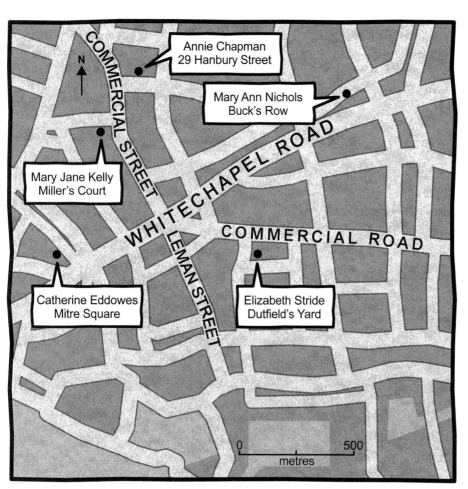

Figure 1: A map of Whitechapel showing where Jack the Ripper's five victims were murdered.

In the 1880s, Whitechapel was a place of tall, overcrowded buildings and dark, dirty alleyways and courtyards. It was where the poorest people in London lived and where crime flourished. A large number of women worked as prostitutes: in 1888, the police estimated that there were over 1000 in the area. There was also a large workhouse in Whitechapel that could hold about 400 inmates, that was usually full. Whitechapel was also the centre of the Jewish community in London.

Jack the Ripper's victims

Eleven prostitutes were murdered in Whitechapel between April 1888 and February 1891. The police believed that the same person, given the name 'Jack the Ripper', had murdered five of them because of the way in which they had been killed.

Date	Victim	Location	How was she murdered?
Friday 31 August	Mary Ann Nichols	Buck's Row	Throat cut and abdomen slashed open
Saturday 8 September	Annie Chapman	Near some steps in a yard off Hanbury Street	Strangled, throat cut and intestines pulled out of her body
Sunday 30 September	Elizabeth Stride	Dutfield's Yard, outside a theatre where Jewish socialists had been meeting	Throat cut. Probably the killer was disturbed before he could do anything more, because he killed again almost immediately
Sunday 30 September	Catherine Eddowes	Mitre Square	Throat cut, intestines pulled out of her body, part of her nose and an ear taken
Friday 9 November	Mary Jane Kelly	Inside her room in Miller's Court	Throat cut, parts of her body cut out and spread around the room

Did anyone see Jack the Ripper?

Inquests* were held into all the deaths. At the inquests, witnesses gave detailed descriptions of a man they had seen talking to the victims just before they were found dead. Was this Jack the Ripper?

Source A: Part of a statement made by Elizabeth Long, who worked on a market stall, at the inquest into the death of Annie Chapman.

He was dark and wearing a hat. I think he was wearing a dark coat but I cannot be sure. He looked shabby but respectable. He was a man over forty, as far as I could tell. He looked to me like a foreigner.

Source B: Part of a statement made by George Hutchinson, an unemployed labourer, at the inquest into the death of Mary Kelly.

He was aged 34–35 years old and about five feet six inches tall, with a pale complexion, dark eyes and hair and a little moustache that curled up at the ends. He wore a long dark coat with a dark jacket underneath, with dark trousers and button boots. His shirt was white and his black tie was fastened with a horseshoe shaped pin. He had a dark hat, turned down in the middle. He was Jewish in appearance and respectable.

Source C: Part of a statement made by William Marshall, a labourer, at the inquest into the death of Elizabeth Stride.

The man was middle-aged and fat, about five foot six inches tall, respectably dressed in a small cut-away coat and dark trousers, wearing a small peaked cap like that worn by sailors.

Key term

Inquest*: A legal enquiry into an incident – usually a death.

Your turn!

1 Using the information on these pages, write down three problems the police faced in their hunt for Jack the Ripper.

2 Read Sources A, B and C. How far would these be useful to the police in their investigation? Discuss this in your class.

3 Nowadays, police often use evidence about a criminal's behaviour to create a profile of who they are looking for. Imagine the police in 1888 asked you to draw up a profile of Jack the Ripper. What would you tell them – and why?

The police investigation

In the 1880s, the police had very limited scientific help in their investigations. There was no fingerprint or blood group analysis, and the importance of photographs of crime scenes was only just beginning to be understood. The police's best hope of making a successful arrest was either to catch someone committing a crime or to extract a confession from a suspect.

Following up leads given by the public
Hundreds of suggestions were made. The police followed 300 lines of enquiry suggested to them and arrested 80 people for further investigation.

Asking for help
The police had over 8000 posters and handbills printed, asking for anyone with information to come forward.

Following up evidence from postmortem examinations
A doctor who examined Annie Chapman's body suggested that the Ripper was left-handed and had an understanding of anatomy. This led to investigations and interviews in slaughterhouses, butchers' shops, vets' surgeries and hospitals.

Making house-to-house enquiries
Hundreds of house-to-house enquiries were made in the houses and workplaces close to where the five victims were found. Over 2000 people were questioned in this way.

Interviewing witnesses
The police interviewed everyone who claimed to have seen one of the victims just before they were murdered.. Some were unreliable witnesses and were later found to be lying. Nevertheless, all the clues they gave the police were followed up.

Visiting psychiatric hospitals
The murders were so horrific that the police decided the Ripper must be seriously mentally disturbed. Psychiatric hospitals, called 'lunatic asylums' in Victorian times, were visited and patients, nurses and doctors interviewed.

Opening soup kitchens
The police were not allowed to pay informants. Instead, they opened soup kitchens, hoping that the offer of hot food would encourage people to come forward with information.

Figure 2: Police investigations during the Ripper inquiry.

Source D: A cartoon from the *Illustrated Police News*, October 1888.

Police rivalry

The Metropolitan Police force, under the command of Chief Commissioner Sir Charles Warren, was responsible for policing most of London. In order to do this effectively, London was split up into a number of divisions. All the Ripper murders, except one, took place in H division. In order to help with the investigations, police were drafted in to H division from the other London divisions. Catherine Eddowes, however, was murdered in the City of London, which had its own police force under the command of Major Henry Smith. While the police and detectives from the Metropolitan Police and City Police worked well together, the two commissioners did not.

Part of Catherine Eddowes' bloodstained apron was found under an archway, half a mile away from where she was murdered. Some anti-Jewish graffiti was chalked over the archway (see Figure 3).

Major Henry Smith ordered a City policeman to wait by the graffiti until it could be photographed. Sir Charles Warren, afraid of anti-Jewish rioting in his area, wrote down what the graffiti said and ordered it to be wiped off. This was done. It resulted in a breakdown in the relationship between the two commissioners and, later, the resignation of Charles Warren.

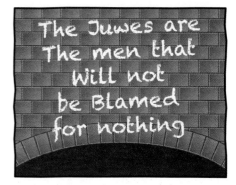

Figure 3: A copy of the graffiti seen above the archway where part of Catherine Eddowes' bloodstained apron was found.

Key term

Home Office*:
The government department responsible for the police.

Source E: From a report written by Charles Warren and sent to the Home Office* on 6 November 1888, shortly before his resignation.

It was just getting light; the public would be in the streets in a few minutes, in a neighbourhood very much crowded with Jews and Christians and the writing would be visible to anybody in the street. After taking into consideration the strong feelings that existed in the area against the Jews, and fearing a riot, I ordered the writing to be wiped away. I took a copy of it and this I enclose.

Source F: From a book, *From Constable to Commissioner*, written by Major Henry Smith, published in 1910.

The writing on the wall may have been written – and, I think, probably was written – to throw the police off scent, to throw suspicion upon the Jews. It may have been written by the murderer, or it may not. To wipe out the words that might have given us a most valuable clue, more especially after I had sent a man to stand over them until they were photographed, was totally unreasonable.

Your turn!

1   Imagine you are in control of the police inquiry. You have 100 policemen and 10 detectives under your command.

   a   Look carefully at Figure 2. Put the types of investigations in order of priority and allocate a number of policemen and detectives to each action.

   b   For each action, say what you hope it will achieve.

   c   Are there any actions you would like to add? What do you hope they will achieve?

2   Read Sources E and F. How far do you agree that Charles Warren did the right thing in ordering the graffiti to be wiped out?

What slowed down the police investigation?

Source G: A cartoon, published in the magazine *Punch* in 1888, showing a blindfolded policeman being taunted by Ripper suspects. 'Blind-Man's Buff' is a children's game in which one child is blindfolded and tries to catch other children.

As the police had not caught Jack the Ripper in the act of murdering a prostitute, they had to rely on painstakingly interviewing everyone even remotely connected to the murders in the hope of finding clues. The actions of some people, however, distracted them from following genuine leads.

The press

Exciting stories sell newspapers, and there was fierce competition between the 13 daily and nine evening papers on sale in London in 1888 to get the 'best' Ripper stories. The police released as few details of the murders as possible – it was left to the newspapers to build sensational stories on the little information they had. Journalists, for example, interviewed people who had given evidence at the inquests, and who then usually changed what they had said in order to make it, and themselves, more interesting. The press paid money for good stories! This created new (but usually false) leads that the police had to follow up.

When the investigation failed to find the Ripper, the press turned on the police. The press argued that it had provided the police with so much information (though most of it was false) that the police must be really stupid not to have found the Ripper. Most of the public agreed, and this made the job of the police even more difficult.

The 'Ripper' letters

A letter, dated 25 September 1888 and signed 'Jack the Ripper', was received by the Central News Agency in London. The agency had a reputation for stories which were not always completely true. However, the police took the letter seriously, and copies were published in every national newspaper in the hope that someone would recognise the handwriting. This led to hundreds of letters arriving with the police and press, all claiming to be from the Ripper. Although these were hoaxes, a lot of police time was wasted following them up.

Source H: Part of the first letter signed 'Jack the Ripper' and sent to the Central News Agency. Some people believe that this was a hoax, made up by a journalist who wanted a sensational story.

I keep on hearing that the police have caught me but they wont fix me just yet. I have laughed when they look so clever and talk about being on the right track. I am down on whores and shant stop ripping them up till I do get caught. Grand job the last job was. I gave the lady no time to squeal. How can they catch me now? The next job I do I shall clip the lady's ears off and send to the police officers. My knife's so nice and sharp I want to get to work right away if I get the chance.

The Whitechapel Vigilance Committee

A group of Whitechapel businessmen were worried about the impact of the Ripper killings on local trade and angry at what they thought was the lack of police progress. They formed the Whitechapel Vigilance Committee, led by a builder called George Lusk. Committee volunteers patrolled Whitechapel at night, hoping to catch the murderer. They published posters offering rewards for information and hired two private detectives to follow up clues.

Source I: Members of the Whitechapel Vigilance Committee stalk a suspect. This picture was published in the *Illustrated London News* in October 1888.

The Committee's activities often cut across and confused lines of enquiry being followed by the police. For example, George Lusk was sent a letter claiming to come from the Ripper. It was in a package that contained half a human kidney that the letter said had been taken from Catherine Eddowes. This could have been genuine: the kidney showed evidence of the same kidney disease from which Catherine Eddowes suffered. However, a medical student or doctor could have sent it as a hoax.

There were no more Ripper murders after November 1888. This should have been a significant clue. Was the killer dead? Had he gone abroad? Was he in prison for other, different crimes? Even so, and despite the best efforts of the police over several years, Jack the Ripper was never caught.

Your turn!

1 Look at Source G.
   a What is the message of the cartoon?
   b Use your own knowledge of the investigation to explain whether or not you agree with the cartoonist.

2 Think about the ways in which the police investigation was slowed down. On a scale of 1–5, where 5 is 'a lot' and 1 is 'hardly at all', assess the effect of:
   a the press
   b the Ripper letters
   c the Whitechapel Vigilance Committee.
   Explain your reasons for the highest score.

3 You have answered a lot of small questions about the Whitechapel murders and the police investigation. Now is the time to put all your thinking together, and write an answer to the big question: 'Why was Jack the Ripper never caught?'

Glossary

Abbot: The head of an abbey.

Abolition: Banning or getting rid of something.

Abolitionist: Someone who campaigns for something to be banned or stopped. In this case, someone who campaigns for the slave trade to be brought to an end.

Absolution: The forgiving of a person's sins.

Absolutist: An absolutist ruler is one who has supreme authority and power.

Act of Supremacy: An act passed by parliament in 1534 which made Henry and his successors Supreme Head of the Church of England. It was abolished by Queen Mary and a new Act of Supremacy was passed under Elizabeth I in 1559.

Annexed: Territory taken over without the owner's permission.

Annulment: Declaration that something is invalid.

Apprentice: A person who agrees to work for an employer for a fixed period while learning a trade.

Arsenic: A white powder that had no taste or smell. It could easily be put in food or drink. It builds up in a body and eventually causes multiple organ failure.

Baggage train: People, wagons and supplies that the army needed on campaign. As well as basics, the baggage train could contain expensive personal items and plunder from previous battles.

Basilica: A type of building, usually a church, given special status by the pope.

Bill: The draft of a proposed law.

Boycott: When people refuse to buy something as a protest.

British Overseas Territory: The name given to the parts of the British Empire that remain ruled by Britain to this day.

Cash crop: Crop grown and sold for profit rather than grown as food for local people.

Caste: Class of person within Hindu society.

Coffer: A strong box used to store money or valuable items.

Colony: An area of land settled by and under the control of people from another country.

Compensate: Give money to make up for the loss of something.

Counter-Reformation: Reforms to the doctrine and beliefs of the Catholic Church in response to the Protestant Reformation, starting in 1545. It also involved attempts to enforce Catholic practices and convert Protestants back to Catholicism.

Domestic slaves: Slaves who performed household jobs such as cooking and washing. These were usually female slaves. They would work in the homes of their owners.

Dominican friar: Monk following the rule of St Dominic. Friars were monks who could travel around, instead of staying in a monastery.

Emancipation: Freedom from slavery.

Empire: A group of states or countries ruled over by one monarch or government.

Enlightenment, the: New ways of thinking that emerged in the 18th century which emphasised reason and logic over tradition and superstition.

Enslaved: Made into a slave.

Excommunicated: Cut off or banished from a religious group, in this case, the Catholic Church.

Field slaves: By far the largest percentage of slaves in the Americas, field slaves would work in the fields on the plantations. They were more commonly, but not always, men.

Garrison: A base for soldiers.

Gentry: People of high social status, just below the nobles, and usually landowners.

Globalisation: The world becoming more interconnected.

Governor: Most British colonies had a governor who was responsible for ruling on behalf of the monarchy. As they were so far from London, they had a lot of power and independence.

Governor-general: The chief representative of the British in India.

Heretic: A person with religious views that disagree with official Church teaching.

Home Office: The government department responsible for the police.

Inference: Something that can be learned from a source, which goes beyond the surface detail of what the source says, to what it suggests.

Inquest: A legal enquiry into an incident – usually a death.

Irrigation: Supplying water to dry areas of land so that they can be farmed.

Joint-stock company: A company where a group of investors share the cost and the profits of their business between them.

Legacy: Something handed down from the past.

Legal rights: Rights that a person has according to the laws of a country: for example, the right to be protected from harm, the right to an education, and so on.

Litany: A long prayer, usually led by a priest but also involving responses from worshippers.

Lock: When canals had to cross hilly land locks were dug in sections at different levels. They enabled barges to move from one level of water to another.

Miasma theory: The idea that disease is caused by bad air, called miasma.

Middle-class: The social group between the upper and working classes.

Missionary: A person sent on a religious mission, often to convert other people to Christianity.

Monopoly: A business or person with the exclusive right to do or sell something.

Mutiny: A revolt by the military. The Indian Rebellion is often known as the Indian Mutiny, but some historians say that it is wrong to call it a mutiny as it was not just a military revolt. Sometimes the Rebellion is described as being India's First War of Independence, as it can be viewed as an attempt to overthrow British rule.

Nawab: An Indian prince or ruler.

New World: A name given to the Americas during the colonisation by Europeans in the 16th century.

Nonconformist: A Protestant who does not follow the teachings of the Church of England. Examples are Quakers, Baptists and Methodists.

Patent medicine: Cheap medicine that does little to cure disease.

Patriotic: To be very loyal and devoted to your own country.

Patronage: The power to appoint people to jobs and positions. Sometimes this was in return for money or favours, or because they were relatives or friends.

Petition: A list of requests or demands signed by many people.

Plantation: A large farm or estate where one main crop is grown.

Plunder: To steal goods by force.

Popery: Catholic religious practices.

Popular movement: Where a large proportion of the general public support a cause.

Prince of Wales: Since the 13th century, this title has been given to the eldest son of the monarch, who is the heir to the throne.

Privateer: A naval captain who has permission from their government (in the form of a document called a 'letter of marque') to attack and rob the ships of another country.

Proclamation: An official announcement on an important issue.

Puppet ruler: An official ruler who has little political power because they are controlled by someone else.

Quack doctor: Someone who pretends to have medical skills.

Raj: An Indian word meaning 'ruler'. It is often used to describe the period from 1858 to 1947 when the British government ruled India.

Reformation: A movement in the 16th century which led to the founding of Protestantism. A Protestant is a type of a Christian whose beliefs are different from those of the Catholic Church.

Regent: A person appointed to rule, normally while a monarch is abroad, ill or too young to rule.

Relic: Part of the body or clothing of a holy person.

Republic: A country that has no monarchy, and in which supreme power is held by an elected body.

Republican: A person living in, or wanting to live in, a republic.

Rood screen: A screen in a church that separates the area around the altar from the congregation.

Rosary: A string of beads used to help Catholics to follow a set sequence of prayers, each bead corresponding to part of the prayer cycle.

Royal Navy: The official naval fighting force of Britain.

Safety bicycle: A bicycle with a comfortable saddle that looks a bit like a modern bike. Women could ride it and be thought respectable.

Salvation: Deliverance from sin and its consequences.

Slums: Overcrowded and filthy houses lived in by very poor people.

Smuggler: Someone who trades goods illegally.

Tariff: A tax paid on goods that are imported.

Thirteen Colonies, the: The British colonies established in North America between 1607 and 1732.

Toll: A fee charged for using a stretch of canal or a lock, relating to the weight of goods carried. Tolls were also charged on some roads.

Trading factory: A building or settlement where people could meet to carry out trade.

Transatlantic slave trade: The forced movement of around 12 to 15 million Africans across the Atlantic Ocean to the Americas and the West Indies, where they were used as slaves. It occurred between the 16th and 19th centuries.

Transubstantiation: A belief held by Catholics that, when a priest blesses the bread and wine during mass, they transform into the physical body and blood of Christ.

Vagrancy: Wandering and begging because a person is homeless.

Answers

Chapter 1

Page 38
1. Martin Luther
2. So he could marry Anne Boleyn
3. Acts of Supremacy
4. Edward VI
5. Edward VI, Lady Jane Grey, Mary I
6. Elizabeth I
7. The Armada
8. Elizabeth had no children, and James was the son of Mary, Queen of Scots – a relative of Henry VII
9. The 'Monteagle' letter
10. They were hanged, drawn and quartered

Chapter 2

Page 66
1. She was Catholic
2. Archbishop Laud
3. He introduced a new prayer book
4. The 'Personal Rule'
5. He arrived at the House of Commons with 300 soldiers and tried to arrest five MPs
6. The New Model Army
7. Treason
8. It was cold, and he didn't want people to think he was shivering from fear

Chapter 3

Page 94
1. Need for stable government, but could be broken down into, for example, lack of an acceptable successor to Oliver Cromwell, acceptance of Declaration of Breda, fear of power of army.
2. An MP, who became Chief Secretary to the Admiralty, and diarist
3. Epidemic that killed thousands of people
4. The Great Fiire of London
5. Willliam and Mary
6. Two from: gravity; colours of the spectrum; calculus; that the universe worked according to mathematical rules.
7. Microscope
8. First prime minister
9. Men with wealth or property
10. None

Chapter 4

Page 128
1. From West Africa to the Caribbean and the Americas
2. Approximately 12 million
3. Although slaves worked in many roles, the vast majority worked as field hands on plantations (often sugar, tobacco or cotton). Female slaves were also commonly domestic servants.
4. William Wilberforce – led the abolition campaign in parliament
   Thomas Clarkson – led the propaganda campaign for abolition
   Olaudah Equino – wrote an autobiography of his experiences as a slave
   William Pitt – the British prime minister who supported abolition
   Hannah More – wrote poems and play to support abolition
5. 1807
6. 1833 (although 'apprenticeships' continued until 1837)

Chapter 5

Page 156
1. The Mughal Empire
2. Indian craftsmen produced very fine quality cloth.
   India had supplies of spices that Europe did not.
   The Mughal Empire was very wealthy and English traders wanted to share in this wealth.
3. Robert Clive
4. Military conquest
   Doctrine of lapse
   Princely states
   Puppet rulers
   Alliances with Indian princes
5. An export market for British-manufactured goods
   Imports of goods, especially cotton
   People to serve in the armies of the British Empire
   Taxation from the lands ruled in India
   British dominance and profit from Indian trade and industry
6. Introduction of technological developments, such as the railways
   Employment in British-owned industries
   Spread of team sports, such as cricket

(continued)

(Chapter 5 continued)

7   Famine
Loss of liberty and right to self-rule
British domination of Indian trade and industry
High taxation
Lack of respect for local culture and religion

8   The period from 1858 to 1947 when India was directly ruled by Britain

Chapter 6

Page 188

1   Selective breeding and crop rotation
2   They needed to use water power
3   Growth of the railways
4   Factories could be built in towns and fewer workers were needed
5   People who broke machines that they thought were going to put them out of work
6   Children couldn't work for more than 10 hours a day in a factory
7   That cholera was a water-borne disease
8   To show the world England's superiority
9   Holidays at the seaside; fresh food transported to inland towns
10 Enabled elementary education for all children

Index

Acknowledgements

The authors and publisher would like to thank the following individuals and organisations for their kind permission to reproduce copyright material.

Photographs

(Key: b-bottom; c-centre; l-left ; r-right; t-top)

Alamy Stock Photo: Archivart 6l, 92t, Granger Historical Picture Archive 6c, 10, 64, 87b, 93t, 109, 110tl, 118, 132, 135, 148, 149, 152, Ian Dagnall 6-7, 45, 74, 77, 78, Guildhall Library & Art Gallery/Heritage Image Partnership Ltd 7r, 181, Art Collection 2 9b, 146, Archive Images 11, Annie Eagle 15t, SOBERKA Richard/hemis.fr 15b, Collection/Active Museum/Le Pictorium 16, World History Archive 17, 18, 44, 54, 62, 70, 166, 174, 175, 178, 186c, Paul Fearn 19, 46, 145b, 163, 171b, Heritage Image Partnership Ltd 20, Mike Kipling/LOOP IMAGES 21, Alastair Balderstone 22, Pictorial Press Ltd 23, 27, 141, 160, Fine Art Images/ Fine Art Images 26, Peter Horree 30, Julia Gavin 34, Classic Image 35, 155, De Luan 43, FineArt 48, Timewatch Images 49, Art Collection 3 50, Neil Holmes/Holmes Garden Photos 51, Hilary Morgan 63, Pictorial Press Ltd 68, 91t, 176, GL Archive 69, 94, 110tr, NMUIM 71, Photo Researchers/ Science History Images 75, Martin Shields 79, Antiqua Print Gallery 80, INTERFOTO/ Personalities 84t, Lordprice Collection 87t, Niday Picture Library 89, Lebrecht Music and Arts Photo Library 90, Anna Stowe 91b, The National Trust Photolibrary 92b, PAINTING 93b, Chronicle 96, 127, 164b, 167, 173, 182, INTERFOTO 111l, 126, ART Collection 115b, North Wind Picture Archives 120, 137, Lebrecht Music and Arts Photo Library 122, Fine Art Images/Heritage Image Partnership Ltd 134, Olaf Kruger/ imageBROKER 145t, The Print Collector 147, The Granger Collection 154, 195, Jesse Willcox Smith 169b, John Frost Newspapers 171t, The Keasbury-Gordon Photograph Archive 183l, 192t, The Artchives 186t, Vintage Book Collection 194; **Bridgeman Art Library:** English School, (17th century) (after)/Private Collection 37, Cope, Charles West (1811-90)/Houses of Parliament, Westminster, London, UK 40, Gow, Andrew Carrick (1848-1920)/Imperial Defence College, Camberley, Surrey, UK 65, Wren, Christopher (1632-1723)/St. Paul's Cathedral Library, London, UK 81, American School, (18th century)/Historic New England, Boston, Massachusetts, USA/Gift of Bertram K. and Nina Fletcher Little 83t, Kneller, Godfrey (1646-1723)/The Crown Estate 84bl, 84br, English School, (18th century)/Private Collection 88, American School, (19th century)/Private Collection/Courtesy of Swann Auction Galleries 108, Beastall, W.E. (fl. 1806) (after)/Private Collection/© Michael Graham-Stewart 110b, Duperly, Adolphe (1801-65)/Private Collection/Photo © Christie's Images 121, Moses, Henry (1782-1870)/Private Collection/© Michael Graham-Stewart 128, Boultbee, John (1745-1812) (after)/Private Collection 158, Shepherd, Thomas Hosmer (1792-1864) (after)/London Metropolitan Archives, City of London 162, Cruickshank, George (1792-1878) (after)/Private Collection/© Look and Learn 169t, Universal History Archive/UIG 180, Durand, Godefroy (b.1832)/Private Collection/© Look and Learn/ Illustrated Papers Collection 183r, Crowe, Eyre (1824-1910)/Manchester Art Gallery, UK 186b; **British Museum:** ©The Trustees of the British Museum 83b; **Getty Images:** Hulton Archive 111r, CherryMarch 37, Hulton Archive 111r, Corbis Historical 124t, English School 192b; **Mary Evans Picture Library:** 103, 115t, 124b, 164t, The National Archives, London. England 123, ©Antiquarian Images 136; **Shutterstock:** Kevin Eaves 5, 8, Everett Historical 7l, 106, 119b, Watchara Panyajun 112, larry1235 119t; **TopFoto.co.uk:** 56, Granger, NYC 100

All other images © Pearson Education

Text

Page 33 Interpretation 2: © History Extra/Immediate Media.
Page 38 Interpretation 2: Used by the permission of the publisher, History Today.